The BOOK of MORMON

A PATTERN FOR PARENTING

The BOOK *of* MORMON

A PATTERN FOR PARENTING

GERI BRINLEY

Covenant

Covenant Communications, Inc.

Cover image © 2006 Stockbyte Platinum/Getty Images

Cover design copyrighted 2006 by Covenant Communications, Inc.

Published by Covenant Communications, Inc.
American Fork, Utah

Printed in Canada
First Printing: February 2006

11 10 09 08 07 06   10 9 8 7 6 5 4 3 2 1

ISBN 1-59811-061-6

I'd like to dedicate this book to my hero and forever sweetheart, Doug. He has been a wonderful support and a source of inspiration as well as editing expertise, never too busy to help me through this entire project.

Acknowledgements

I am grateful to Mormon, Moroni, Nephi, and Jacob for their faithful record-keeping and their desire to share the principles of the gospel we'd need to rear a special generation in this last dispensation. Though not many would at first see the Book of Mormon as a parenting guide, the principles laid out in this sacred volume, though written so very long ago, can help modern parents meet the challenges of parenting today.

Nephi was right: "Feast upon the words of Christ; for behold, the words of Christ will tell you *all things what ye should do*" (2 Nephi 32:3, emphasis added). That includes parenting, as I hope to point out.

To my husband, children, and grandchildren, I express my deepest love and devotion and wish for them to experience the same love of the Book of Mormon that I have, all the days of their lives. And to my husband, a special thanks for his continued support of this effort and some editing ideas.

I would like to acknowledge the contribution of our six children who taught me everything I know about parenting and served as guinea pigs while I struggled to learn. And happily they have all turned out to be much better at parenting than I was and are doing a great job raising our nineteen grandchildren.

My thanks to all those individuals who graciously allowed me to record their experiences for the good of others. (Out of respect, those quotes will be anonymously rendered.) Also thanks to Covenant Communications, Inc. Angela Eschler was especially patient as I reworked this material that is so dear to my heart. Though many voices contributed to the process, I, alone, am responsible for its final contents.

Geri Brinley

TABLE OF CONTENTS

INTRODUCTION

I always felt early in life that, after marriage, parenting would be the greatest adventure of all. I somehow knew that caring for the very special children God assigned to me would be of utmost importance to both Him and me. I looked forward to the privilege, as I think all potential mothers do, and yet, despite all my anticipation, I was not prepared for its realities. No matter how well you think something through, to imagine yourself in a specific role, it never turns out quite as you saw it in your own mind.

Just as my husband and I were getting used to living together as a couple, and our newly formed marriage was developing fairly well, along came what proved to be an interloper—this third party who was capable of disrupting our marital bliss. And it was a little difficult to just ignore him! Yet, I knew in my heart that one of the primary reasons marriage was commanded in the first place was to have posterity, if we were able. Before long, however, I found myself wanting to know who it was that said parenting would bless our lives. Well, of course it does, but you don't always know that early in the game.

Another paradigm shift for which we are unprepared is that children are given to us to teach *us* about life. Yes, we teach them a few things, but in the end it is really the children who teach their parents how to refine their own souls, bringing parents a maturity that can be gained in few other ways.

But this journey is often long and difficult. As children move out of the "feed 'em and change 'em" stages, it hits us that these are real people, that we are rearing the very spirit children of God. Yet He provides us with no manual for what to do with these characters once we get them, and the last place most of us would probably look for parenting help is in the Book of Mormon. We don't normally think of this text as a parenting commentary, even though it begins with a story of a family that manifests dysfunctionality rather quickly after departing Jerusalem!

My own story on coming to appreciate the Book of Mormon as a parenting guide did not come about naturally or easily. Let me share a little of its beginnings. It began as my children and I came to grips with the reality of Sunday church services and my having to wrestle my way through a three-hour block of meetings without my husband's help. Oh yes, I am married, but this Church has a way of splitting you up with different assignments so that you have to parent alone on many occasions. My frustrations came to a head one day during a Relief Society lesson. Here's what I heard, and I'm sure it will sound familiar to all mothers.

"Now, sisters," the teacher said, wrapping up her lesson, "let's review the principles. What must we do if we want to have the inspiration of Father in Heaven as wives and mothers?" And of course, we provided the usual cliché answers: "We must *pray, study the scriptures daily,* and *live the commandments.*"

"That's correct," acknowledged the instructor. "If we will do these three things, the Lord has promised He will be with us in our time of need." Then she bore testimony concerning the three principles, invoking the Lord as her authority, and punctuating her statement with an "Amen."

Well, how could I disagree with her? How could anyone disagree? It sounded good; it made sense. I had a good feeling about it, too, as I gathered up my baby's toys and Cheerios and hurried from the Relief Society room to check on my two-year-old in the nursery.

Relief Society always made me feel good, especially the "spiritual living" lesson. However, the trick to it was making the lesson last through the whole day, to say nothing of the entire week. With three preschoolers and a Sunday-absentee husband, it was hard to stay on a spiritual high very long. Most of the week, it seemed, I just rushed from one crisis to the next, barely finding time to read the instructions on the detergent box, let alone delve into sacred text. Sundays, it seemed, were always the worst. It was a rush to get myself and the kids ready and off to church on time with our nine-to-twelve schedule. Usually by the time I got the last one dressed, the first one had soiled, torn, or taken off his Sunday attire and I had to start all over again.

Four-year-old David was finally old enough to go to his Primary class alone, but his two-year-old sister, Terri, never gave me up without a struggle at the nursery door. Invariably, it seemed, I found myself slipping into a seat at the back of the Relief Society room somewhere in the middle of the lesson. If I was lucky, six-month-old Becky would play quietly near me, but more often than not I spent a good part of the meeting entertaining her so she wouldn't disturb others with her vocal demands. Things didn't get much better during Sunday School either. Becky usually wouldn't let me stay in the class long enough to find out if we were studying the New Testament, the Old Testament, or *The Wizard of Oz.*

And even if I was able to hold things together during the first two meetings, it all came apart during sacrament meeting. I always tried to sit somewhere near the back so I could slip out quietly if the children got too restless before the meeting concluded. We generally made it through the sacrament part of the service (probably because there was bread and water coming), but not much longer. One time I was so determined to feel the spirit of the sacrament service that I actually closed my eyes and tried to meditate on the Savior's life and death as I waited for the deacons to approach our row. When I opened my eyes, to my horror I saw David trotting up the aisle, on his way, apparently, to check the piano's tuning. Perhaps he intended to lend a soothing hymn to the atmosphere of the occasion, but I couldn't take a chance to wait and see. In my frantic mind I had two choices. I could either gather up the other two children and leave the building immediately, disclaiming the young pianist as any relation of mine, or I could walk all the way up that long aisle, leaving my other children behind, and put a stop to the possible concert by dragging David, kicking and screaming, out the nearest exit, and then go home—never to return again until the children were in their teens and could be trusted to sit with their friends' families. I was still in that state of indecision when a kindly brother on the stand gently lifted

David from the piano bench and held him firmly on his own lap for the remainder of the meeting. At first David was too surprised to protest, and then he became so enthralled with some finger game this Good Samaritan taught him that he was perfectly content to remain right where he was for the rest of the meeting.

Even at home the remainder of the Sabbath day didn't go much better. My spirit desperately needed nourishment, but Sunday afternoons were long and dragging and it seemed as if the children needed constant direction and supervision if the day was to be a happy one for them. I usually lay down with them at nap time, intending to tell them a story and then slip out once they fell asleep, to do my own gospel study. More often than not I fell asleep before they did and I woke to find myself the only one on the bed!

Weekdays were busy and full of household tasks and church responsibilities. They didn't seem as discouraging as Sundays because I didn't expect much from them. I met the children's demands and needs with a happy heart because I knew this was what the Lord wanted from me at this time of my life. Wasn't I doing everything expected of me? Well, then where were the blessings? The joy? The peace of mind? What spiritual growth comes from mopping the bathroom floor or changing diapers? Reading *Little Red Ridinghood* might be great for the kids, but it didn't do a thing to stimulate my intellect. I knew there was a sacred and a profane side to every vocation, but must there be such a wide gap between the two, I mused. How could I blend the day-to-day chores and responsibilities of child-rearing with the personal celestial instruction for which my spirit hungered?

I had two problems: (1) I needed inspiration on how to be a better mother to my children, and (2) I was spiritually starving because of my inability to find time to dig into the scriptures. I knew the solution to both issues; I just didn't know how to make it work. The cliché answers I had heard a hundred times in a hundred different lessons kept dancing in my mind: *pray always, read the scriptures, keep the commandments.*

Okay, let's see: I was keeping the commandments. I was praying, or thought I was. And I was trying to read the scriptures whenever time permitted. It's just that time didn't permit it very often, and anyway, what did Lehi's journey to the promised land or Alma's conversion have to do with my problems? Show me a chapter or verse in the Book of Mormon that tells you how to toilet train a stubborn two-year-old or get a four-year-old to pick up his toys. I was sure I had more relevant things to worry about than who was going to win the next Nephite-Lamanite war when I had my own three children warring right in front of me. I was struggling to win some of my own battles.

Something had to be done. My spirit was dying. I was desperate. It seemed the only quiet time I had to myself was in the bathroom—the one door in the house I could lock. Once I realized this inner sanctum existed, I began locking myself in briefly two or three times a day so I could have a heart-to-heart talk with the Lord—in private. I really poured my heart out to Him during these sessions and pleaded for His help with my problems.

As usually happens, it wasn't long after my sincere pleadings that an inspired bishop called me into his office. He wanted *me* to serve as the spiritual living leader in Relief Society! What? Me? Can you believe it? This wasn't the kind of help I expected. At first I was dumbfounded. I had a "No way" right on the tip of my tongue. However, growing up in the Church, I was trained to be obedient, so my final thought was to accept the call. I stumbled out of his office wondering what I had just agreed to, and more importantly, how in the world I was going to pull it off.

In hindsight I confess that the Lord knew what He was doing. That call to teach Relief Society literally *changed my life*. The study and preparation it took for me to give those lessons taught me three things. One, if you know you have a serious calling, you will find time late at night or early in the morning to prepare; two, if the incentive is strong enough—in this case, *fear*—you don't fall asleep reading scriptures; and three, I discovered the difference between just reading scriptures and *searching* scriptures, feasting upon them, as Nephi called it. His words rang true: "Feast upon the words of Christ," he said, "for behold, the words of Christ will *tell you all things what ye should do*" (2 Nephi 32:3, emphasis added). Maybe the Relief Society teacher's counsel was right: perhaps the answers to my parenting questions really were in the scriptures. Then, as if to confirm my new insight, I found Alma's profound declaration: "And now, as the preaching of the word had a great tendency to lead the people to do that which was just—yea, it had had more powerful effect upon the minds of the people than the sword, or anything else [that] had happened unto them—therefore Alma thought it was expedient that *they should try the virtue of the word of God*" (Alma 31:5, emphasis added).

That statement was not unlike another witness from a modern prophet: "It is not just that the Book of Mormon teaches us truth, though it indeed does that. It is not just that the Book of Mormon bears testimony of Christ, though it indeed does that, too. But there is something more. *There is a power in the book which will begin to flow into your lives the moment you begin a serious study of the book*" (Ezra Taft Benson, *The Teachings of Ezra Taft Benson* [Salt Lake City, UT: Bookcraft], 1998, 54, emphasis added).

There. I had it from three credible witnesses that when you prayerfully search the scriptures, you find that they can tell you what to do in every dilemma, and from them it is possible to gain power to do those things.

"Well," I thought to myself, "if the scriptures claim to do all this, why not put the promise to the test?" So I began reading the Book of Mormon; I had a good commentary by authors I respected, a notebook at hand, and now, for the first time, a real purpose in reading it. I began seeing all kinds of insights into parenting, both positive and negative. I began to write down the scriptural references with a brief note about the account. When I had finished the entire book (and it is amazing how interesting it became when I learned to study it as a resource book rather than a novel), I organized the examples I'd discovered into parenting principles and added my own applications to each principle.

Let me give you an example of what I found: I was having a hard time getting my children to cooperate with me and with each other. They would fight, ignore my requests to help with small jobs until I became insistent and angry, or they would act out or show off at the most inconvenient times. Does that sound familiar? Alma's interview with each of his sons in Alma 36–42 helped me realize how well he knew each one of them as individuals and how crucial a one-on-one relationship is with each child. I began holding personal interviews periodically with each, doing things solely with that child. I had special days or dates with each one, enjoyed an activity together that he or she chose, or made bedtime routines more personal. In short, I began treating my children as individuals with different needs rather than lumping them together as "our kids." They, in return, responded with less need to seek my attention in negative ways. As they became more confident in their own abilities and found their roles in the family, they became more cooperative both at home and in public.

I also discovered an excellent model for any family found in Mosiah 18, which gives an account of Alma establishing the Lord's Church at the waters of Mormon. He taught his disciples the importance of being united. As I read those verses, the thought occurred to me that this would also be an excellent model for a righteous family. (I suggest you read this section aloud as a family, brainstorming ways to apply it to your own family.)

As I began making scripture study a part of my daily routine, I also began looking at the way I was keeping the commandments. By gaining new scriptural insights, I was able to view homemaking and parenthood not as a duty that fell to me, but as a blessing and opportunity to learn more about parenthood in this life as a preparation for eternity. "So this is what Heavenly Parents go through," I found myself saying out loud. It isn't always easy to keep this perspective in mind when a two-year-old makes a mess again and the stack of laundry is matched only by the stack of dirty dishes. But these occasional setbacks become easier to face if you aren't suffering from spiritual malnutrition.

Now when I have a Relief Society lesson to give I use those same cliché answers because they have much more meaning to me. I can bear testimony with conviction to the sisters I teach that these three principles do work if we are willing to pay the price to understand them. And I, too, have learned that the prophets are right: there isn't a problem we encounter that isn't answered for us if we will search the scriptures.

In putting my discoveries in book form, my hope is that as a parent facing the typical challenges we all face in these tumultuous days, you will be able to study this Book of Mormon parenting commentary and (1) identify principles of parenting, (2) understand how the Lord and His prophets use these principles to govern His people, and (3) discover how you, with inspiration, can find ways to become a more effective parent. The principles here, however, are not exhaustive, because the Book of Mormon's message changes as your own situation changes. But these principles will start you on your way to becoming a better parent to the special children God has assigned to you in this final dispensation, and reading the Book of Mormon in this way will bring power to your life—power to cheerfully endure and conquer any challenge, especially parenting.

Teach Your Children

Principle 1
The Importance of Teaching—Why and When to Teach

Why Teach Our Children

We have been commanded to teach our children the first principles of the gospel (See D&C 68:25–28), to teach them to pray, to walk uprightly before God, and to teach them by the Spirit of the Lord (See D&C 42:13–14). This commandment places responsibility and accountability for their spiritual instruction squarely upon our shoulders as parents. Children need direction, and they need to know their parents care enough about them to offer them guidance whether they are in or outside of our homes. The best way to accomplish these sacred obligations is to do what the prophets have pled for years that we do as parents: be consistent in having family home evening, family scripture study, and family prayer. Having a set time during the day or week for instruction, visiting, gospel study, sharing life events, and general quality time is crucial for family unity in a day when families are so mobile that some days they hardly see each other. President Joseph F. Smith, as far back as 1904, even before family home evening was suggested, counseled parents:

> There is too little religious devotion, love, and fear of God in the home; too much worldliness, selfishness, indifference, and lack of reverence in the family, or these never would exist so abundantly on the outside. Then, the home is what needs reforming. Try today, and tomorrow, to make a change in your home. . . . Do not let your

> children out to specialists in these things, but teach them by your own precept and example, by your own fireside. Be a specialist yourself in the truth. ("Worship in the Home," *Improvement Era*, Dec. 1904, 135)

More recently, under the signatures of Presidents Gordon B. Hinckley, Thomas S. Monson, and James E. Faust, parents were reminded of what must be a high priority:

> We call upon parents to devote their best efforts to the teaching and rearing of their children in gospel principles which will keep them close to the Church. The home is the basis of a righteous life, and no other instrumentality can take its place or fulfill its essential functions in carrying forward this God-given responsibility. We counsel parents and children to give highest priority to family prayer, family home evening, gospel study and instruction, and wholesome family activities. However worthy and appropriate other demands or activities may be, they must not be permitted to displace the divinely appointed duties that only parents and families can adequately perform. ("Policies, Announcements, and Appointments," *Ensign*, June 1999, 80)

Speaking to the members of the Salt Lake Valley Stake, President Hinckley pleaded:

> I just want to make a plea to you people here, you parents who have young families, many of you, in this stake: Take advantage of the great responsibility and opportunity that you have to teach your children, to rear them in the light of the gospel, to build faith in their hearts, to sit down with them. If you can't do it at the dinner table, and I'm sorry if you can't, then you have a family home evening, and don't miss it. Talk with them about these things. Let them feel of your love for the Lord. Let them hear you testify of the truth of

> this work. Let them partake of the good that comes from a father and a mother who seek to do the right thing and do it while they're young.
>
> Parents should talk with their children about the blessing that the Word of Wisdom is, about the good that comes from paying tithes and fast offerings, about missionary work and how they might share the gospel, about the welfare plan and what it seeks to accomplish. . . .
>
> *I want to tell you—I want to promise you—you fathers and mothers, if you will do that, your children will grow up with love for the Lord, and the greatest reward you can have in this life, nothing excepted, will be to see your children walk in truth before the Lord.* ("Special Visitor Attends Stake Conference," *Church News*, Nov. 16, 2002, 3, emphasis added)

Despite decades of warnings and assistance in the past century, many LDS families still ignore that inspired counsel. General Authority Emeritus H. Burke Peterson tells of a troubled young man from a "good" LDS home where these opportunities to teach were not taken:

> On one occasion my young friend told me he was sure that his parents loved him, but, oh, how he wished they cared about him! You know, to a young person there can be a difference. He said he wished just once as he went out the door they would ask him where he was going and when he would be home. He wanted them to give him some guidelines. He confessed that he wasn't always sure of the judgments that were left to him. If only they had cared enough. Now, years later, the offspring of this family have experienced the birth of illegitimate children, divorce in their own marriages, runaways, drug addiction, and most everything else that can be tragic in our lives. ("Help for Parents," *Ensign*, May 1975, 52–54)

The most effective fathers in the Book of Mormon are the ones who taught their children. From his son's account, imagine the family home evenings Enos must have had with his father:

> Behold, it came to pass that I, Enos, knowing my father that he was a just man—for he taught me in his language, and also in the nurture and admonition of the Lord—and blessed be the name of my God for it—
>
> And I will tell you of the wrestle which I had before God, before I received a remission of my sins.
>
> Behold, I went to hunt beasts in the forests; and the words which I had often heard my father speak concerning eternal life, and the joy of the saints, sunk deep into my heart. (Enos 1:1–3)

Nephi too was taught by his father:

> I, Nephi, having been born of goodly parents, therefore I was taught somewhat in all the learning of my father; and having seen many afflictions in the course of my days, nevertheless, having been highly favored of the Lord in all my days; yea, having had a great knowledge of the goodness and the mysteries of God, therefore I make a record of my proceedings in my days. (1 Nephi 1:1)
>
> And now I, Nephi, do not make a full account of the things which my father hath written, for he hath written many things which he saw in visions and in dreams; and he also hath written many things which he prophesied and spake unto his children, of which I shall not make a full account. (1 Nephi 1:16)

Even when we do teach our kids, sometimes as parents we become discouraged in thinking that our children are not listening, or not heeding our counsel. Lehi surely felt that way as he observed his two oldest sons (see 1 Nephi 15:2–3). Parents can only do their best, of course, to implore, plead, and gently teach by the Spirit. Most children will respond favorably—if not immediately, then at a later time. We should never give up on them. When parents discover a truth or insight that brings them joy, they naturally want to share it with their children. An example of this is when Lehi shares with his family his vision of the tree of life: "And as I partook of the fruit thereof it filled my soul with exceedingly great joy; wherefore, I began to be desirous that my family should partake of it also; for I knew that it was desirable above all other fruit" (1 Nephi 8:12).

There are many ways and opportunities to teach gospel principles besides the "big three"—family home evening, family scripture study, and family prayer. Parents also teach by example, by informal instruction, by asking questions formally and informally, by listening, and by establishing righteous traditions. In fact, parents are always teaching children something—it just may not be what they thought they were teaching, or what they intended to teach. Example is certainly one of the best ways to help children learn to cope successfully with the world around them.

A juvenile-court judge once told me that many of the children who come before her bench to be tried for some societal offense were not always there because their parents hadn't instructed them properly, but because the parents' *behavior* had actually taught them a far different message.

Why teach? I think the following song by Natalie Sleeth answers this question very well:

How Will They Know?
How will they know, the ones for whom we care,
That God is love and with us ev'rywhere,
That life is good with blessings all can share?
How will they know unless we teach them so?

How will they learn that though they go astray,
God will forgive and help them find the way?
How will they feel the Spirit day by day?
How will they unless we teach them so?

How will they grow in wisdom and delight?
How will they choose to follow what is right?
How can they trust the future will be bright?
How will they know unless we show them?

How will they live when they at last are grown?
What will they give to children of their own?
Will they reflect the values we have shown?
How will they know, as on through life they go?
How will they know unless we strive to teach them so?
(*Children's Songbook*, 182)

For the following three chapters I will discuss separate elements of teaching that I found displayed in the Book of Mormon by prophets and by the Lord Himself—the best teacher of all. There is a wealth of information from their examples on *when* to teach, *what* to teach, and *how* to teach. I'll discuss these topics extensively, with additional helps and examples in an appendix at the end, but I hope you will look for additional examples as you study the writings of Book of Mormon prophets in order to receive inspiration concerning your own family.

When to Teach

As you study the Book of Mormon, you will be inspired when to teach; there is a time to teach and a time to listen. For more help in recognizing such opportunities, you would benefit from reading "Teaching Moments in Family Life," a section in *Teaching, No Greater Call: A Resource Guide for Gospel Teaching* (published by The Church of Jesus Christ of Latter-day Saints, see pages 140–41; also see later sections of this book). Regardless of our need to be aware of the correct setting for this or that lesson, there is a general approach concerning when we should teach our children core values. The prophets have warned us that children do not grow up in a vacuum—they are always learning something and it may not always be something good. Parents would do well to teach their children wholesome values while they are young and pliable, eager to learn and please, and while lifelong habits are being formed. Elder Henry B. Eyring expressed his feelings this way:

> We have the greatest opportunity with the young. The best time to teach is early, while children are still immune to the temptations of their mortal enemy, and long before the words of truth may be harder for them to hear in the noise of their personal struggles.
>
> A wise parent would never miss a chance to gather children together to learn of the doctrine of Jesus Christ. Such moments are so rare in comparison with the efforts of the enemy. For every hour the power of doctrine is introduced into a child's life, there may be hundreds of hours of messages and images denying or ignoring the saving truths. ("The Power of Teaching Doctrine," Ensign, May 1999, 74)

We haven't a moment to lose. Alma pleaded with his young son, "And now, O my son Helaman, behold, thou art in thy youth, and therefore, I beseech of thee that thou wilt hear my words and learn of me" (Alma 36:3). And again from Alma: "O, remember, my son, and learn wisdom in thy youth; yea, learn in thy youth to keep the commandments of God" (Alma 37:35).

The stripling warriors were taught by their mothers in their youth. Later this teaching proved invaluable to them and their countrymen, perhaps saving their own lives and the lives of the Nephites (see Alma 53:20–21).

On their missions, Helaman's two sons Nephi and Lehi recalled the things they learned at the knee of their father when they were young. As you read the account (see Helaman 5:5–14), note how many times the word *remember* appears. They were admonished to "remember, remember"—one of the prerequisites of gratitude. *Remember* your ancestors and the legacy they left you, *remember* the Savior and what He did for you, and *remember* the blessings you enjoy because of them and Him.

From all the above examples we learn that parents must teach their children in the home, for children can't be expected to remember something they've never been taught. How important it is that young adults who leave the home for school, marriage, or to serve missions have a reserve of memories to bless them.

In my own family we tried very hard to regularly gather our family of six children around us every Monday night for family home evening, but we often wondered just what they were retaining. Our youngest boy, for instance, often appeared to be dozing or uninterested during our study sessions. Was any of this reaching him? we wondered. We were both surprised and delighted, however, when, years later while serving a mission, he wrote home about how those family home evening lessons and scriptures came to him as he was teaching others, and he found himself quoting his father on many points of the gospel. We rejoiced. His mind had absorbed more than we gave him credit for; we were grateful we hadn't become discouraged and given up.

One last point. Be sensitive to your child's readiness to learn. Look at the example in 1 Nephi 11–14. Here we find a good example of a father responding to a child's need to know. Nephi went to his Father in Heaven for understanding. He was not put off with "I'm too busy right now" or "Go ask someone else." His inquiry was not ignored or belittled. He was not told he was too young to understand. He was taught. Not only was he shown what his father saw, but he was taught the plan of salvation, including the history of mankind from the beginning of the world to its end. He was taught the difference between good and evil, that he could make wise choices. The Lord knew Nephi's heart and knew what he was capable of absorbing. The Lord recognized a teaching moment when He saw one. What other lessons come to your mind from this account?

Principle 1
The Importance of Teaching—What to Teach

Sadly, there are some who feel they do their children a disservice by so-called "brainwashing them" with a certain religious or moral set of values while they are young. They think they should let their children make those discoveries as they mature. Of this philosophy President David O. McKay chided parents: "There are parents who say: 'We will let our children grow to manhood and womanhood and choose for themselves.' In taking this attitude, parents fail in the discharging of a parental responsibility. . . . It is the responsibility of parents to teach religion to their children" (*Treasures of Life*, comp. Clare Middlemiss [Salt Lake City, UT: Deseret Book], 1965, 74). President Brigham Young gave this caution, "If we do not take the pains to train our children, to teach and instruct them concerning these revealed truths, the condemnation will be upon us, as parents, or at least in a measure" (*Discourses of Brigham Young*, sel. and arr. by John A. Widtsoe [Salt Lake City, UT: Deseret Book], 1954, 207).

Perhaps this disregard of parental responsibility comes because some parents themselves are not entirely sure where truth is anymore. They aren't sure what to teach. The philosophies of men have muddied the water, blurred the vision—made us doubt those things our parents and grandparents were so sure of.

Though countless lessons will jump out at you as you read from the Book of Mormon, in this chapter I will discuss a few principles that are taught repeatedly and with great forcefulness. They include love and service, gratitude, the use of agency, tolerance, valuing scripture, prayer, obedience, pure doctrine, and the joy of work. The plan of salvation is repeatedly explained, as are the first principles of the gospel: faith in Jesus Christ, repentance, baptism, and the gift of the Holy Ghost; thus they are also important concepts to teach our children.

Teach Love and Service

King Benjamin gave the scriptural injunction to teach children love and service. "But ye will teach them to walk in the ways of truth and soberness; ye will teach them to love one another, and to serve one another" (Mosiah 4:15).

Teach children to love and serve one another, and they will discover the great key to personal joy, self-worth, and effective ways to build relationships. We learn to love the ones we serve. All parents know this, for surely the one who needs nurturing the most—the sick one, the lonely one, or the sad one—is the one our heart goes out to at that particular time. The more of ourselves we invest in another human being, the more our love for that person grows.

I gained this insight from an experience we had with our daughter. She was just a few months short of the qualifying age for going to youth conference. As she sat in sacrament meeting and heard all the wonderful things the youth would be doing that weekend, she couldn't help feeling a little sorry for herself; however, when she learned that an acquaintance of hers was unable to go because of finances, she determined she could do something about that.

In her mind, helping another girl to go would be the next best thing to actually going herself. She worked hard all week, earning and saving money. When she told us her plan, we were more than happy to help her find jobs to do. This friend never knew where the funds came from, but she went to the conference that year and had a wonderful time. Terri didn't go, but she too had a wonderful time. And the strangest thing happened. Somehow, though this young woman never found out about Terri's efforts, she and Terri became best friends that year. It was the beginning of a friendship that lasted throughout junior high and high school. Terri had invested something of herself in a friend, and this young woman had sensed her love and responded.

Our missionaries are another good example of how service helps love develop. Have you ever listened to missionary reports and not heard them say how much they learned to love the people they served? We read over and over again in Alma how much joy he and the sons of Mosiah felt as they worked to serve the Lord by serving His children as missionaries (see Alma 26:30; 29:9; 34:28; 36:24–25).

In the following scripture, one can't help but be impressed with how much Mormon, like the parent of an erring child, loved his people because he had served them all his life in spite of their wickedness and hard-heartedness. "Behold, I had led them, notwithstanding their wickedness I had led them many times to battle, and had loved them, according to the love of God which was in me, with all my heart; and my soul had been poured out in prayer unto my God all the day long for them; nevertheless, it was without faith, because of the hardness of their hearts" (Mormon 3:12).

Even though we are sinful and make mistakes, our Savior loves us because we are His children, and because of the investment He made in us long ago, and which He continues to make as He intercedes in our behalf with the Father. Parents can teach a child to love an unkind sibling or peer by providing opportunities for them to serve the erring individual. Eventually that sibling or friend will respond to the love directed toward him.

Teach Gratitude

In Amulek's great sermon to the people of Ammonihah, he admonishes his brethren to be thankful: "Humble yourselves even to the dust, and worship God, in whatsoever place ye may be in, in spirit and in truth; and that ye live in thanksgiving daily, for the many mercies and blessings which he doth bestow upon you" (Alma 34:38).

President Gordon B. Hinckley commented on gratitude in this way: "Absence of gratitude is the mark of the narrow, uneducated mind. It bespeaks a lack of knowledge and the ignorance of self-sufficiency. It expresses itself in ugly egotism and frequently in wanton mischief. . . . Where there is appreciation, there is courtesy, there is concern for the rights and property of others. Without appreciation, there is arrogance and evil" ("With All Thy Getting Get Understanding," First Presidency Message, *Ensign*, Aug. 1988, 2). Interestingly, the Roman orator Cicero declared that gratitude was "not only the greatest of virtues, but the parent of all the others" (cited in Joseph B. Wirthlin, "Living in Thanksgiving Daily," *Ensign*, Sept. 2001, 6).

A grateful person is a happy person. Test this axiom yourself. You simply cannot be unhappy while you are counting your blessings and giving thanks. But sometimes, when the days are dark, we need a reminder that the sun did shine once and that it will shine again. And sometimes we are so busy managing all the positive blessings in our lives we forget to recognize them as such and return thanks. Here's a small example: the day before my forty-fifth birthday I suddenly realized my vision was blurry when I tried to read. For the next ten years I fought the verdict that I truly needed glasses and murmured every time I had to put them on, or worse yet, had to go find them. Finally, it dawned on me that my glasses were not my enemy, but my blessing. What on earth did people do before they had glasses to complain about? Now when I go look for them, I am thankful I have them—somewhere. All I have to do is find them!

Teach that Agency and Accountability Go Together

The Jaredites desired a king to rule over them and even though Jared and his brother felt it unwise, the people were so insistent on having a king that the brothers relented. Even though Jared did not approve of the decision, he did not become angry and leave them to ruin, but he tried to support their decision by providing the best possible candidate for king (see Ether 6:22–24).

Ann Pritt sheds light on this perspective:

> Moral agency is an integral part of our mortal experience—indeed, it is a central feature of our Heavenly Father's plan. Our purpose in mortality is to exercise our agency in ways that lead us back to Christ. Yet some individuals use their agency to make evil choices, and others suffer deeply as a result.
>
> In most cases Heavenly Father does not prevent individuals from accomplishing evil; to do so would compromise the agency of all of His children [as illustrated in Alma 14:11]. He knows that moral agency is a precious gift that must be protected, for the proper and best use of it will result in the greatest gift of all—exaltation and eternal life. ("Healing the Spiritual Wounds of Sexual Abuse," *Ensign*, Apr. 2001, 60–61)

The Lord respects agency, but He also establishes laws to assist us in returning to Him. There are important "teaching" consequences for every law. Jacob's "conference address" in 2 Nephi 9:28–29 goes into great detail about the need for laws and punishment and the wisdom of "hearkening to the counsels of God." In this address he lists ten temptations and their consequences. Look for them as you read this passage in your own scriptures. After reading the section, note Jacob's closing statement on the topic: "Therefore, cheer up your hearts, and remember that ye are free to act for yourselves—to choose the way of everlasting death or the way of eternal life" (2 Nephi 10:23).

Teaching this principle to our children goes a long way toward helping them be responsible and toward helping us let go of self-negativity while our children are experimenting with their agency. In Ether 12:35–37, Moroni expresses his fear that the Gentiles would fail in charity because of his weakness in not being able to write powerfully enough (see verses 24–26). But the Lord taught him that his task was to teach; the Gentiles would have to decide if they would obey, as the choice was theirs. Like Moroni, our job as parents is to teach our children. It's their job to choose whether they will accept or reject that which we teach them. We cannot make that decision for them, nor are we accountable for their decisions or the consequences that follow. We are held accountable only if we do not teach them.

Teach Tolerance

How does a child learn hate and fear, or prejudice and intolerance towards those who are different than they are? Mostly from the example of those closest to him. A child picks up attitudes at a very young age by observing and listening to the actions and words of parents and family members. As children mature and begin to form ideas of their own, they also learn to be tolerant or intolerant of others' ideas based on how their parents react when faced with compromises or different ideals. In a tolerant, nonjudgmental atmosphere, a child is more apt to feel safe in expressing his ideas without ridicule or condemnation; thus the lines of communication will remain open. As your child communicates with you openly and honestly, opportunities to teach become more apparent. A parent and child can look at an idea and discuss its merits and pitfalls objectively, thereby assisting a child in making wise decisions.

When we tell our children of the persecutions to early Latter-day Saints, we might also take the opportunity to point out that if others had been tolerant of the Saints' beliefs, all the pain, death, and misery experienced by the Saints might have been avoided. Therefore, we, of all people, should be sensitive to the rights of others to worship or think as they desire. Along these lines, the Nephites had legal precedents. Alma 30:11 explains: "For there was a law that men should be judged according to their crimes. Nevertheless, there was no law against a man's belief; therefore, a man was punished only for the crimes which he had done; therefore all men were on equal grounds." And King Mosiah, in Mosiah 27:2–4, expresses this thought:

> And it came to pass that king Mosiah sent a proclamation throughout the land round about that there should not any unbeliever persecute any of those who belonged to the church of God.
>
> And there was a strict command throughout all the churches that there should be no persecutions among them, that there should be an equality among all men;
>
> That they should let no pride nor haughtiness disturb their peace; that every man should esteem his neighbor as himself.

Teach the Value of the Scriptures

President Hinckley counseled parents:

> Read to your children. Read the story of the Son of God. Read to them from the New Testament. Read to them from the Book of Mormon. It will take time, and you are very busy, but it will prove to be a great blessing in your lives as well as in their lives. And there will grow in their hearts a great love for the Savior of the world, the only perfect man who walked the earth. He will become to them a very real living being, and His great Atoning sacrifice, as they grow to manhood and womanhood, will take on a new and more glorious meaning in their lives. ("Excerpts from Recent Addresses of President Gordon B. Hinckley," in *Ensign*, Apr. 1998, 74)

Quoting President Marion G. Romney, President Ezra Taft Benson echoed the above sentiment:

> If we would avoid adopting the evils of the world, we must pursue a course which will daily feed our minds . . . and call them [our thoughts] back to the things of the Spirit. I know of no better way to do this than by reading the Book of

> Mormon. I counsel you . . . to make reading in the Book of Mormon a few minutes each day a lifelong practice. I feel certain that if, in our homes, parents will read from the Book of Mormon prayerfully and regularly, both by themselves and with their children, the spirit of that great book will come to permeate our homes and all who dwell therein. ("Cleansing the Inner Vessel," *Ensign*, May 1986, 5)

We have been counseled by our Church leaders in almost every conference to read the scriptures daily with our children. Like many good LDS parents, we resolve each October and April to start over again. And we may even succeed for a few days or even weeks. Then things start to fall apart. Somebody's schedule changes and it's just too hard to find a time to get everyone together, so we drop it—meaning to get back to it soon. But in many cases it just doesn't happen. Some of us get discouraged because, for all our efforts, the children just don't seem to understand the words anyway and we wonder if it's worth it. Sometimes we just get distracted with other pressures, and our good intentions go down the drain. What message does this inconsistency send to the children? How can we teach them to truly love and value our precious scriptures? The advice of the prophet is to never give up. We haven't failed until we've quit trying. Our good intentions may get derailed time and time again, but we shouldn't let it be for long. We should jump right back in with a new plan, a new time, and renewed determination.

In April conference of 1975, Elder H. Burke Peterson told of his own family's struggle to consistently read the scriptures together. They were confronted with the same challenges and obstacles we all are, but they persisted in trying. Looking back on that experience and the blessings received from being obedient he concluded, "There shouldn't be—there mustn't be—one family in this church that doesn't take the time to read from the scriptures every day. Every family can do it in their own way. I have a testimony of this" ("Help for Parents," *Ensign*, May 1975, 52–54).

President Marion G. Romney taught in this personal example that even very young children benefit from reading scripture:

> I urge you to get acquainted with [the Book of Mormon]. Read it to your children; they are not too young to understand it. I remember reading it with one of my lads when he was very young. . . . I lay in the lower bunk and he in the upper bunk. We were each reading aloud alternate paragraphs of those last three marvelous chapters of Second Nephi. I heard his voice breaking and thought he had a cold. . . . As we finished, he said . . . "Daddy, do you ever cry when you read the Book of Mormon?"
>
> "Yes, son . . . sometimes the Spirit of the Lord so witnesses to my soul that the Book of Mormon is true that I do cry."
>
> "Well," he said, "that is what happened to me tonight." (Conference Report, Apr. 1949, 41, quoted by Elder Richard G. Scott, "The Power of a Strong Testimony," *Ensign*, Nov. 2001, 88)

President Romney's experience with his son reveals the power that can come even to the young when we read with them—even when the words are difficult to understand. I too had a similar experience. Years ago, when our children were very small, we determined, once again, that we would take the counsel of the Brethren and start a daily scripture program. My husband got our little ones out of bed at six o'clock every morning, gathering them up in their night clothes—even bedding if it was a cold morning—and deposited them on the couch in the family room. Then, facing them, he presented a large, illustrated Book of Mormon story, and paraphrased the text associated with the picture. That's the way we began. After going through the entire Book of Mormon, we went through the Church history series and then came back to the Book of Mormon without the pictures this time. We didn't know if they understood any of what we were reading, but we did feel good about being obedient and trying.

Years later when Becky, one of the youngest of our children at the time, was a grown mother, she told me of a visiting teaching experience she'd had recently. She and her companion were teaching a single mother who was trying to get her kids to cooperate with a daily scripture-reading program. This young mother was very discouraged, she confided, because her children just didn't seem to get anything out of it. Our daughter said to her, "Keep trying. Don't give up. When I was a little girl my family read the scriptures together early every morning and I didn't understand them either, but I do remember the feeling it gave me. I knew they must be important for my dad to get us up early every morning, and I loved the way it felt to be snuggled up all together on the couch while he read to us. That was the beginning of my love for the scriptures. To this day, whenever I open my scriptures to read, I remember that feeling."

So much for children being too young to understand! What about busy schedules? If you talk to your family about the importance of the scriptures and ask for their cooperation, then pray together as a family for the Lord's help, you will find a way. And while you're having this discussion, share with them just why reading the Book of Mormon is so important.

"For behold, it is as easy to give heed to the word of Christ, which will point to you a straight course to eternal bliss, as it was for our fathers to give heed to this compass, which would point unto them a straight course to the promised land" (Alma 37:44).

Elder Carlos E. Asay summed up the importance of reading scripture: "Few of us would go astray or lose our way if we regarded the scriptures as our personal guide or compass. The iron rod is the word of God, and if held to, we will not fail" ("Opposition to the Work of God," *Ensign*, Nov. 1981, 68).

Teach the Value and Power of Prayer

The Lord commanded us to "watch and pray always" (2 Nephi 32:9; Alma 34:27; 3 Nephi 18:15, 18) and to teach our children to pray (see D&C 68:28). When children grow up in a home where mother, father, brother, and sister kneel together each night and morning in prayer, where they offer their own prayers alone in secret, they receive two legacies: one is a trust in and appreciation for the Lord and His willingness to listen to our concerns, and second is a love and appreciation for family members as they support each other and hear one another open their hearts to the heavens. Knowing they are never alone, that they always have the Lord to turn to, and that no matter where they are, someone at home is praying for them, are some of the great realizations a child takes with her as she faces the trials and temptations of life.

Our children will follow our lead. If they see and hear us praying for power in our own lives to resist temptation (see 3 Nephi 18:15, 18), for personal inspiration (see 3 Nephi 14:7–8; Moroni 10:3–5), for strength and peace of mind (see Alma 58:10–12), for our loved ones (see Enos 1:9; Mosiah 27:11–17), for our enemies (see Alma 10:22–23; 3 Nephi 12:44), for those who haven't yet received the gospel (see Alma 6:6), for gratitude for our blessings (see Alma 34:38) and especially for our children, their hearts will be softened.

Elder Loren C. Dunn tells this powerful story of his father's impact on him:

> When I sat across from President David O. McKay and was first called to this calling [member of the Seventy] some 32 years ago, I remember that after he discussed with me what would be expected, he then charged me to serve by asking me to carry out this calling in a way that would be pleasing to my own father. That was enough of a challenge for a lifetime. President McKay knew my father, who had been a stake president for 20 years, and I looked on my father as one of the greatest men I knew. My first understanding of how

> important I was to my father and how real the Savior was, was when I heard him pray for us in family prayer. ("Because My Father Sent Me," *Ensign,* May 2000, 81)

The Lord expects us to speak to Him regularly, just as any parent wants to hear from his children to know how they are doing, to hear words of gratitude, to give them counsel when needed, and to offer forgiveness when forgiveness is needed. Communication between parent and child is essential, and it is essential that we speak to our Father in Heaven. Recall His chastisement of Jared for his failure to call upon the name of the Lord (see Ether 2:14).

The Lord taught us how to pray (see 3 Nephi 13:6–13) and then showed us; one of the most touching passages in the Book of Mormon is the account of the Savior Himself kneeling in prayer to the Father in behalf of His children (see 3 Nephi 17:14–21; 19:17–28, 31–33). What a great example of love and humility and the importance of prayer—if the Savior prays, then it is important that we do so too.

Jeffrey R. Holland declared:

> The praying Christ. That is the example to which we are to point others. . . . The Christ who is one with the Father in at least one way that we may be united with him as well—through prayer. . . . Give your (children) this promise as Christ gave it to the Nephite multitude—"And whatsoever ye shall ask the Father in my name, which is right, believing that ye shall receive, behold it shall be given unto you" (3 Nephi 18:20). They need to believe that. And they will if you believe it. (CES Symposium, BYU, Aug. 9, 1994, 21)

Teach the Wisdom of Obedience

There are many examples of obedience throughout the Book of Mormon, and just as many examples of the folly of disobedience.

If Lehi hadn't been obedient to the Lord's counsel, his family would have suffered the same fate as those who laughed at and scorned him and were destroyed along with the city (see 1 Nephi 2:2–3; 17:14). If Nephi hadn't been obedient in obtaining the plates and then later in writing their history, the family and the generations that followed would not have had the plates of brass, nor would we have the Book of Mormon (see 1 Nephi 4; 9:5–6). If the sons of Helaman had not been obedient, they would not have been victorious in battle (see Alma 57:21; 58:40). The list goes on.

Henry B. Eyring warns:

> When we reject the counsel which comes from God, we do not choose to be independent of outside influence. *We choose another influence.* We reject the protection of a perfectly loving, all-powerful, all-knowing Father in Heaven, whose whole purpose, as that of His Beloved Son, is to give us eternal life, to give us all that He has, and to bring us home again in families to the arms of His love. In rejecting His counsel, we choose the influence of another power, whose purpose is to make us miserable and whose motive is hatred. . . .
>
> Every time in my life when I have chosen to delay following inspired counsel or decided that I was an exception, I came to know that I had put myself in harm's way. Every time that I have listened to the counsel of prophets, felt it confirmed in prayer, and then followed it, I have found that I moved toward safety. ("Finding Safety in Counsel," *Ensign*, May 1997, 24, emphasis added)

Teach the Doctrine

"And now, as the preaching of the word had a great tendency to lead the people to do that which was just—yea, it had had more powerful effect upon the minds of the people than the sword, or anything else, which had happened unto them—therefore Alma thought it was expedient that they should try the virtue of the word of God" (Alma 31:5).

Alma believed, as President Boyd K. Packer does, that "true doctrine, understood, changes attitudes and behavior. The study of the doctrines of the gospel will improve behavior quicker than a study of behavior will improve behavior" ("Do Not Fear," *Ensign*, May 2004, 79).

When Alma's son Corianton came home from his mission because of misconduct, his father was directed by the Spirit to bring his son to repentance by explaining the role of the Savior in his son's life (see Alma 39:15–19), the importance of his decisions, agency and accountability (see 40:6–15), the resurrection and final judgment (see 40:2–5,16–23; 41:2), the necessity of an Atonement (including the justice and mercy of God), and the necessity of repentance (see Alma 42). In other words, he reviewed for him the entire plan of salvation—pure doctrine.

President Ezra Taft Benson taught this principle:

> The Lord works from the inside out. The world works from the outside in. The world would take people out of the slums. Christ takes the slums out of the people, and then they take themselves out of the slums. The world would mold men by changing their environment. Christ changes men, who then change their environment. The world would shape human behavior, but Christ can change human nature. ("Born of God," *Ensign*, Nov. 1985, 5)

The Lord has a plan for His children, and He has gone to a lot of trouble to see that we understand its provisions. In His wisdom He knows that if a child can be led to understand the reasons behind a law or rule, he is more apt to accept and follow it. When Nephi asked for an understanding of his father's insistence that the family leave Jerusalem, he was given instruction by the Lord on the entire plan of salvation (see 1 Nephi 13). Not only did he try to teach it to his rebellious brothers on many occasions, but he wrote it down for us to read two thousand years later (see 1 Nephi 19). Alma and Amulek changed Zeezrom's heart by teaching him the plan of salvation (see Alma 11:39–45). Samuel the Lamanite called the wicked Nephites to repentance by teaching them the doctrines of salvation (see Helaman 14:15–19), and Christ taught the Nephites His gospel after His resurrection (see 3 Nephi 12).

Other important components to the plan that are taught throughout the Book of Mormon include repentance (see Mosiah 4; Alma 3:33; Ether 11:20; 12:3–22; Moroni 8:25–26, 29), faith (see Alma 32; Mormon 9:25; Moroni 7:25–26), baptism (see 2 Nephi 9:23) by one having authority (see Mosiah 18:17–18), covenants (see 2 Nephi 7–8; 9:1), the need for charity (see 2 Nephi 26:30; Alma 7:23–24; Moroni 7), and the wonder of the Atonement (see 2 Nephi 25:13).

Teach the Joy of Work

Elder Neal A. Maxwell shared the following thoughts on the importance of work:

> Though I murmured as a young man at times with chores, I have acquired in this passage of time a hardened view of the spiritual necessity of work. Even if work were not an economic necessity, it is a spiritual necessity. If I have any concern about the younger generation, speaking collectively, it is that a few of our wonderful youth and young adults in the Church are unstretched—they have almost a free pass. Perks are provided, including cars complete with fuel and insurance—all paid for by parents who sometimes listen in vain for a few courteous and appreciative words. What is thus taken for granted, however innocently, tends to underwrite selfishness and a sense of entitlement. Selfishness and a sense of entitlement don't need any transfusions in our society today. As I look at the rising generation, the gospel of work, which is part of the fulness of the gospel, will need more attention, not less. ("Insights from My Life," *Ensign*, Aug. 2000, 7)

President Gordon B. Hinckley, in a BYU fireside in March of 1992, said of work:

> I believe in the gospel of work. There is no substitute under the heavens for productive labor. It is the process by which dreams become realities. It is the process by which idle visions become dynamic achievements.
>
> Most of us are inherently lazy. We would rather play than work. We would rather loaf than work. A little play and a little loafing are good. But it is work that spells the difference in the life of a man or woman. It is stretching our minds and utilizing the skills of our hands that lifts us from mediocrity. It is work that provides the food we eat, the clothing we wear, the homes in which we live. We cannot deny the need for work with skilled hands and educated minds if we are to grow and prosper individually and if our nation is to stand tall before the world.
>
> When Adam and Eve were expelled from the garden, Jehovah declared: "In the sweat of thy face shalt thou eat bread, till thou return unto the ground" (Gen. 3:19). ("I Believe," *Ensign*, Aug. 1992, 4)

As a parent I've discovered, as I'm sure you have, that there are several reasons to insist children participate in "home work." Nephi figured it out when he taught his little band of "children" to work:

> And I did teach my people to build buildings, and to work in all manner of wood, and of iron, and of copper, and of brass, and of steel, and of gold, and of silver, and of precious ores, which were in great abundance.
>
> And it came to pass that I, Nephi, did cause my people to be industrious, and to labor with their hands.

> And it came to pass that we lived after the manner of happiness. (2 Nephi 5:15, 17, 27)

The first reason to teach work is that successful living takes hard work. Many times I see parents who think they are doing their children a favor by not insisting they help at home. Some feel their children should be allowed to play and be idle because they'll have to work soon enough when they grow up. I feel sorry for those children. They are never allowed to experience the joy of a job well done, of feeling needed in the family, of developing the confidence that they can do something helpful and productive. I often wonder if this void in the life of many of our young people plays a part in some of the depression and teen suicides we see today. Could it be they simply do not feel needed and are starving for a sense of worth? The Lord has no place for the idler in His kingdom. Children love to help when they are little and should be allowed to do what they can at a very early age. These responsibilities can increase as the child's ability increases. There is a correlation between work and happiness.

The second reason is because busy hands stay out of trouble.

> And this city became an exceeding stronghold ever after; and in this city they did guard the prisoners of the Lamanites; yea, even within a wall which they had caused them to build with their own hands. Now Moroni was compelled to cause the Lamanites to labor, because it was easy to guard them while at their labor; and he desired all his forces when he should make an attack upon the Lamanites. (Alma 53:5)

Children who are working are not only happier but less apt to get into trouble than children who have little or nothing to do. Years ago, when our children were young and we lived in a neighborhood of working mothers, our children's friends would often come home from school in the afternoon, finding no one home and nothing to do. Their next stop was our house to see if our children could play. We had a rule that family chores had to be done before play or TV, so often our children were busy. I found that rather than go home and be bored, the neighborhood children chose to stay and work. They enjoyed having something useful to do, and perhaps, had they been left to their own devices, they might have created some mischief as bored children often do.

As I did some babysitting for one or two of the working mothers, I found that babysitting was much easier if I could keep them busy with small jobs or projects. Again I found that bored children often quarreled or got into mischief. If I heard quarreling, I assumed they were not enjoying their free play time and immediately found a job for them to do.

Reason number three for having your children work is that you need the help.

> Therefore, all the prisoners of the Lamanites did join the people of Ammon, and did begin to labor exceedingly, tilling the ground, raising all manner of grain, and flocks and herds of every kind; and thus were the Nephites relieved from a great burden; yea, insomuch that they were relieved from all the prisoners of the Lamanites. (Alma 62:29)

Sometimes teaching young children to work seems to take more time and effort than it's worth, but if you take the time while they are young and still eager to help, the benefits will pay off as they mature and are able to work on their own.

And that brings us to reason number four—which is probably one of the most important reasons: a crucial bonding takes place as parent and child work together. Children mimic what they see their parents doing. They want to be with them, to be like them. Wise parents will take advantage of this innate desire and, rather than sending a child off to complete a chore, will invite the child to help do the chore well, teaching and training by example. A child will grow up equating the good feelings she had working with her mom or dad with the work itself; and as she matures, she will find joy and take pride in accomplishing tasks alone. She will also feel a certain respect for the work itself. Children will realize that if it is important enough for their parents to do it, it must be important (see Alma 1:25–28).

When our grown children get together and talk about their memories, some of the happiest they recall are the times Dad went on the paper route with whoever had it at the time (we seemed to have passed that job down from child to child as each outgrew the need), or the times we had what we called a "Super Saturday" and all worked in the yard together raking, weeding, picking the fruit, or whatever was needed at the time. We often ended these Saturday work marathons with a barbecue in the backyard or a swim party at the local pool.

Work is food for the soul, and the Lord will not tolerate an idler. In the Book of Mormon idleness is coupled with wickedness (see 1 Nephi 12:23; Alma 1:32; 22:28; 24:18; 38:12). Ours is a gospel of work; let's teach our children to enjoy it. "Yea, and all their priests and teachers should labor with their own hands for their support, in all cases save it were in sickness, or in much want; and doing these things, they did abound in the grace of God" (Mosiah 27:5).

Principle 1

The Importance of Teaching—How to Teach

In the scriptures we have numerous examples of how to teach children and how not to teach them. On the positive side, the Lord asks us to teach "by persuasion, by long-suffering, by gentleness and meekness, and by love unfeigned" (D&C 121:41). By example we teach character traits such as "kindness, and pure knowledge, which shall . . . greatly enlarge the soul" (D&C 121:42). "Each mother and father should lay aside selfish interests and avoid any thought of hypocrisy, physical force, or evil speaking," said Elder Russell M. Nelson ("Set in Order Thy House," *Ensign*, Nov. 2001, 71). We are to teach topics by inspiration, and teach them so plainly that there will be no misunderstanding in a child's mind as to the meaning of a precept. Of course, we must always keep in mind a child's stage of development and ability to understand our explanations. The Book of Mormon helps us discover appropriate and helpful teaching techniques that include repetition, question/answer, story, allegory, the use of incentives, the importance of "likening" scriptures to present situations to help children identify essential life lessons, the importance of commitment and participating in the learning process, and the importance of speaking softly rather than emotionally and harshly (as we may be prone to do).

In this section we'll cover all of these concepts in detail, but first let's look at an overall teaching perspective found in Alma 38:2–11. Let's explore the model Alma used with his son Shiblon.

Verses 2–3: Alma expressed confidence in his son's abilities and spirituality.
Verse 4: Alma showed understanding and empathy for his son's experiences.
Verse 5: Alma reminded Shiblon of the power that comes to us through our covenants with God.
Verse 6: He shared his own testimony with his son.
Verses 7–9: He admitted his own past mistakes to Shiblon, hoping his son would learn from them and not duplicate them.
Verses 10–14: He counseled Shiblon as a tender father.
Verse 15: Alma blessed his son and sent him on his mission.

We would do well to look closely at the steps Alma took and the order in which they came. Sometimes when we're very excited/anxious about the message we want to get across to our children, we forget the preparatory steps that are essential to soften hearts and prepare loved ones for counsel. Ideally we should plead with the Lord as Alma did for help in talking to his son before the confrontation.

Teach by the Spirit

In Alma 39, Alma used a different approach in his interview with Corianton than he did with Helaman or Shiblon. In fact, his comments seem to contradict the principles mentioned previously. When you first examine what Alma said to Corianton, the reaction might be, "Oops! He broke all the rules of good parenting." He appeared to compare him with his brothers, and then he went straight to the problem—confronting Corianton about the serious sins he committed while serving a mission. That approach would normally cause a child to immediately put up a defensive stance. A less humble son might have been tempted to stalk off angrily and be discouraged as well as defensive. However, further reading into the interview reveals that Alma was teaching his son by the Spirit as it dictated to him what he should say. With Corianton, he used the counsel in D&C 121:43–44, wherein the Lord says there are times when we must reprove "with sharpness" as "moved upon by the Holy Ghost" and quickly thereafter "showing forth an increase in love." The Spirit knew Corianton's heart. A wise parent will always take time to seek heavenly wisdom for direction when correcting a child. Then they are prepared to proceed with confidence to teach or discipline their children.

Notice the word *command* in Alma's counsel. We are not often directed to command children, but rather to exhort, plead, and entreat (see D&C 121:41–42), but Alma is repeating verbatim what inspiration dictated to him: "And now the Spirit of the Lord doth say unto me: Command thy children to do good, lest they lead away the hearts of many people to destruction; therefore I command you, my son, in the fear of God, that ye refrain from your iniquities" (Alma 39:12).

There are more clues in this story that Alma is teaching by the Spirit. How did Alma perceive his son's concerns? Did he know Corianton well enough to know what troubled him? Or was he enlightened by the Spirit when he said, "Now my son, here is somewhat more I would say unto thee; for I perceive that thy mind is worried concerning the resurrection of the dead" (Alma 40:1). And again, "And now, my son, I have somewhat to say concerning the restoration. . . . And I perceive that thy mind has been worried also concerning this thing. But behold, I will explain it unto thee" (Alma 41:1). Then, once more, further along in the discussion, "And now, my son, I perceive there is somewhat more which doth worry your mind, which ye cannot understand" (Alma 42:1).

It's important to remember that while there are general guidelines, each child is a unique combination of many factors. They come with a different set of DNA, physical and emotional psyches, challenges, temperaments, weaknesses, and gifts. Isn't that what makes parenting so interesting and challenging? That's also what makes it so important that we rely on the Lord for inspiration, for He is the only one who really knows our child's—His child's—heart.

You can see why it is important to spend time with each child. There are no shortcuts to understanding a child's unique personality package. No wonder prophets plead for mothers to be with their children. It takes time and observation, playing, working, studying together, and sharing a multitude of experiences together. Alma, as a great father-leader, set an effective example for us to emulate.

In Alma 4:17–20 we learn that the Nephites (a symbol of family) are falling apart, and that wickedness, pride, and contentions are overtaking them. By the spirit of revelation, Alma is moved to leave the judgment seat to another and go among the people to teach and review with them basic gospel principles, give feedback, bear testimony, and recommit them to their covenants. Parents must be careful not to neglect their family; things can fall apart rather quickly when we fail to monitor each child. We too must pray, and seek help, and listen to divine counsel as Alma did. Our most important responsibility in mortality is our family, and we must not allow other distractions to take precedence. At times we may find it necessary, as Alma did, to stop, pull back from too many extracurricular activities that take us from home, delegate what we can to others, and spend more time with our family teaching or reteaching, establishing a closer relationship, reviewing values, bearing testimony, "sharpening the saw," and recommitting ourselves as a couple and as a family to gospel principles. Later we'll discuss the importance of spending time with children in more depth. Here, the focus is on the importance of parenting by the Spirit.

The Spirit inspires parents to take advantage of teaching moments as they occur. Some of the best sermons are taught spontaneously, when children least expect it, as this young woman describes:

> We always had family home evening and family scripture study, as well as monthly personal interviews with Dad, but I remember some small moments where I wasn't expecting

to be taught and I was. For example I remember that when I was in junior high I passed through a stage where I didn't like my mom and didn't treat her well. I also wasn't approachable. One night my dad had me fill up some water balloons with him. He and my brother were always playing tricks on each other. We went and sat on the roof and waited for my brother to come home to throw the balloons at him. While we were waiting, we looked at the stars and my dad said, "You know sweetheart, I don't know anyone in the world who loves you as much as your mom loves you. She would do anything for you." I started to cry, and I changed my behavior from that day.

In the following scripture we see Lehi taking the opportunity to teach his children, including the need to be firm with them when they are out of line:

> And when my father saw that the waters of the river emptied into the fountain of the Red Sea, he spake unto Laman, saying: O that thou mightest be like unto this river, continually running into the fountain of all righteousness!
>
> And he also spake unto Lemuel: O that thou mightest be like unto this valley, firm and steadfast, and immovable in keeping the commandments of the Lord!
>
> And it came to pass that my father did speak unto them in the valley of Lemuel, with power, being filled with the Spirit, until their frames did shake before him. And he did confound them, that they durst not utter against him; wherefore, they did as he commanded them. (1 Nephi 2:9, 10, 14)

My friend in the above story talked about having family home evening regularly, and that is certainly one of the best times to teach children in a more formal, consistent setting. But sometimes if not handled right, it can turn into a "family fight that begins and ends with prayer." Moroni teaches us: "And their meetings were conducted by the church after the manner of the workings of the Spirit, and by the power of the Holy Ghost; for as the power of the Holy Ghost led them whether to preach, or to exhort, or to pray or to supplicate, or to sing, even so it was done" (Moroni 6:9).

This scripture refers to Church meetings, but family home evening is one of the most important of all meetings. Its preparation should be accompanied by prayer as a parent seeks inspiration as to what to teach and how to present it to the family.

Here are more examples of prophet-fathers who taught by the Spirit: 1 Nephi 10:17; 2 Nephi 1:6; 25:11; Jacob 1:5–6; 2:7–11; Mosiah 1:6–8; Alma 5:43–48; 38:9. (This sequence would provide a good discussion for a family home evening.) Latter-day Saints also have the ability to receive inspiration for their own family members. As a parent reads scripture seeking answers to concerns about his children, the Lord can speak to him through the Spirit, helping him interpret a particular scripture in a way that is meaningful to him and his present concern. Doctrine and Covenants 46:15 and 1 Corinthians 12: 4 refer to this inspiration as "differences in administration" of the Spirit. The Prophet Joseph Smith taught that "this is the principle on which the government of heaven is conducted—by revelation adapted to the circumstances in which the children of the kingdom are placed" (*Teachings of the Prophet Joseph Smith*, sel. and arr. by Joseph Fielding Smith, Jr. [Salt Lake City, UT: Deseret Book], 1972, 256). We should work to enjoy the power of the Holy Ghost in our homes.

Teach with Love and Service

Closely related to teaching by the Spirit is teaching with love. President Howard W. Hunter points out that Heavenly Father's chief way of acting toward His children is by persuasion, patience, and long-suffering, "by gentle solicitation and by sweet enticement. He always acts with unfailing respect for the freedom and independence that we possess" ("The Golden Thread of Choice," *Ensign*, Nov. 1989, 17).

This was Jacob's approach when he said, "Wherefore we labored diligently among our people, that we might persuade them to come unto Christ, and partake of the goodness of God. . . . Wherefore, we would to God that we could persuade all men not to rebel against God" (Jacob 1:7–8).

What more poignant pleas can we read than that of Lehi trying to persuade his wayward sons to "shake off the awful chains by which [they] were bound" (2 Nephi 1:13–28)? Lehi might have easily become discouraged and given up because some of his sons would not listen to his counsel (see 1 Nephi 15:2–3), but he continued to love and entreat them. He never gave up. Most children will respond, in time, if our expressions are of love and are soft and inviting rather than harsh and angry.

Alma implored his people with his love and testimony (see Alma 13:27–30). We have great examples of missionaries being successful because they taught out of a love for their brethren and by giving genuine service (see Alma 17–18; 28:8). Missionaries today have far more success when they serve their investigators lovingly while presenting them the gospel (see also Alma 31:32–36).

Teaching with love is discussed more thoroughly in later sections of this book.

Teach through Righteous Family Traditions

Establishing family traditions is important for family unity. Simply going to church every Sunday as a family, for example, is a strong tradition that implants in the hearts of children what Latter-day Saints do and require for spiritual nourishment. A friend told me that her brother, although currently inactive, nevertheless still attends the general conference priesthood session with his father and brothers twice a year because it is a family tradition. That may well be the one thing that eventually draws him back into Church activity. Another individual disclosed that though he is far from home, he knows at a certain time each night his parents and brothers and sisters will be kneeling in prayer on his behalf.

President Spencer W. Kimball suggested giving father's blessings to family members at appropriate times. That's an appropriate tradition. He said, "A child leaving to go away to school or on a mission, a wife suffering stress, a family member being married or desiring guidance in making an important decision—all these are situations in which the father, in exercise of his patriarchal responsibility, can bless his family" (*The Teachings of Spencer W. Kimball,* [Salt Lake City, UT: Deseret Book], 1982, 506).

Another friend described a family tradition important to him: "Every weeknight, and especially Sunday evenings, we ate a meal together and we would talk and laugh long after the last person finished eating. Looking back, I know this was a crucial time for us to discuss family matters and bond together as family members." Other examples of helpful traditions include consistent family home evenings, daily scripture reading, and family prayer, morning and night.

Ammon's life might well have been saved because of the righteous traditions Lamoni learned from his fathers about God:

> And now, when the king heard these words, he said unto them: Now I know that it is the Great Spirit; and he has come down at this time to preserve your lives, that I might not slay you as I did your brethren. Now this is the Great Spirit of whom our fathers have spoken.
>
> Now this was the tradition of Lamoni, which he had received from his father, that there was a Great Spirit. (Alma 18:4–5)

Reading the scriptures together daily can be a great family tradition. King Benjamin taught his sons to read and love the scriptures (see Mosiah 1:2–4). We learn in Mosiah how not reading the scriptures leaves a void for unrighteous traditions to fill.

> I say unto you, my sons, were it not for these things, which have been kept and preserved by the hand of God, that we might read and understand of his mysteries, and have his commandments always before our eyes, that even our fathers would have dwindled in unbelief, and we should have been like unto our brethren, the Lamanites, who know nothing concerning these things, or even do not believe them when they are taught them, because of the traditions of their fathers, which are not correct. (Mosiah 1:5)

> They were a wild, and ferocious, and a blood-thirsty people, believing in the tradition of their fathers, which is this—Believing that they were driven out of the land of Jerusalem because of the iniquities of their fathers, and that they were wronged in the wilderness by their brethren, and they were also wronged while crossing the sea. (Mosiah 10:12)

> And thus they have taught their children that they should hate them, and that they should murder them, and that they should rob and plunder them, and do all they could to destroy them; therefore they have an eternal hatred towards the children of Nephi. (Mosiah 10:17)

Evil, unrighteous traditions teach just as effectively as do righteous traditions and can damage generations as it did the Lamanites. There was more mercy extended the Lamanites, in the long run, however, because of the false traditions that were handed down. "Behold, can you suppose that the Lord will spare you and come out in judgment against the Lamanites, when it is the tradition of their fathers that has caused their hatred, yea, and it has been redoubled by those who have dissented from us, while your iniquity is for the cause of your love of glory and the vain things of the world" (Alma 60:32).

Another person described how grateful she was that her parents were able to break some bad family characteristics or traditions they'd grown up with. They became what is called "transitional characters." They refused to carry on the negative family traditions of the past. She says:

> My parents each came from dismal family backgrounds where there was little positive communication or [any] expressions of love and trust. Breaking the chains of her family's tense and insincere traditions, my mom somehow became the most empathetic communicator I've ever known. She has the uncanny ability to make everyone feel like she understands them completely and that she is their closest friend. She possesses the Christlike qualities of love and sincerity, and you would never guess she came from a distant and strained family. My mom is my best and most loyal friend. My dad's home was full of disagreement and contention, but my dad is the ultimate example of righteous and peaceful leadership in our home. He is passionate about being good, standing up for right, and about loving and being there for his family. My dad has a light about him that tells you he is good. He doesn't seek for power or praise. He leads at work, at church, and in the home, through love, the way the Savior would lead. My dad is my hero; he is the type of person I hope to become. My parents have formed a very close-knit family by establishing their own traditions, habits, and patterns. We cherish family vacations, conversations on the phone, and we work to keep our family bonds tight. I know our family has been blessed because of my parents' righteousness.

In October conference 2000, Elder Donald Hallstrom chose family traditions for the theme of his address. He reminded parents everywhere of the power of cultural and family traditions in the lives of their children. "Unwanted traditions are those which lead us away from performing holy ordinances and keeping sacred covenants." This seems simple enough, but we live in a world where traditions often fail to separate right from wrong. For instance, one family tradition might be to spend Sundays together on the lake with the family boat, or on the ski slopes. While these normally wholesome family activities might have value in establishing family bonds, they also lead the family away from the Lord's commandments regarding the Sabbath day. Elder Hallstrom adds:

> Of all the traditions we should cultivate within ourselves and our families, a "tradition of righteousness" should be preeminent. Hallmarks of these traditions are an unwavering love for God and His Only Begotten Son, respect for prophets and priesthood power, a constant seeking of the Holy Spirit, and the discipline of discipleship which transforms believing into doing. A tradition of righteousness sets a pattern for living which draws children closer to parents, and both closer to God, and elevates obedience from a burden to a blessing. ("Cultivate Righteous Traditions," *Ensign*, Nov. 2000, 27–28)

Parents might ask themselves: "What are we doing as a couple and family that our children will look back on in our home with some nostalgia?" "Are the traditions we are setting righteous or unrighteous?"

Teach Plainly

A good friend told me that from the time her children were little, she always gave them household chores—make beds, clear the table after a meal, empty the dishwasher, pick up toys, etc., and then later as they grew older, cleaning bathrooms, bedrooms, and other rooms in the house, washing dishes, etc. She found that if sh sent a child to do a chore with only vague orders, for exam "Clean the bathroom," she was often disappointed in the r The child's perception of a clean bathroom was not the hers. She learned that if she gave them a list of specific s lead to a clean bathroom, their performance came much closer to meeting her expectations. For instance: scour the sink and tub with cleanser, wipe off the counters with the appropriate rag, polish the mirrors with this cleaner, scrub the floor with this material, hang up towels and washcloths this way, empty wastebaskets in the garbage container, etc. They could then check off each item, and when they finished the job she could be fairly certain, as could they, that it would pass inspection and they'd be free to play.

The Lord teaches that way—clearly and specifically—so there is no doubt in the minds of His children. He is especially clear regarding the performance of ordinances (see 3 Nephi 11:22–28, 32–35, 39–41).

Our Father did not want us to be confused about how we are to live the gospel: "For my soul delighteth in plainness; for after this manner doth the Lord God work among the children of men. For the Lord God giveth light unto the understanding; for he speaketh unto men according to their language, unto their understanding" (2 Nephi 31:3; see also 31:21).

Nephi demonstrated his commitment to this principle as he explained Isaiah's message to his people:

> Wherefore, hearken, O my people, which are of the house of Israel, and give ear unto my words; for because the words of Isaiah are not plain unto you, nevertheless they are plain unto all those that are filled with the spirit of prophecy. But I give unto you a prophecy, according to the spirit which is in me; wherefore I shall prophesy according to the plainness which hath been with me from the time that I came out from Jerusalem with my father; for behold, my soul delighteth in plainness unto my people, that they may learn. (2 Nephi 25:4)

Be simple and clear in what you say and expect of your children. You might even have them repeat instructions back to you to ensure that they've interpreted your words correctly.

Use Appropriate Teaching Techniques

When I was a graduate student I learned there are some teaching techniques that help cement lessons in a child's mind. "To help others want to learn, our teaching must be interesting. To help them understand, our teaching must be clear. To help them retain and ponder what they learn, our teaching must be memorable" (*Teaching, No Greater Call: A Resource Guide for Gospel Teaching*, published by The Church of Jesus Christ of Latter-day Saints, 88). In the Book of Mormon I found a number of teaching techniques used by prophet-fathers and the Lord, who is the master teacher. In my mind two obvious examples such as *teaching by example* and *getting a commitment* were stressed sufficiently to warrant a chapter of their own (discussed in detail later).

Closely related to obtaining a commitment is *personal involvement*—getting children involved through active participation on their part helps them commit to a value or cause (i.e., missionary work). Lehi sent a clear message to his sons concerning the value of scriptures when he sent them back to secure the brass plates (see 1 Nephi 3:2–4).

It's always a good idea to get the child's attention before you begin teaching something you want him to remember. The Lord has shown His own way of doing this.

> And he did straiten them [the Israelites] in the wilderness with his rod; for they hardened their hearts, even as ye have; and the Lord straitened them because of their iniquity. He sent fiery flying serpents among them; and after they were bitten he prepared a way that they might be healed; and the labor which they had to perform was to look; and because of the simpleness of the way, or the easiness of it, there were many who perished. (1 Nephi 17:41)

Although our Father does not intend for us to use a rod or send a plague of fiery serpents on our children, we can learn an important principle from this example—get their attention. The

Lord certainly got everyone's attention in 3 Nephi 8 when "a great storm arose . . . and a terrible tempest . . . [and] exceedingly sharp lightnings . . . [and] fire . . . [and cities sinking and mountains rising] . . . [and] the whole face of the land was changed . . . [and] whirlwinds [came] . . . [and there was] quaking of the whole earth. Highways [were] broken up . . . rocks were rent in twain . . . [and there were] three days that there was no light seen" (8:5–18, 23).

After you have taught, and are sure the child has heard you, be still and let the child ponder what has been said.

> And it came to pass that there was a voice heard among all the inhabitants of the earth, upon all the face of this land, crying:
>
> Wo, wo, wo unto this people; wo unto the inhabitants of the whole earth except they shall repent; for the devil laugheth, and his angels rejoice, because of the slain of the fair sons and daughters of my people; and it is because of their iniquity and abominations that they are fallen! (3 Nephi 9: 1–2)
>
> And now behold, it came to pass that all the people of the land did hear these sayings, and did witness of it. And after these sayings there was silence in the land for the space of many hours. (3 Nephi 10:1)

Another way to get a child's attention is to suddenly speak softly and deliberately so he has to strain to hear what you're saying:

> And it came to pass that while they were thus conversing one with another, they heard a voice as if it came out of heaven; and they cast their eyes round about, for they understood not the voice which they heard; and it was not a harsh voice, neither was it a loud voice; nevertheless, and notwithstanding it being a small voice it did pierce them

> that did hear to the center, insomuch that there was no part of their frame that it did not cause to quake; yea, it did pierce them to the very soul, and did cause their hearts to burn. (3 Nephi 11:3)

There is another example of this principle in Helaman 5:30. The Lord wanted the attention of the wicked Nephites who were persecuting Nephi and Lehi: "It was not a voice of thunder, neither was it a voice of a great tumultuous noise, but behold, it was a still voice of perfect mildness, as if it had been a whisper, and it did pierce even to the very soul."

I learned quite by accident the value of this approach when I taught school before our children were born. One morning I woke up to find that my voice was gone. I wondered how I'd get through the day. I could just barely speak above a whisper. Interestingly enough, that day turned out to be a wonderful, quite productive experience. The children were calm and quiet, having to listen carefully to hear my instructions. Prior to this, when I found the children becoming overly excited or noisy, my first inclination was to speak louder, trying to shout above their voices in my attempt to regain control of the class. It rarely worked. Later, remembering what my laryngitis had taught me, I began speaking in a very soft tone so that only the children on the first row could hear. The others soon stopped their own talking to hear what was going on, and soon I was in control again. My tone of voice not only aroused their curiosity, but seemed to calm them.

Following the sequence of both the events in 3 Nephi as well as Helaman 5, we learn still another method used by the Lord—repetition. "And again the third time they did hear the voice, and did open their ears to hear it" (3 Nephi 11:5). "And behold the voice came again. . . . And also again the third time the voice came" (Helaman 5:32, 33).

The Lord uses this approach several other times in the Book of Mormon (see 3 Nephi 10:4–6; 11:37–38; 18:15, 18). He had Moroni come into Joseph's room three times in one night and repeat the same message. He taught the Twelve that way after His resurrection (see John 21:15–17). He uses it when He asks us to partake of the sacrament once a week and return to the temple often to hear and renew our understanding of the plan of salvation.

One afternoon I was ironing—watching TV to entertain myself—and I noticed how often the same commercial was repeated over and over. True, it got to be annoying, but I remembered that commercial for days. Perhaps you have had the same experience. We don't want to annoy our children, but repetition is a good technique for producing a lasting message.

The Lord also used incentives to encourage His children to make righteous decisions: "Wherefore, ye must press forward with a steadfastness in Christ, having a perfect brightness of hope, and a love of God and of all men. Wherefore, if ye shall press forward, feasting upon the word of Christ, and endure to the end, behold, thus saith the Father: Ye shall have eternal life" (2 Nephi 31:20).

We will discuss this in more detail later, but God always presents Plan A—the positive, righteous plan—for us to choose, and then Plan B—the consequences should we make poor choices. When planning a family workday, for instance, build a reward into the plan—an ice-cream cone, a free afternoon, a family picnic, etc.—and see how much happier children work. I read somewhere that if you wanted to provide an incentive for a child to do a particularly good job dusting the living room, for instance, tell that child to dust everywhere, even under the lamp or table runners because a surprise was hiding somewhere, just waiting to be found. It could be just a quarter or a small treat planted earlier, but it would make the job more fun and it would provide the incentive to do the job more thoroughly.

Another way to help children pay attention is to give them a hint that important information is coming. "Yea, and the Lord said also that: After ye have arrived in the promised land, ye shall know that I, the Lord, am God; and that I, the Lord, did deliver you from destruction; yea, that I did bring you out of the land of Jerusalem" (1 Nephi 17:14). Can you see what technique the Lord is using here? He was preparing Lehi's family by telling them ahead of time what they were going to learn. Children don't always recognize a lesson when they see one, and sometimes a good technique is to help the child identify the lesson. When reading the scriptures together, for instance, a parent might say, "Now, in this next scripture we are going to learn about something important. See if you can find it." You can identify the intended lesson ahead of time and help the child focus on what he's reading or hearing so his mind won't wander. You can identify the lesson after you've read by asking questions like this: "What does this scripture (story or experience) teach us?" We don't always want to use the same technique every time, so vary it.

Nephi taught another way to identify and remember lessons in the scriptures. He counseled us to "liken all scriptures unto us" (1 Nephi 19:23). Sometimes when my husband read the scriptures to our children, he'd replace a prophet's name with one of the children's names. This simple technique seemed to grab their attention and made the scripture somehow more applicable as well as memorable.

Notice in Alma 5 how Alma uses a series of "thinking questions" as he expounds on the principles he wants to teach. This is a good technique in the classroom as well as in personal interviews with a son or daughter. It pulls them mentally into the discussion and helps them clarify in their own minds just how they stand in relation to that principle. In this way you are helping them teach themselves or to identify what the Spirit is trying to teach them.

The Lord often uses symbols, parables, and analogies to teach His children profound lessons from everyday experiences (see 3 Nephi 27:14–15). We see much of this in the New Testament with parables. Parents can also use this technique to help their little ones understand and remember concepts. Tell simple stories to them, help them recognize common symbols, and point out life's lessons in everyday experiences. For instance, I know a family who, when their children were old enough to think abstractly, for family home evening collected common objects around the house, put them in a paper sack, and asked the children to draw one out of the bag and think of an object lesson that could be taught the family from those items. They enjoyed this activity, and it taught them to be alert to other learning opportunities. Also, when reading scriptures together, help your children see the connection between what they have read and what they might do, asking "How does this scripture relate to you?" or "What gospel principle does this scripture (or story) teach?"

For some children, the only way to get their attention, even though your instructions have been clear and simple, is to let them experience the consequences of their disobedience, hopefully humbling them enough to open their ears. As discussed in detail later, one of the most effective teaching techniques is to let consequences teach. Sometimes the Lord allows the wicked to punish the wicked (see Mormon 4:5). If your children continue to fight and bicker with one another, withdraw and let them work it out between themselves; let them experience the consequences of their refusal to be peacemakers. They'll punish each other far more effectively than you would have. Then you might try sending the misbehaving children to separate rooms to calm down and think about their actions and possible consequences before you go in to speak to them. (This gives parents an opportunity to calm down too, get under control, offer a prayer, and collect their thoughts.)

Good Parenting

Principle 2
Parental Responsibility Involves Both Parents

Ideally, parenthood requires the unique gifts and abilities of both father and mother. President Gordon B. Hinckley charged fathers:

> Yours is the basic and inescapable responsibility to stand as head of the family. That does not carry with it any implication of dictatorship or unrighteous dominion. It carries with it a mandate that fathers provide for the needs of their families. Those needs are more than food, clothing, and shelter. Those needs include righteous direction and the teaching, by example as well as precept, of basic principles of honesty, integrity, service, respect for the rights of others, and an understanding that we are accountable for that which we do in this life, not only to one another, but also to the God of heaven, who is our Eternal Father. ("Bring Up a Child in the Way He Should Go," *Ensign*, Nov. 1993, 54)

He also reviewed with mothers the importance of their calling: "I remind mothers everywhere of the sanctity of your calling. No other can adequately take your place. No responsibility is greater, no obligation more binding than that you rear in love and peace and integrity those whom you have brought into the world" (ibid., 54).

All of this takes individual time with a child. President Howard W. Hunter told husbands and fathers: "A righteous father protects his children with his time and presence in their social, educational, and spiritual activities and responsibilities" ("Being a Righteous Husband and Father," *Ensign*, Nov. 1994, 51).

Turning to the Book of Mormon, we find several good examples of fathers carrying out their divinely charged mandate. Probably because we only have male "journals" of the time, little is mentioned about mothers and their role. Many of the "parenting" scriptures herein pertain to parenting in a very generic sense that includes both father and mother. There is no reason why a mother cannot teach her children gospel principles or a father can't teach domestic skills. Both are responsible for preparing their children to live both inside and outside of the home. Note this example: Jacob and Joseph were consecrated priests and teachers to the Nephites; one can't help but notice the similarity in a priest (spiritual leader) and a teacher. It seems as if they had the same responsibility as a parent. "And we did magnify our office unto the Lord, taking upon us the responsibility, answering the sins of the people upon our own heads if we did not teach them the word of God with all diligence; wherefore, by laboring with our might their blood might not come upon our garments; otherwise their blood would come upon our garments, and we would not be found spotless at the last day" (Jacob 1:19).

Helaman's two thousand stripling warriors were taught by their mothers. "Now they never had fought, yet they did not fear death; and they did think more upon the liberty of their fathers than they did upon their lives; yea, they had been taught by their mothers, that if they did not doubt, God would deliver them. And they rehearsed unto me the words of their mothers, saying: We do not doubt our mothers knew it" (Alma 56:47–48).

What do you think these mothers taught their sons? Faith? *How* do you suppose they taught them? Wouldn't you like one of their lesson plans? How do you teach faith to your children? Personal experience? Example? Kneeling in prayer with your children and letting them experience how you obtain answers from the Lord? By relating faith-promoting experiences of prophets, missionaries, and those searching ancestral records, or of those who work in the temple? Reading scripture and introducing children to God and His Son are crucial elements in the teaching process. We don't have the lesson plan, but we know those mothers spent a significant amount of time teaching these young men.

Be United As Parents in Your Parenting Philosophy

One area where problems often arise is in different parenting philosophies. Children have a way of dividing and conquering parents when they are not united in their approach. They can turn spouses against each other should the parents not be on the same page. Elder Henry B. Eyring explained the need for spousal unity: "At the creation of man and woman, unity for them in marriage was not given as hope, it was a command! 'Therefore shall a man leave his father and his mother, and shall cleave unto his wife: and they shall be one flesh' (Genesis 2:24). Our Heavenly Father wants our hearts to be knit together. That union in love is not simply an ideal. It is a necessity" ("That We May Be One," *Ensign*, May 1998, 66).

Being united as parents is another important element of effective parenting. Men and women are different in natural talents and abilities, but that very difference is of divine origin. Differences between males and females can strengthen marriages and families in a complementary way. Elder Neal A. Maxwell commented on President Harold B. Lee's daughter: "More parents should be remembered as a prophet's daughter, Helen Lee Goates, remembers hers: 'A father who was gentle beneath his firmness, and a mother who was firm beneath her gentleness'" ("Take Especial Care of Your Families," *Ensign*, May 1994, 90).

A man and woman from completely different backgrounds are inevitably going to have different parental approaches. Such disparity can be muted or resolved, but it doesn't happen automatically in the marriage ceremony or when you suddenly become a parent. Such togetherness involves a substantial amount of talking together, listening, understanding, and cooperation—if not outright compromise. Elder M. Russell Ballard strongly suggested that we counsel in family councils (see "Counseling with Our Councils," *Ensign*, Nov. 1994, 24). That council ought to begin before children come into the family, and it should continue after. Husband and wife have a number of issues and topics that need their mutual attention. Parenting should be on that agenda. Then, when the two add children to their union, they have already established a format, a regular way to resolve concerns and review family policies. The children will be much more secure and compliant if they know their parents support one another and can't be divided. One young woman revealed how this works in her family:

> Mom was usually the one to discipline us since she was the one that was around, but if she ever said that she was going to bring Dad into it, then we knew we'd goofed up. Punishments were usually given by both of my parents together, although I don't think that it had to be that way. My mom and dad were perfectly capable of doing it on their own, but I just think they chose to do it together.
>
> In our family, if you ever wanted to go do something, or if you had a favor to ask, it was best to go talk to Mom. Mom was more likely to listen and take your side, but she would always go talk to Dad and then give you a decision if it was something important.
>
> As I think back I cannot remember a time when my parents fought. I can never remember an argument, and I can never remember my dad or mom treating each other in a way that they shouldn't have. My dad would always come and give my mom a hug before he left for work and then a kiss. When he came back, it was straight to my mom again for a hug and kiss. He sometimes would hold her around the waist and nibble on her neck as she was getting dinner ready. My parents were always loving towards one another and they showed it in their actions.

A young student friend of mine said:

> One area that I really consider a strength in my parents' marriage is their oneness. Even though their approach to parenting differs somewhat—my dad tends to be more lenient and my mother more strict—they have made these differences a strength, complementing and tempering one another. After many years together and countless trips to the temple, both have a strong desire for the family to be eternal and they work hard to make that possible.

A young husband shared this observation:

> One strength I see in the relationship I have with my wife is that we like to decide on issues in a way that benefits both of us. We have seen from the examples of others, including our parents, that if a husband and wife do not make decisions together, the marriage becomes strained. My wife and I hope to retain the mutual respect we feel for each other's opinion at this point in our marriage and plan to include each other in all marital decisions. I don't feel threatened if I'm not always right, and neither does my wife. A wise man once said, "It's better to be loved than to be right."

Too often a parent vents frustrations over a spouse by complaining to the children. "Your father never . . ." or "I wish your mother would . . ." Children should never be the sounding board for marital complaints. Though marital disagreements and disputes may be inevitable, the point is to resolve them as a couple rather than go behind each other's backs to the children. How much better to resolve grievances privately—humbly, prayerfully, respectfully—arriving at a peaceful solution or compromise together. You'll need that united front in dealing with your children.

The Book of Mormon provides a classic example of a marital conflict and its resolution. Sariah was so concerned over the safety of her sons that she began to doubt Lehi's prophetic leadership; to her credit, she went directly to him with her concerns. Notice how their interaction played out: "For she had supposed that we had perished in the wilderness; and she also had complained against my father, telling him that he was a visionary man; saying: Behold thou has led us forth from the land of our inheritance, and my sons are no more, and we perish in the wilderness. And after this manner of language had my mother complained against my father" (1 Nephi 5:2–3). Notice Lehi's reaction when he understood her anguish and empathized with her. He did not meet her accusations with defensive anger, but he responded to her with empathy, reason, understanding, and humility.

> And it had come to pass that my father spake unto her, saying: I know that I am a visionary man; for if I had not seen the things of God in a vision I should not have known the goodness of God, but had tarried at Jerusalem, and had perished with my brethren.
>
> But behold, I have obtained a land of promise, in the which things I do rejoice; yea, and I know that the Lord will deliver my sons out of the hands of Laban, and bring them down again unto us in the wilderness.
>
> And after this manner of language did my father, Lehi, comfort my mother, Sariah, concerning us, while we journeyed in the wilderness up to the land of Jerusalem, to obtain the record of the Jews. (1 Nephi 5:4–6)

Sariah was also humbled and quick to admit that her husband was inspired after the boys were safely back in camp: "Now I know of a surety that the Lord hath commanded my husband to flee into the wilderness" (1 Nephi 5:8). They were again unified in their perspective and faith. From the record, it seems a fight was not had in front of the children and the parents maintained a unified front;

however, if children do witness or hear of a conflict, as was obviously the case with Nephi, it is important that they then also witness the resolution of that conflict. Cleary Nephi was privy to this resolution. There are many children who are lacking in communication/marital skills because they either never saw their parents have or resolve a conflict, or they only saw conflict and never resolution. The goal for parents is to someday emulate the perfect example of unity before us—the unity of the Godhead.

Principle 3
Parenting One-On-One

It has been said, and wisely so, that a child, or anyone for that matter, doesn't care how much you know until he knows how much you care. Parents cannot hope to effectively teach children what they want them to know until they first establish a loving and trusting relationship with each one.

Elder H. Burke Peterson suggested:

> May I suggest that we give more of ourselves, that we give more good experiences to our children, experiences that are love-producing and family-solidifying. . . . It may be five minutes at a child's bedside each night or a fifteen minute walk in the evening. It may be a day in the hills or a three-minute phone call from the office at midday. It may be a clever love note to a little girl or a night out to a ball game with a boy. . . . Simple experiences with children develop unbreakable ties that will endure forever. ("Harmony in the Home," *Ensign*, Jan. 1973, 114)

Obviously those ties cannot develop if you aren't there! Elder Richard G. Scott said, "When, as mothers, you are consistently in the home, at least during the hours the children are predominantly there, you can detect the individual needs of each child and provide ways to satisfy them. Your divinely given instincts help sense a child's special talents and unique capacities so that you can nurture and strengthen them" ("The Power of Correct Principles," *Ensign*, May 1993, 32).

Years ago a stake president shared a meaningful story with parenting applications. He began by telling of an elderly woman (Golda) in the stake who was an extraordinary gardener. She could coax magnificent blossoms out of her plants when no one else could. Her back and front yard always had something colorful blooming, and she always had a bouquet to share with a neighbor, or for sacrament meeting decor, or any special occasion. Appropriately enough, she was called to be the "beautification specialist" in Relief Society. Golda and this stake president were neighbors, and one day while working in his garden, an activity he admitted he did very little of, he asked his neighbor Golda her secret. She didn't discuss soil acidity, special fertilizers, or insect sprays, but responded simply:

> "I stay close to the garden." And then she explained, "I go into my garden every day, even when it isn't convenient, and I pick a bouquet of flowers every day, even when I don't need one, and I thank my flowers for their blossoms. Flowers do better when they are appreciated. The more you pick," she said, "the more they flourish and bloom [a scientific fact]. And while I'm out there," she went on, "I look for little signs of possible problems, things like weeds and insects and soil conditions that are simple to correct if caught in time, but can become overwhelming if left unchecked."

The stake president continued the story, suggesting that our families are much like our gardens: "If we want them to flourish and bloom, we need to spend time every day with them, talk to them, express appreciation often, and without being critical, look for little telltale signs of potential problems that can be corrected or attended to before they become overwhelming. In other words, 'stay close to the garden.'"

This reminded me of all the times I'd stuck a plant or two in the soil and left it unchecked only to discover weeks later that it had disappeared. I simply hadn't taken the time to check its progress daily, and when I did get around to it, it was too late. Then I thought of all the opportunities to express love and appreciation to one of our children that I'd let pass unfulfilled. Since hearing this story about gardens I've become a better gardener and a better parent.

This reference to tending family gardens conjures up a picture of a gardener tenderly weeding and tending each plant; it must be so for children also, for children, like plants, do not survive without personal attention. And personal revelation for one of her children would not be possible for a parent who does not first know the special needs and personal traits and challenges of each child. Without that information, how would a parent know what to pray for relative to that child?

The inescapable lesson here is that if we spend time with our children, teaching, playing, working, expressing appreciation, talking and listening to them, getting to know their friends and making sure they are comfortable bringing friends home, the harvest will be fruitful.

You cannot hope to influence a child's thinking and the values he embraces unless you two have a warm and happy relationship. Some individuals maintain that parents have no influence on the course their children take in life, but Elder James E. Faust disputed that line of reasoning:

> Generally, those children who make the decision and have the resolve to abstain from drugs, alcohol, and illicit sex are those who have adopted and internalized the strong values of their homes as lived by their parents. In times of difficult decisions, they are most likely to follow the [religious] teachings of their parents rather than the example of their peers or the sophistries of the media which glamorize alcohol consumption, illicit sex, infidelity, dishonesty, and other vices. ("The Greatest Challenge in the World—Good Parenting," *Ensign*, Nov. 1990, 34)

From personal experience and scripture, it is obvious to me that our Father knows each one of us individually and is mindful of our needs and innermost desires. He answers prayers and blesses our lives in very specific ways unique to the situation (see Ronald A. Rasband, "One by One," *Ensign*, Nov. 2000, 29–30).

The following examples from the Book of Mormon illustrate the importance of having a close relationship between parent and child, and suggests how the Lord and successful fathers taught or influenced each of their children "one by one."

1 Nephi 16:23. Nephi broke his hunting bow, then made another one and asked his father where he should go to find food. Even though Lehi had earlier grumbled and complained to the Lord because of their dire circumstances, Nephi respected his father and sought direction from him. He could have asked the Lord himself, but he honored the patriarchal line: "I said unto my father: Whither shall I go to obtain food?" If you are grumpy or upset, do your children come to you for help or advice? Would they want to? Nephi loved and respected his father despite Lehi's weaknesses because of the great spiritual experiences they shared.

2 Nephi 1:28; also chapters 2–4. In these chapters Lehi calls each of his sons by name and gives each a blessing, pointing out weaknesses and strengths, and blessing each according to his righteous potential. It is evident that this father was aware of his boys' qualities—good or bad.

Alma 35:16. "Therefore, he caused that his sons should be gathered together, that he might give unto them every one his charge, separately, concerning the things pertaining unto righteousness. And we have an account of his commandments, which he gave unto them according to his own record."

Many fathers find that having a personal priesthood interview with their children, individually, is an effective way to stay close, open or continue dialogue, and learn what's going on in their lives. Dad can counsel, give a blessing, or a brief lesson, but his first task might be to listen. Alma had a personal interview with each of his sons—Helaman (Alma 36–37), Shiblon (chapter 38), and Corianton (chapters 39–42). Corianton required a little more attention!

In Alma 4:17–20, we learn how Alma appointed Nephihah chief judge so he could attend to more important matters—providing spiritual leadership. "And this he did that he himself might go forth among his people, or among the people of Nephi, that he might preach the word of God unto them, to stir them up in remembrance of their duty, and that he might pull down, by the word of God, all the pride and craftiness and all the contentions which were among his people, seeing no way that he might reclaim them save it were in bearing down in pure testimony against them" (verse 19).

Alma demonstrated how a leader (or parent) must relate to his people (children) eye to eye—speaking, teaching, learning from them, and influencing them through his witness and testimony. That responsibility he could not abdicate to others. There are some things parents simply cannot leave to schools, peers, or even the Church to teach. Time with children, whether it be working on a project or just enjoying a leisure activity together, can be a special time, a sacred time to reinforce a cherished value, teach a principle, or bear testimony of some gospel principle.

My husband and our oldest son seemed to have their best talks during Ping-Pong games in our family room. My neighbor related to me one day how close his son and he had become since they began jogging together each morning before work and school. The more time you spend together in a relaxed and comfortable atmosphere, the more apt your children are to share personal thoughts, feelings, desires, concerns, and worries, which will provide you with clues to their social and spiritual development.

King Lamoni thanked God for softening his heart and the hearts of his people so they could communicate with their brethren, the Nephites. "And behold, I thank my great God that he has given us a portion of his Spirit to soften our hearts, that we have opened a correspondence with these brethren, the Nephites. And behold, I also thank my God, that by opening this correspondence we have been convinced of our sins, and of the many murders which we have committed" (Alma 24:8–9).

Effective parenting requires a soft heart and an ability to soften the hearts of any rebellion-prone children before those children can be taught. This teaching can only be done when a close and personal relationship is developed between a parent and a child. This is easier said than done; it can be a challenge when one or more children are testing you in your parenting skills!

The Lord also uses a "one-on-one" principle with His children. He knows every flower in his garden, is aware of every sheep in his flock, as these scriptural examples indicate:

> *Mosiah 27:14.* "And again, the angel said [unto Alma the Younger]: Behold, the Lord hath heard the prayers of his people, and also the prayers of his servant, Alma, who is thy father; for he has prayed with much faith concerning thee that thou mightest be brought to the knowledge of the truth; therefore, for this purpose have I come to convince thee of the power and authority of God, that the prayers of his servants might be answered according to their faith."

> *3 Nephi 11:15.* In this inspiring setting, the Lord patiently allowed each individual to come forth and satisfy himself/herself that He was the resurrected Christ. "And it came to pass that the multitude went forth, and thrust their hands into his side, and did feel the prints of the nails in his hands and in his feet; and this they did do, going forth one by one until they had all gone forth."

3 Nephi 17:9. "And it came to pass that when he had thus spoken, all the multitude, with one accord, did go forth with their sick and their afflicted, and their lame, and with their blind, and with their dumb, and with all them that were afflicted in any manner; and he did heal them every one as they were brought forth unto him."

3 Nephi 17:21. "And when he had said these words, he wept, and the multitude bare record of it, and he took their little children, one by one, and blessed them, and prayed unto the Father for them."

3 Nephi 18:36. "And it came to pass that when Jesus had made an end of these sayings, he touched with his hand the disciples whom he had chosen, one by one, even until he had touched them all, and spake unto them as he touched them."

From this verse we learn that the Lord touched each of his newly called disciples. Probably this touch has a deeper, more significant purpose, possibly as a priesthood ordinance, but we can apply the principle of touch here as well. As we speak with our children, especially when teaching or reprimanding them, we would do well to follow this model: stand close, put an arm around them, touch, look into their face and eyes, and speak softly. This approach helps them know that despite the need for the reprimand, your love is still reaching out to them.

3 Nephi 28:1. "And it came to pass when Jesus had said these words, he spake unto his disciples, one by one, saying unto them: What is it that ye desire of me, after that I am gone to the Father?"

Jesus singled out His disciples and spoke to them one by one, asking each to respond to His query. What if a father or mother were to speak with each child during a private moment about their parenting abilities, asking, "How can I be a better mother/father to you? What would you have me do?" Would that not be a positive experience in the life of a child? Try it, and it will pay great dividends.

Principle 4
Know Your Child's Readiness Stages

The last chapter dealt with the importance of having a personal relationship with each child. Principle 4 is similar to and in some cases intertwined with Principle 3, but here we will specifically focus on the need parents have to acquaint themselves with the physical and cognitive developmental stages and capabilities of their children. Though not every child follows a developmental chart exactly, each parent ought to be familiar with the general stages through which children pass.

Inspiration will come to you also, for the Lord knows you and the events and circumstances you will face with this child. Being a fair and gracious Father, He will not give you more than you can handle, nor condemn you for not perfectly handling things you are unprepared to understand. As parents, we need to both study our own children and study about children in general. As we spend time talking to them, listening to them, and learning from them, we can determine where they are in their physical, mental, and spiritual development, and what reasonable expectations we can have for them behaviorally and emotionally, given their age.

A child's cognitive and physical maturation is both systematic and developmental. Each phase of growth prepares her for the next stage. For example, an infant first learns to hold her head up, then sit up, then stand up. Generally an infant learns to crawl before she learns to walk. Cognitively, a child learns to communicate with body language before she masters the finer art of speech. Later she'll be able to transfer language meaning to the symbols on the written page as she learns to read. As her intellect develops, her ability to understand more complex ideas develops as well.

Perhaps you've heard the story of the mother who became upset at her four-year-old for wandering out the door and down the street to the corner of the block. The mother had repeatedly warned her daughter to never go to the corner alone. Rushing down the street to rescue her child from imminent danger, she grabbed her by the shoulders and angrily demanded, "Why did you disobey me? Why did you go to the corner by yourself?" The bewildered child looked up innocently at her angry mother and asked, "Mommy, what's a corner?" Be aware of your child's level of cognitive development and ability to comprehend, and talk at the child's level of understanding. "For my soul delighteth in plainness; for after this manner doth the Lord God work among the children of men. For the Lord God giveth light unto the understanding; for he speaketh unto men according to their language, unto their understanding" (2 Nephi 31:3).

Generally we assume that all behavior in children (as well as adults) has a reason or purpose. As we mature, those reasons may become more complex, but with young children they are fairly simple and straightforward. First, their behavior may indicate a stage of the growth cycle. Knowing the normal growth patterns of children enables a parent to relax and enjoy each stage, patiently allowing the child to work through each one. These stages may be referred to as needs. An infant first has a need to trust those who care for him. A child needs to be physically close to other human beings. A child needs to feel worthwhile. A child needs stimulating experiences of a wholesome nature. Another need of children is to have order in their lives, to be able to make sense out of their experiences. And a child needs to feel that he has control of his life. It would be well for mom and dad to read a good child-development book together so they can be prepared to recognize and wisely deal with their child's stages of growth. Even now I am speaking of generalities, because every child is unique. The more time a parent spends with a child, the better he will be able to understand the child's needs and temperament, and where the child is developmentally.

The Lord is very much aware of how much His children can understand and absorb, and He taught His prophets and people accordingly. He never dumped the whole gospel at once, but rather did so line upon line, in small increments.

> For behold, thus saith the Lord God: I will give unto the children of men line upon line, precept upon precept, here a little and there a little; and blessed are those who hearken unto my precepts, and lend an ear unto my counsel, for they shall learn wisdom; for unto him that receiveth I will give more; and from them that shall say, We have enough, from them shall be taken away even that which they have. (2 Nephi 28:30)

> And behold, I, Nephi, am forbidden that I should write the remainder of the things which I saw and heard; wherefore the things which I have written sufficeth me; and I have written but a small part of the things which I saw. (1 Nephi 14:28)

Though we think we are sufficiently mature enough to know everything, the Lord knows our limitations.

How is a parent to know when her child is ready to learn a particular concept? Waiting for a child to ask a question is a good indicator, though not the only one. Having said this, it is important for parents to be on the alert for other signs of readiness. This is particularly true of children who are naturally quiet and less inclined to verbally express their concerns and feelings. If, for instance, a child is twelve years old and has not yet asked about human reproduction, a parent might want to feel out the situation to make sure that whatever information he has received (and he surely will have by twelve) is accurate and in keeping with the spiritual nature of this wondrous gift.

Most often the Lord waited for a question before He gave an answer (i.e. Joseph Smith in the grove; numerous sections of the Doctrine and Covenants). There are many similar examples in the Book of Mormon.

> And it came to pass that I beheld my brethren, and they were disputing one with another concerning the things which my father had spoken unto them.
>
> For he truly spake many great things unto them, which were hard to be understood, save a man should inquire of the Lord; and they being hard in their hearts, therefore they did not look unto the Lord as they ought.
>
> And I said unto them: Have ye inquired of the Lord?
>
> And they said unto me: We have not; for the Lord maketh no such thing known unto us. (1 Nephi 15:2–3, 8–9)

Laman and Lemuel were too hard-hearted to ask, but the Lord is willing to teach as soon as we are ready:

> And Ammon said: I will go and inquire of the Lord, and if he say unto us, go down unto our brethren, will ye go?
>
> But the king said unto him: Inquire of the Lord, and if he saith unto us go, we will go; otherwise we will perish in the land.
>
> And it came to pass that Ammon went and inquired of the Lord, and the Lord said unto him:
>
> Get this people out of this land, that they perish not; for Satan has great hold on the hearts of the Amalekites, who do stir up the Lamanites to anger against their brethren to slay them;

> therefore get thee out of this land; and blessed are this people in this generation, for I will preserve them. (Alma 27:7, 10–12)

The Lord waited for Ammon's people to ask Him for help. He knew that Ammon needed to move the people of Anti-Nephi-Lehi for their own safety, but he gave Ammon a chance to figure out the logistics himself. Maybe parents need to be less anxious to give advice and wait instead until the child asks for help so they know the child is ready to receive it and has done all he can for himself. Is it possible that we sometimes jump in too soon with help and advice when our children need the opportunity to make choices and experience the consequences?

If your child is quiet and reserved and doesn't verbally communicate a great deal with you, it would be wise to spend extra time with that child, listening and observing and being more involved in her life to learn what's in her heart.

The Lord knows what's in our hearts because He knows us well. "And he gathereth his children from the four quarters of the earth; and he numbereth his sheep, and they know him; and there shall be one fold and one shepherd; and he shall feed his sheep, and in him they shall find pasture" (1 Nephi 22:25).

Knowing your children as individuals at different stages means you also have to be willing to treat each one uniquely. "For behold, the Lord doth grant unto all nations, of their own nation and tongue, to teach his word, yea, in wisdom, all that he seeth fit that they should have; therefore we see that the Lord doth counsel in wisdom, according to that which is just and true" (Alma 29:8).

In his interview with his son Corianton, Alma jumps right into his concerns. He did something different with both Shiblon and Helaman. He held Corianton's older brothers up as models, something you would not normally do. Yet he seems to know his son pretty well, what his needs are, and how Corianton feels about what he's done as it relates to justice and mercy. We gain an understanding of Alma's insight from his opening line: "I perceive thy mind is worried" (Alma 39:17; 40:1; 42:1).

The Savior is an impressive teacher. He manifested a spirit of compassion for His children and their weaknesses. If only we as parents could be as perceptive and value our children and their feelings as we teach them. It helps to look into their eyes and truly listen to their responses when you teach. Help them feel you care more about them than about getting the lesson taught. A child may not remember every thing you say, but he will long remember how it made him feel.

> I perceive that ye are weak, that ye cannot understand all my words which I am commanded of the Father to speak unto you at this time.
>
> Therefore, go ye unto your homes, and ponder upon the things which I have said, and ask of the Father, in my name, that ye may understand, and prepare your minds for the morrow, and I come unto you again.
>
> And it came to pass that when Jesus had thus spoken, he cast his eyes round about again on the multitude, and beheld they were in tears, and did look steadfastly upon him as if they would ask him to tarry a little longer with them.
>
> And he said unto them: Behold, my bowels are filled with compassion towards you. (3 Nephi 17:2–3, 5–6)

Aside from your love, one of the needs children have is the need for approval. Sometimes the naughty things our children do for attention make us doubt this principle, but a child would much rather have a positive affirmation than a negative one.

Our Father offers challenges just within our reach to help us grow, knowing what we are capable of achieving. It is obvious that the Lord understands the pure nature of children. A wise parent will likewise provide or at least allow a variety of challenges to a growing child, but not those beyond his reach, knowing that it is the natural inclination of children to want to please their parents. Children become discouraged and frustrated when that approval is always beyond them, and they will turn to creative ways to get your attention, even negative attention if that's what it takes. Most often you may safely assume that a misbehaving child is a discouraged child. We get an insight into the nature of children when the Lord admonishes us, "And [become] as a child, submissive, meek, humble, patient, full of love, willing to submit to all things which the Lord seeth fit to inflict upon him, even as a child doth submit to his father" (Mosiah 3:19).

Adults often forget that children aren't as sophisticated in the way they choose to obtain this approval, and we often misunderstand their motives. Before reacting to what you perceive to be misbehavior, ask yourself what could possibly be going on in the child's life or mind to cause him to behave in this way. Sometimes it is because the parents' marriage is not good; sometimes it is because Dad is away from home too much; sometimes it is because of a peer relationship that is not going well.

In Alma 60, there is a scathing letter from Moroni to Pahoran. This account tugs at our heartstrings because we know Pahoran is innocent of all Moroni's accusations. Children are innocent too. Many times they are hurt when we assume they meant to be naughty, just as Moroni assumed Pahoran was ignoring his pleas for help. An example I recall is when our daughter Becky, as a first grader, was told to get in the hot-lunch line. She got confused about what the teacher meant. The teacher assumed Becky's hesitation was a sign of stubbornness or disobedience and scolded her in front of everybody. Years later Becky still remembers how frightened she was of that teacher and how unsure of herself she felt in her presence.

The Lord taught us that children are not capable of sin until age eight. They make mistakes—not intentionally or willfully, but playfully or inquisitively. Remember it is the nature of a young child to please his parents. He wants their love and approval. Satan cannot influence them to do evil:

> Listen to the words of Christ, your Redeemer, your Lord and your God. Behold, I came into the world not to call the righteous but sinners to repentance; the whole need no physician, but they that are sick; wherefore, little children are whole, for they are not capable of committing sin; wherefore the curse of Adam is taken from them in me, that it hath no power over them; and the law of circumcision is done away in me.
>
> Behold I say unto you that this thing shall ye teach—repentance and baptism unto those who are accountable and capable of committing sin; yea, teach parents that they must repent and be baptized, and humble themselves as their little children, and they shall all be saved with their little children.
>
> And their little children need no repentance, neither baptism. Behold, baptism is unto repentance to the fulfilling the commandments unto the remission of sins. (Moroni 8:8, 10–11)

In helping children grow and mature, parents can arrange or plan successful experiences to build their confidence. The Lord always prepares His children to receive what He is about to give them. He plans for their success.

> The Lord did pour out his Spirit on all the face of the land to prepare the minds of the children of men, or to prepare their hearts to receive the word which should be taught among them at the time of his coming—
> That they might not be hardened against the word, that they might not be unbelieving, and go on to destruction, but that they might receive the word with joy, and as a branch be grafted into the true vine, that they might enter into the rest of the Lord their God. (Alma 16:16–17)

A wise parent will allow their child room to grow but not to continually fall short to the point of becoming discouraged. The Lord allowed the Lamanites to persecute the Nephites in order that the Nephites might be humbled and repent. However, when they did well, He blessed them. It takes wisdom and self-control for a parent to know when to step in and help a child who has stumbled, and when to step back and let the child pick herself up.

I saw this illustrated by my own daughter-in-law one Sunday afternoon while we were all gathered at home watching general conference. While the rest of us were engrossed in the remarks of one of the Brethren, our twelve-month-old granddaughter was attempting to climb up onto a chair just a foot or two away from her mother. The task was difficult enough for her short little legs, but doubly so because of the long dress she was wearing. As she struggled in climbing, it looked at times like she might lose her balance and fall, with the potential of hitting her chin or head on the chair seat. Denise, our daughter-in-law, was watching carefully, but wisely allowed little Katy to fight her own battle with the chair and the bothersome dress. However, every time the venture looked precarious, the ever-vigilant motherly hand automatically shot forward protectively to break the fall, should it come, to soften the possible consequences. It was obvious that her motherly instincts urged her to lift her child and place her on the desired seat, but in that instance it was time to let little Katy solve her problem in her own way.

The Lord's hand is ever ready to reach out to us, but He wisely withholds His help when the struggle will help us grow and become stronger.

> And now the Lord was slow to hear their cry because of their iniquities; nevertheless the Lord did hear their cries, and began to soften the hearts of the Lamanites that they began to ease their burdens; yet the Lord did not see fit to deliver them out of bondage.

> And it came to pass that they began to prosper by degrees in the land, and began to raise grain more abundantly, and flocks, and herds, that they did not suffer with hunger. (Mosiah 21:15–16)

Understanding our capabilities, the Lord is the perfect parent. Following this pattern will greatly assuage our own parenting difficulties.

Principle 5
Be Humble and Teachable

And now I would that ye should be humble, and be submissive and gentle; easy to be entreated; full of patience and long-suffering; being temperate in all things; being diligent in keeping the commandments of God at all times; asking for whatsoever things ye stand in need, both spiritual and temporal; always returning thanks unto God for whatsoever things ye do receive. (Alma 7:23)

This scripture is especially applicable to parents and parenting. You won't be a parent very long before you realize your need for the Lord's help in this great adventure. The Lord knows His children better than we do, and He also knows our strengths and weaknesses. He stands ready to help us raise our families righteously if we will be humble enough to seek His counsel. Our prophet cautioned: "Never forget that these little ones are the sons and daughters of God and that yours is a custodial relationship to them, that He was a parent before you were parents and that He has not relinquished His parental rights or interest in these His little ones" (President Gordon B. Hinckley, "Excerpts from Recent Addresses of President Gordon B. Hinckley," *Ensign*, July 1997, 72). Perhaps children are given to us to keep us humble, to show us our weaknesses. How well they do their job! And our weaknesses are magnified in them if we are not careful. Fortunately, the reverse is also true. Humility is a major ingredient of genuine spirituality—the foundation of a happy home.

> And if men come unto me I will show unto them their weakness. I give unto men weakness that they may be humble; and my grace is sufficient for all men that humble themselves before me; for if they humble themselves before me, and have faith in me, then will I make weak things become strong unto them.
>
> Behold, I will show unto the Gentiles their weakness, and I will show unto them that faith, hope and charity bringeth unto me—the fountain of all righteousness. (Ether 12:27–28)

As parents, we want to seek counsel from the most experienced parent in the universe, the Father of us all: "Counsel with the Lord in all thy doings, and he will direct thee for good; yea, when thou liest down at night lie down unto the Lord, that he may watch over you in your sleep; and when thou risest in the morning let thy heart be full of thanks unto God; and if ye do these things, ye shall be lifted up at the last day" (Alma 37:37).

In the Book of Mormon there are many great father-leaders who were humble and teachable, and their example is inspiring to those who read this sacred text. In the following scripture, Helaman shares with Pahoran how the sons of Ammon are fighting for their lives against the Lamanites. He describes a battle not unlike the battle parents face every day in this age—the battle with Satan over our children. If you will follow Helaman's example of humble service, and try to do your best as a parent now, the Lord will grant you peace of mind, even if you have made mistakes with your children. Some parents find their child has rejected their values as did the prodigal; however, if those parents remain faithful to their covenants and never give up on the child, life may teach the children that which they were unwilling to learn at home. We are never to give up on them. Again, note the similarities between this scripture and the parenting experiences of so many today:

> Therefore we did pour out our souls in prayer to God, that he would strengthen us and deliver us out of the hands of our enemies, yea, and also give us strength that we might retain our cities, and our lands, and our possessions, for the support of our people.
>
> Yea, and it came to pass that the Lord our God did visit us with assurances that he would deliver us; yea, insomuch that he did speak peace to our souls, and did grant unto us great faith, and did cause us that we should hope for our deliverance in him.
>
> And we did take courage with our small force which we had received, and were fixed with a determination to conquer our enemies, and to maintain our lands, and our possessions, and our wives, and our children, and the cause of our liberty.
>
> We trust in our God. . . .
>
> But behold, they have received many wounds; nevertheless they stand fast in that liberty wherewith God has made them free; and they are strict to remember the Lord their God from day to day; yea, they do observe to keep his statutes, and his judgments, and his commandments continually; and their faith is strong in the prophecies concerning that which is to come. (Alma 58:10–12, 33, 40)

Alma, in an earlier time, prayed fervently for the few righteous among the Zoramites. He prayed for comfort, for strength to endure, for power, wisdom, and success in teaching the stubborn and prideful. This is a wonderful missionary scripture, but consider its parenting implications—humility and willingness to seek heaven's help, to learn, and to be led by the Lord. Imagine this prayer on behalf of your children, and learn the humility required to create such faith:

> O Lord, wilt thou comfort my soul, and give unto me success, and also my fellow laborers who are with me—yea, Ammon, and Aaron, and Omner, and also Amulek and Zeezrom, and also my two sons—yea, even all these wilt thou comfort, O Lord. Yea, wilt thou comfort their souls in Christ.
>
> Wilt thou grant unto them that they may have strength, that they may bear their afflictions which shall come upon them because of the iniquities of this people.
>
> O Lord, wilt thou grant unto us that we may have success in bringing them again unto thee in Christ.
>
> Behold, O Lord, their souls are precious, and many of them are our brethren; therefore, give unto us, O Lord, power and wisdom that we may bring these, our brethren, again unto thee.
>
> Now it came to pass that when Alma had said these words, that he clapped his hands upon all them who were with him. And behold, as he clapped his hands upon them, they were filled with the Holy Spirit. (Alma 31:32–36)

Listen to the Spirit

Closely related to the principle of humility is the need to listen to the promptings of the Holy Ghost. Nephi's task was to secure the brass plates, but he was not sure how to do it. He thought it through and tried his own way first (drew straws, took family jewels and wealth to Laban in exchange), but nothing worked. At that point Laman and Lemuel were ready to quit, but Nephi trusted in the Lord to help him. Many times, parents, too, find themselves confronted with a problem concerning a child, and they haven't any idea what to do or say to resolve the issue. I have often gone from my knees into my angry child's room and been inspired on the spot as to what I should say to soften his heart. Through trial and error I learned that you never discipline a child in anger. Calm down, seek divine help, and then you are ready to confront a child. "And I was led by the Spirit, not knowing beforehand the things which I should do" (1 Nephi 4:6).

In an earlier chapter we read the account of a disagreement between Lehi and Sariah. She was worried over her boys' long absence, and in frustration struck out at her husband. He was not defensive but responded to her with reason, understanding, and humility. He couldn't really give her any good reasons for his actions except that he was led by the Spirit (see 1 Nephi 5:2–3).

Apply this principle to parenting. Suppose, for example, that a father insists his teenage daughter not go on a particular outing with some friends. He feels uncomfortable about it for reasons he cannot explain, but he feels the Spirit has directed him to say no. The daughter obeys but is unhappy about the decision. Now we've all either experienced such a situation ourselves, or have heard similar accounts. Sometimes the parent's uneasiness is vindicated when, the next day, word gets out that a terrible tragedy occurred in which some or all of the young people were injured or worse. Thus, the daughter is grateful and the father feels justified. But, what if the report that she hears the next day is positive? The kids had a great time and nothing bad happened. The daughter is even more frustrated because she had to sit home while the others were having a great time. So she passes that along to her father. What might his response be? What would yours be? We can't always give good reasons for what we feel, but neither can we afford to ignore those personalized offerings of divine help.

While the circumstances are different, perhaps the same principle applies in this story:

> After living a few years in a part of the country where we were the only Mormons in the neighborhood, we moved to Provo where suddenly our children had other members of the Church for playmates everywhere they went. This was a

blessing in many ways, but it also presented a few challenges. Prior to this move, when the non-LDS neighbor children came over [on] Sunday to see if our children could play, it was easy to explain to our children why they could not [play] on the Sabbath. I explained to them that our Heavenly Father taught us to keep the Sabbath day holy and we felt playing basketball in the park was not in keeping with that commandment. The children accepted that decision.

But when we moved to Provo and some of their member friends came over to see if they could play basketball on Sunday, the children questioned us. I remember one particular Sunday afternoon the issue came up. I turned the friends away at the door as kindly as possible and invited them to come back the following day, then I turned to face my confused and disappointed son. I didn't want to appear judgmental toward his friends or their parents, who were also friends of mine, but I knew I owed him an explanation.

After a quick prayer for inspiration, I sat with him on the couch and said, "I can't answer for the other children or their parents. They are good people and are doing the best they can. Their children are their responsibility. My stewardship is to parent you the best that I can, and the Spirit tells me that our family will be blessed if we follow divine counsel in this matter. Will you support us in this?"

How would you have handled this event? Would you respond in anger, insisting that you [were] the parent and your word [was] law, with no questions asked? Some parents do operate that way because that was the way they were parented. The Lord teaches us that explaining doctrine sustained by the Spirit is more effective than anger and force.

> We do have some promises about keeping the Sabbath day holy that are more important to our children's spiritual development than what peers would do with them. For example, we have been promised that reading the Book of Mormon together as a family will soften hearts and melt away contention, and what better time to do that than on the Sabbath (see Ezra Taft Benson, *Ensign*, May 1986, 5).

Both parents and children are thus edified: "And now, as the preaching of the word had a great tendency to lead the people to do that which was just—yea, it had had more powerful effect upon the minds of the people than the sword, or anything else, which had happened unto them—therefore Alma thought it was expedient that they should try the virtue of the word of God" (Alma 31:5).

King Benjamin teaches the importance of being humble and submissive, even though the tendencies of the natural man lean toward pride and independence. Some parents were themselves raised in abusive home situations and may repeat such angry responses with their children. The Spirit can help a parent break that chain of abuse and become what is called a transitional character, one who behaves differently than his parents.

> For the natural man is an enemy to God, and has been from the fall of Adam, and will be, forever and ever, unless he yields to the enticings of the Holy Spirit, and putteth off the natural man and becometh a saint through the atonement of Christ the Lord, and becometh as a child, submissive, meek, humble, patient, full of love, willing to submit to all things which the Lord seeth fit to inflict upon him, even as a child doth submit to his father. (Mosiah 3:19)

Soften Your Heart

> And behold, I thank my great God that he has given us a portion of his Spirit to soften our hearts, that we have opened a correspondence with these brethren, the Nephites.

> And behold, I also thank my God, that by opening this correspondence we have been convinced of our sins, and of the many murders which we have committed. (Alma 24:8–9)

A soft heart is a humble heart. It allows us to communicate positively with both spouse and children. When pride or selfishness hardens our hearts, causing us to lean too much on the wisdom of the world or blocking us from seeking divine counsel, we miss information that could have resolved problems earlier and more easily. The scriptures teach us to search the word of God, read and listen to living prophets, and seek our own personal revelation through sincere and humble prayer. "But behold, there are many that harden their hearts against the Holy Spirit, that it hath no place in them; wherefore, they cast many things away which are written and esteem them as things of naught" (2 Nephi 33:2).

Several years ago I was visiting with a family when they expressed their concerns over their teenage son. The parents described how he had become angry, defiant, even verbally abusive to his mother and younger sister, and how he insisted on making poor choices concerning activities and friends—choices that could only lead him further into spiritual trouble. They said that when he walked in the door, the Spirit walked out. They were very distraught. We talked late into the night. In parting, I remembered that we have been promised that if we are righteous parents and do all we can do to bring up our children in light and truth, they may stray from us for a time, but they will return as they recall the teachings of their youth. At every recent conference, one or more of the Brethren had reminded us of the importance of consistently holding family home evening, family prayer, and scripture reading. If we did just those three things, hearts would be softened. I shared this recollection with the parents.

The two parents looked at one another for a moment, then the mother admitted, "We're not doing any of those things." She went on to give all the reasons so many of us give for not doing the things we know in our heart we should do—not enough time, resistance from the children, conflicting schedules, etc. I challenged them to find the time if they wanted any improvement in their home. Perhaps they could review their priorities, cut something out, make some changes in their lifestyle, and try the Lord's way before they turned to outside help. The good news is that they humbled themselves sufficiently to follow the prophet's inspired counsel. They began a family scripture-study program, reading the Book of Mormon together nightly before bedtime. Hearts were softened, contention disappeared and they reported an increase of the Spirit in their home.

President Marion G. Romney made the promise:

> If, in our homes, parents will read from the Book of Mormon prayerfully and regularly, both by themselves and with their children, the spirit of that great book will come to permeate our homes and all who dwell therein. The spirit of reverence will increase; mutual respect and consideration for each other will grow. The spirit of contention will depart. Parents will counsel their children in greater love and wisdom. Children will be more responsive and submissive to the counsel of their parents. Righteousness will increase. Faith, hope, and charity—the pure love of Christ—will abound in our homes and lives, bringing in their wake peace, joy, and happiness. ("The Book of Mormon," *Ensign*, May 1980, 67)

By listening to our Church leaders in semiannual conferences, we have an opportunity to learn better approaches to parenting. But we also have our agency and can choose whether to put into practice their wisdom, or do it our way. If we are humble and teachable parents, the Lord will instruct us—and the more light we accept, the more we'll be given. Are we really listening when the Lord's servants speak? Or, like my friends, do we listen but not hear? Do we take the words of the prophets so much for granted that we don't take them seriously? Do we lack the faith to try it the Lord's way? Is it too difficult to make the changes in our lives necessary to follow the Lord's counsel? If we choose to ignore His counsel—leaning upon our own wisdom and the philosophies of the world—and find we've lost our children, we will look back on what we have done or not done with remorse.

> And therefore, he that will harden his heart, the same receiveth the lesser portion of the word; and he that will not harden his heart, to him is given the greater portion of the word, until it is given unto him to know the mysteries of God until he know them in full. [And what greater mystery is there than why your child behaves the way he does?]
>
> And they that will harden their hearts, to them is given the lesser portion of the word until they know nothing concerning his mysteries; and then they are taken captive by the devil, and led by his will down to destruction. Now this is what is meant by the chains of hell. (Alma 12:10, 14)

The Lord will not force Himself or His blessings upon us. "And because of this their great wickedness, and their boastings in their own strength, they were left in their own strength; therefore they did not prosper, but were afflicted and smitten, and driven before the Lamanites, until they had lost possession of almost all their lands. . . . And it came to pass that they did repent, and inasmuch as they did repent they did begin to prosper" (Helaman 4:13, 15).

The following are additional scriptures that teach of the blessings of the soft heart and the dangers of remaining hard-hearted and unteachable: 1 Nephi 7:4–5; 13; 15:2–3, 8–9; 16:24–25; Alma 24:24; Helaman 12:2–6; 16:15.

Repent and Apologize

Many parents feel they must be right all the time in order to garner respect from their children. Another motive for self-righteously demanding perfection from themselves and their children might be to keep up external appearances in order to impress others outside the family circle. Such parents are often caught up in the pride of materialism, status, and prestige, caring more what the world thinks of them than what the Lord thinks. Such parents have learned to be judgmental and critical of themselves and of others. When their children do not meet their expectations, the fear of looking like bad parents becomes a serious threat to their personal image. Admitting a mistake would be admitting they are not perfect and undermine their authority. What such parents may not remember is that respect and love are not the same thing. You can have great respect for something or someone you fear, but it is difficult to hold love and fear in your heart at the same time. Better to choose love and respect as a basis for a relationship with your children. That may mean being humble enough to admit when you are wrong and to apologize. An example might be when you have overreacted and dealt too harshly with an erring child. Elder Jeffrey R. Holland tells of such an incident when the accumulation of stress throughout the day on one occasion caused him to overreact to his small son's misbehavior one evening.

> One evening I came home from long hours at school, feeling the proverbial weight of the world on my shoulders. Everything seemed to be especially demanding and discouraging and dark. I wondered if the dawn would ever come. Then, as I walked into our small student apartment, there was an unusual silence in the room.
>
> "What's the trouble?" I asked.
>
> "Matthew has something he wants to tell you," Pat said.

"Matt, what do you have to tell me?"

He was quietly playing with his toys in the corner of the room, trying very hard not to hear me.

"Matt," I said a little louder, "do you have something to tell me?"

He stopped playing, but for a moment didn't look up. Then these two enormous, tear-filled brown eyes turned toward me, and with the pain only a five-year-old can know, he said, "I didn't mind Mommy tonight, and I spoke back to her." With that he burst into tears, and his entire little body shook with grief. A childish indiscretion had been noted, a painful confession had been offered; the growth of a five-year-old was continuing, and loving reconciliation could have been wonderfully underway.

Everything might have been just terrific—except for me. If you can imagine such an idiotic thing, I lost my temper. It wasn't that I lost it with Matt—it was with a hundred and one other things on my mind; but he didn't know that, and I wasn't disciplined enough to admit it. He got the whole load of bricks.

I told him how disappointed I was and how much more I thought I could have expected from him. I sounded like the parental pigmy I was. Then I did what I had never done before in his life—I told him that he was to go straight to bed and that I would not be in to say his prayers with him or to tell him a bedtime story. Muffling his sobs, he obediently went to his bedside, where he knelt—alone—to say his prayers. Then he stained his little pillow with tears his father should have been wiping away. . . .

> Later, as [Pat and I] knelt by our own bed, my feeble prayer for blessings upon my family fell back on my ears with a horrible, hollow ring. I wanted to get up off my knees right then and go to Matt and ask his forgiveness, but he was long since peacefully asleep.
>
> [Elder Holland relates how his own sleep was not easy in coming. He slept fitfully and dreamed of Matt.]
>
> The dream ended, and I shot upright in bed. *My* pillow was now stained, whether with perspiration or tears I do not know. I threw off the covers and ran to the little metal camp cot that was my son's bed. There on my knees and through my tears I cradled him in my arms and spoke to him while he slept.

As he held his small son, he wept and told him how much he loved him, that he had made a mistake and expected too much from a five-year-old boy. He asked Matt's forgiveness and promised he would never withhold his love again, and hoped that Matt wouldn't either, and he was honored to be his father and would try with all his heart to be worthy of such a great responsibility (see "Within the Clasp of Your Arms," *Ensign*, May 1983, 36–7).

Such actions took a great deal of humility, but it was essential if he was to have the Spirit sustain his parenting methods. He learned the simple principle that when we offend our little ones, we offend the Spirit as well.

Most often this lesson comes to us from parent-prophets. King Benjamin was a powerful leader because of his humility not only as a king, but as a parent. We are parents, yes, and we need to take our charge seriously, but we must not forget that these little ones we nurture and raise are our equals in the sight of the Lord, and their spirits may even be older, age-wise, than ours. They deserve respect and consideration. When your parental authority is challenged by a child struggling to develop independence before he is ready to use it wisely, you might explain, "I've never been a parent before this life and I'm learning, the same as you. For some reason the Lord saw fit to make me the parent and you the child in this family, and I am accountable to Him for this responsibility. I no doubt make some mistakes, but I must do what I feel is best for you. When you are old enough to make your own decisions in matters as important as this, I pray you will be guided by the Spirit too."

> I have not commanded you to come up hither that ye should fear me, or that ye should think that I of myself am more than a mortal man.
>
> But I am like as yourselves, subject to all manner of infirmities in body and mind; yet I have been chosen by this people, and consecrated by my father, and was suffered by the hand of the Lord that I should be a ruler and a king over this people; and have been kept and preserved by his matchless power, to serve you with all the might, mind and strength which the Lord hath granted unto me.
>
> And I, even I, whom ye call your king, am no better than ye yourselves are; for I am also of the dust. (Mosiah 2:10–11, 26)

When you make mistakes in parenting, as with anything else in life, be humble enough to take responsibility and apologize. Being able to admit mistakes is a sign of great character and meekness. We all make errors in judgment. President Howard W. Hunter devoted an entire conference address to this very issue. He said:

> For every set of parents there are many "first-time" experiences that help to build wisdom and understanding, but each such experience results from the plowing of new ground, with the possibility that errors might be made. . . .

> It is a rare father or mother indeed who travels the difficult path of parenting without making errors along the way, especially at these first-time milestones when experience and understanding are somewhat lacking. Even after the parent has gained experience, the second-time and third-time occurrences of these milestones are sometimes not much easier to handle, nor do they come with much less chance of error. ("Parents' Concern for Children," *Ensign*, Nov. 1983, 65)

The scriptures also emphasize this same principle:

> And again, believe that ye must repent of your sins and forsake them, and humble yourselves before God; and ask in sincerity of heart that he would forgive you; and now, if you believe all these things see that ye do them.
>
> And again I say unto you as I have said before . . . even so I would that ye should remember, and always retain in remembrance, the greatness of God, and your own nothingness, and his goodness and long-suffering towards you, unworthy creatures, and humble yourselves even in the depths of humility, calling on the name of the Lord daily, and standing steadfastly in the faith of that which is to come, which was spoken by the mouth of the angel. (Mosiah 4:10–11)

Alma told his son Shiblon of his own past mistakes and of the awful feeling of remorse he endured until he repented and sought God for peace of soul. It is not always wise to tell your children of all your past sins, but when moved upon by the Spirit, you might bear testimony of a principle or ease a pain a child might be carrying. Sometimes a child needs to know it is okay if he's not perfect if he's willing to repent and has a desire to do better—to know that others have made mistakes and recovered.

Perhaps Alma was following the example of his father who also had cause to repent when he served in the court of King Noah. He shared his past and his remorse with his sons. His purpose was to teach his sons and to offer comfort and direction regarding the Lord's role in our lives.

To have access to the blessings the Lord offers, He requires humility of all His servants, but most especially from those who parent His precious little ones.

> And it came to pass that after Aaron had expounded these things unto him, the king said: What shall I do that I may have this eternal life of which thou hast spoken? Yea, what shall I do that I may be born of God, having this wicked spirit rooted out of my breast, and receive his Spirit, that I may be filled with joy, that I may not be cast off at the last day? Behold, said he, I will give up all that I possess, yea, I will forsake my kingdom, that I may receive this great joy.
>
> But Aaron said unto him: If thou desirest this thing, if thou wilt bow down before God, yea, if thou wilt repent of all thy sins, and will bow down before God, and call on his name in faith, believing that ye shall receive, then shalt thou receive the hope which thou desirest. (Alma 22:15–16)

Isn't this what we desire most—joy and eternal life for ourselves and our children? The scriptures clearly point the way we should go.

Principle 6
Teach by Example

Therefore I would that ye should be perfect even as I, or your Father who is in heaven is perfect. (3 Nephi 12:48)

The Lord came to the earth for a number of reasons, among them, to set an example of gospel living before men. Our Father in Heaven thought it important for His children to have an example before them, someone they could emulate and follow, someone like us, but who would show us the way to live in a fallen world. He sent His beloved Son to suffer for our sins if we repent, not because Jehovah needed to be tested, but because we needed Him to set an example before us. In his April 1999 conference address, Elder Jeffrey R. Holland taught us of the relationship that exists between God the Father and Jesus Christ as an example of fatherhood. Speaking of their relationship Elder Holland said:

> To those who wanted to see the Father, to hear from God directly that Jesus was what He said He was, He answered, "If ye had known me, ye should have known my Father also: . . . he that hath seen me hath seen the Father." When Jesus wanted to preserve unity among His disciples, He prayed using the example of His own relationship with God: "Holy Father, keep through thine own name those whom thou hast given me, that they may be one, as we are [one]." ("The Hands of the Fathers," *Ensign*, May 1999, 15)

One of the primary purposes for Christ condescending to come to earth was to teach us what Heavenly Father is like so that we could relate to Him, to know Him, and thus keep His commandments. Of earthly fathers Elder Holland said, "In any case, we do know that a young person's developing concept of God centers on characteristics observed in that child's earthly parents" (ibid.). What an awesome responsibility that places on mortal parents. Elder Holland quotes a personal acquaintance of his who grasped that connection and felt that same responsibility:

> Often as I watch my son watch me, I am taken back to moments with my own dad, remembering how vividly I wanted to be just like him. I remember having a plastic razor and my own can of foaming cream, and each morning I would shave when he shaved. I remember following his footsteps back and forth across the grass as he mowed the lawn in summer.
>
> Now I want my son to follow my lead, and yet it terrifies me to know he probably will. Holding this little boy in my arms, I feel a "heavenly homesickness" a longing to love the way God loves, to comfort the way He comforts, to protect the way He protects. The answer to all the fears of my youth was always "What would Dad do?" Now that I have a child to raise I am counting on a Heavenly Father to tell me exactly that. (ibid., 16)

President James E. Faust gave an illustration of one young woman who became much more aware of the wonderful relationship we have to our Heavenly Father when she left home for the first time to go to college. Her father gave her a blessing and expressed his love. She wrote:

> I clung to his words of love and support as I said a painful good-bye to my family. I felt alone and scared in those uncharted waters. Before I left the apartment that morning, I

> knelt down to ask for help. Desperately I pleaded with my Heavenly Father for strength to be able to face the college world all alone. I had left my family and friends and everything familiar the day before, and I knew I needed His help.
>
> My prayers were answered as I reflected on the tender experience with my father the day before. A wave of comfort fell over me as I realized that I had not come to college with the blessing of just my earthly father. I suddenly felt that one day, not so long ago, my Heavenly Father had held me close in His arms. Perhaps He gave me words of advice and encouragement and told me that He believed in me, just as my earthly father had. And at that moment, I knew that I am never without the perfect love and endless support of my Father in Heaven. ("What It Means to Be a Daughter of God," *Ensign*, Nov. 1999, 100)

In a general conference message, Elder Loren C. Dunn pleaded with fathers throughout the Church to step forward and be committed to this most important calling. He told of the wonderful example his own father was to him, but added, "If the example has not been set in your life, then reach out and try to help establish it, and resolve that that example will begin with you, if there is no one else. If all is not perfect in your home, then let it begin with you" ("Because My Father Sent Me," *Ensign*, May 2000, 81).

The Book of Mormon is full of great fathers who fulfilled the role of father admirably, but it also has some not-so-perfect fathers who, by their wicked example, taught their children and/or followers wickedness. For purposes of comparison and to emphasize the great impact parental example has on our children, I have included in this chapter wicked and righteous examples from the Book of Mormon.

Be Trustworthy

Children often resist parental advice and counsel, not being quite willing to trust in parental wisdom. For example, moving away from a comfortable home and friends is usually hard for children, and they often put up resistance, asking "Why do we have to move?" Nephi was a typical young man who must have resisted the idea of moving; we assume this because he asked the Lord to soften his heart so he could be obedient. "I did cry unto the Lord; and behold he did visit me, and did soften my heart that I did believe all the words which had been spoken by my father" (1 Nephi 2:16).

But the account also says something about Lehi and the example he set for his family. The verse above tells us that Nephi was taught to pray when confronted with difficult decisions.

I've discussed the importance of both parent and child having a soft heart, but I think the point there is that while Nephi learned to trust his father, he also wanted an independent witness of his own. Lehi was able to engender trust in this young son's heart. How does that happen in a family? It happens in the same way we learn to trust our Father in Heaven, through personal experience. It is important that a child knows his father will ask nothing of him he is not willing to ask of himself, that his father holds himself up to the same standards he expects of his children.

When I was very young I remember an acquaintance of my father commenting to him, "I really admire you. You don't just send your children to church, you take them." That impressed me because I'd never really thought about it before. I just took it for granted that my parents would attend church with us. Observation and experience have taught me this is not always the case.

This principle applies to most everything one could teach a child: don't send your young children out to rake the leaves or pick the fruit, but rather go with them; don't shout at them to calm down, be calm; don't restrict them from watching movies you watch, or drinking drinks that you drink. Don't set standards you aren't willing to keep.

> Verily, verily, I say unto you, this is my gospel; and ye know the things that ye must do in my church; for the works

> which ye have seen me do that shall ye also do; for that which ye have seen me do even that shall ye do;
>
> And know ye that ye shall be judges of this people, according to the judgment which I shall give unto you, which shall be just. Therefore, what manner of men ought ye to be? Verily I say unto you, even as I am. (3 Nephi 27:21, 27)

A loving and wise father leads the way, and gives support rather than shoves: "And they shall go out from all nations; and they shall not go out in haste, nor go by flight, for I will go before them, saith the Father, and I will be their rearward" (3 Nephi 21:29). Neither did the Savior allow us to come to earth without being willing to join us, show us the way, and set the example. We can more easily accept our challenges here on earth because we know our Savior came and endured the same difficulties. We trust Him when He says, "This is the way," for He knows the way from personal experience. He suffered, was persecuted, and yet He loved the sinner and forgave His enemies—thus He can ask that of us, as well.

The Book of Mormon is full of the Savior's leadership example: He was willing to submit to baptism though He was perfect (see 1 Nephi 11:27; 2 Nephi 31:5–6, 9–13, 17); use the power of the priesthood to bless others (see 3 Nephi 26:15); pray for His children (see 3 Nephi 19:20, 23, 27–28, 31); be a light to others in darkness (see 3 Nephi 18:16, 24); be consistent, dependable, and trustworthy (see 2 Nephi 10:14).

The Book of Mormon is replete with good father-leaders who set the example for their children; they practiced what they preached. We should apply this principle even to marital conflicts as did Lehi. Boys tend to husband and father as did their father before them. Girls tend to be the kind of wives and mothers their mothers were. Not only did Lehi set the example of humility and patience, he was also an example of obedience. Given the discord and arguments he faced from his children, coupled with the distress of his wife, it would be natural for Lehi to doubt himself and the Lord, to give in to their complaints and demands, and to forsake the journey. It would have been easier for him to just pack up and go back home. Occasionally a father may be tempted to forsake his role as leader in the home and give in to the wheedling of a disgruntled wife or child for the sake of peace and harmony. Elder Russell M. Nelson warns fathers: "As we go through life, even through very rough waters, a father's instinctive impulse to cling tightly to his wife or to his children may not be the best way to accomplish his objective. Instead, if he will lovingly cling to the Savior and the iron rod of the gospel, his family will want to cling to him and to the Savior" ("Set in Order Thy House," *Ensign*, Nov. 2001, 69).

Sharon Larsen, former counselor in the Young Women general presidency, reminds us, "If we are going to lead in righteousness, there can't be any question where we stand. Small uncertainties on our part can produce large uncertainties in our youth" ("Fear Not, For They That Be with Us Are More," *Ensign*, Nov. 2001, 68).

It is parents who must set the example of obedience as Lehi did, even if we don't fully understand the Lord's purposes (see 1 Nephi 9:3, 5–6). By doing so, Lehi honored his wife, his children, and the Lord all his life. "I have spoken these few words unto you all, my sons, in the last days of my probation; and I have chosen the good part, according to the words of the prophet. And I have none other object save it be the everlasting welfare of your souls. Amen" (2 Nephi 2:30).

Contrast that example with fathers and husbands who were not so valiant. The Lord, through Jacob, condemned the Nephites for not being a good example for their wives and children.

> And now behold, my brethren, ye know that these commandments were given to our father, Lehi; wherefore, ye have known them before; and ye have come unto great condemnation; for ye have done these things which ye ought not to have done.

> Behold, ye have done greater iniquities than the Lamanites, our brethren. Ye have broken the hearts of your tender wives, and lost the confidence of your children, because of your bad examples before them; and the sobbings of their hearts ascend up to God against you. And because of the strictness of the word of God, which cometh down against you, many hearts died, pierced with deep wounds. (Jacob 2:34–35)

Jacob chastised the Nephites for their wickedness and the poor example they set for their families. "Wherefore, ye shall remember your children, how that ye have grieved their hearts because of the example that ye have set before them; and also, remember that ye may, because of your filthiness, bring your children unto destruction, and their sins be heaped upon your heads at the last day" (Jacob 3:10).

Turn to Alma 5:43–48 and read his example of effective fathering/leadership. Read Alma's testimony to his Nephite "family." He didn't just tell them they needed to fast and pray to gain a testimony, but he was willing to pay that price so that he could bear his own testimony with confidence. We also have this description of King Mosiah:

> And it came to pass that King Mosiah did walk in the ways of the Lord, and did observe his judgments and his statutes, and did keep his commandments in all things whatsoever he commanded him.

> And king Mosiah did cause his people that they should till the earth. And he also, himself, did till the earth, that thereby he might not become burdensome to his people, that he might do according to that which his father had done in all things. And there was no contention among all his people for the space of three years. (Mosiah 6:6–7)

Read Mosiah 2:14–18. King Benjamin's great address illustrates what a good example of service he was to his son Mosiah, and to all his people. No wonder these two great father-leaders were so successful and beloved. Who wouldn't follow such examples?

Be Honest with Yourself and Your Children

We are fighting a war with Satan over the very souls of our children! Alma tells us how to win that war. In Alma 59 there is a clue about how to lose the war.

> And now, when Moroni saw that the city of Nephihah was lost he was exceedingly sorrowful, and began to doubt, because of the wickedness of the people, whether they should not fall into the hands of their brethren.
>
> Now this was the case with all his chief captains. They doubted and marveled also because of the wickedness of the people, and this because of the success of the Lamanites over them.
>
> And it came to pass that Moroni was angry with the government, because of their indifference concerning the freedom of their country (Alma 59:11–13).

Moroni was angry because the Nephites were so corrupt internally that the Lord would not support them in battle. If Satan can't penetrate from the outside, he will fight from within. Every battle is fought first in the heart. That is where it begins. Examine your own heart and motives to ensure their purity. Do you believe and practice what you teach your children? Children are perceptive and can easily spot hypocritical behavior. Do you hold yourself to the same entertainment standards you ask of your children? We cannot afford the cost of hypocrisy where we teach our children one thing and then do another ourselves. Elder Nelson warns, "The seditious evils of pornography, abortion, and addiction to harmful substances serve as termites to erode the undergirding strength of a happy home and a faithful family. We cannot yield to any iniquity without putting our families at risk" ("Set in Order Thy House," *Ensign*, Nov. 2001, 71).

Sometimes without our realizing it, the negative example comes from within our own homes rather than the worldly influences we often credit as the cause. Are your actions and example making it easier for Satan to win over the hearts of your children?

Of course we all make mistakes, but can we admit them and change, seeking forgiveness of the Lord as well as our children?

President Heber J. Grant's daughter related an experience with her father when she was very young that left such an impression on her she remembered the event all her life:

> I used some language father didn't approve of, and he told me he would have to wash such words out of my mouth. He scrubbed out my mouth thoroughly with soap and said, "Now your mouth is clean. I don't ever want you to make it dirty with such words again."
>
> Several days later at the breakfast table, father was telling a story, and in quoting someone else he used a profane expression. I was quick to pick it up.
>
> "Papa," I said, "you washed my mouth out for saying words like that."
>
> "So I did," he answered. "And I shouldn't say them any more than you should. Would you like to wash out my mouth?"
>
> "I certainly would." I got the laundry soap and did a thorough job of it.
>
> My father could have hedged. He could have said he wasn't really swearing, which, of course, was true; but that wasn't his

> way. A little child couldn't tell the difference between a quotation and the real thing, and he realized it. From that moment I knew that my father would be absolutely fair in all his dealings with me, and I never found him otherwise. After that, I never heard him even quote profane things. He loved to tell a lively story and he would say, "John said, *with emphasis,* such and such," but he never said the words. He was a great believer in teaching by example and never asked us to do anything he wouldn't do himself. (*The Teachings of Presidents of the Church: Heber J. Grant,* xvi; The Church of Jesus Christ of Latter-day Saints)

A juvenile judge told me her court is full of young people whose parents insist on one set of rules for the children, but live another themselves. Abinadi found a similar problem in the courts of King Noah:

> Ye have not applied your hearts to understanding; therefore, ye have not been wise. Therefore, what teach ye this people?
>
> And they said: We teach the law of Moses.
>
> And again he said unto them: If ye teach the law of Moses why do ye not keep it? Why do ye set your hearts upon riches? Why do ye commit whoredoms and spend your strength with harlots, yea, and cause this people to commit sin, that the Lord has cause to send me to prophesy against this people, yea, even a great evil against this people? (Mosiah 12:27–29).

Examples of Righteous Traditions vs. Unrighteous Traditions

Helaman was a righteous leader because he followed the example of his father; and his sons, Nephi and Lehi, followed their father's example walking in his ways. What a blessing a righteous example can be to growing children with one generation following the example of the previous one.

> And it came to pass that [Helaman] had two sons. He gave unto the eldest the name of Nephi, and unto the youngest, the name of Lehi. And they began to grow up unto the Lord.
>
> And it came to pass in the fifty and third year of the reign of the judges, Helaman died, and his eldest son Nephi began to reign in his stead. And it came to pass that he did fill the judgment-seat with justice and equity; yea, he did keep the commandments of God, and did walk in the ways of his father. (Helaman 3: 21, 37)

It is important that children understand their heritage, that they feel a part of a family chain. That is another reason to make good choices as parents, to honor the family name, and to follow the example of a grandparent or great-grandparent who began what has become a righteous tradition.

> For they remembered the words which their father Helaman spake unto them. And these are the words which he spake:
>
> Behold, my sons, I desire that ye should remember to keep the commandments of God; and I would that ye should declare unto the people these words. Behold, I have given unto you the names of our first parents who came out of the land of Jerusalem; and this I have done that when you remember your names ye may remember them; and when ye remember them ye may remember their works; and when ye remember their works ye may know how that it is said, and also written, that they were good.

> Therefore, my sons, I would that ye should do that which is good, that it may be said of you, and also written, even as it has been said and written of them. (Helaman 5:5–7)

How do children learn to hate and kill other human beings? How do they learn prejudice against another race or religion? They learn by the example others set for them and through unrighteous traditions as these Lamanite children did:

> They were a wild, and ferocious, and a blood-thirsty people, believing in the tradition of their fathers, which is this—Believing that they were driven out of the land of Jerusalem because of the iniquities of their fathers, and that they were wronged in the wilderness by their brethren, and they were also wronged while crossing the sea. (Mosiah 10:12)

> And thus they have taught their children that they should hate them, and that they should murder them, and that they should rob and plunder them, and do all they could to destroy them; therefore they have an eternal hatred towards the children of Nephi. (Mosiah 10:17)

Future generations are influenced by the character traits and attitudes passed on to them by parents and those who live in their culture. Contrast the attitudes above with those of the people of 4 Nephi when "the people were all converted unto the Lord, upon all the face of the land, both Nephites and Lamanites, and there were no contentions and disputations among them, and every man did deal justly one with another" (4 Nephi 1:2). This level of charity extended for almost two hundred years. They were a Zion people, a people pure in heart, who taught their children to respect others in spite of their differences. Apparently it will take the Millennium to bring that state of charity to the earth once again. Only then will there be peace on earth, this time for a thousand years.

Principle 7
Children Learn Best by Encouragement and Positive Reinforcement

If with pleasure you are viewing
Anything your child is doing,
If you like him, if you love him,
Let him know.

Don't withhold appreciation
Until others give expression—
If he wins your commendation
Tell him so.

More than fame and more than money
Is a disposition sunny,
And some hearty warm approval
Makes one glad.

So if you think some praise is due him,
Now's the time to give it to him;
Tie him close with loving language
From his dad.

(Ezra Taft Benson, "Great Things Required of Their Fathers," *Ensign*, May 1981, 34).

It is a common analogy that kids need encouragement like plants needs water. Children learn faster and perform better in an atmosphere of encouragement and approval than one of criticism and fear of failure. William G. Dyer and Phillip R. Kunz conducted a survey of approximately two hundred successful Mormon families to determine why their children were so exceptional. When asked how they expressed their love and approval to their children, ninety-seven percent said they tell their children they love them. Ninety-six reported that they show them love by doing things for them, and ninety-four percent show their love by hugging their children. Asked how often they exchanged some form of physical affection, eighty-one percent said it was a daily occurrence (see *Effective Mormon Families* [Salt Lake City, UT: Deseret Book], 1986, 80–84).

President Ezra Taft Benson once said, "I am convinced that before a child can be influenced for good by his or her parents, there must be a demonstration of respect and love" ("Great Things Required of Their Fathers," *Ensign*, May 1981, 34). As mentioned before, the old adage "I don't care how much you know until I know how much you care" is especially true in parenting.

Our purpose as parents is to build strong families and encourage our children to reach their highest potential. Encouragement and positive reinforcement build, while physical or emotional abuse, criticism, condemnation, and ridicule discourage, tear down, and defeat.

President Howard W. Hunter explained God's method of encouraging his children. Although cited earlier, this powerful statement merits repeating. "God's chief way of acting is by persuasion and patience and long-suffering, not by coercion and stark confrontation. He acts by gentle solicitation and by sweet enticement. He always acts with unfailing respect for the freedom and independence that we possess. He wants to help us and pleads for the chance to assist us, but he will not do so in violation of our agency" ("The Golden Thread of Choice," *Ensign*, Nov. 1989, 17).

President Gordon B. Hinckley shared his thoughts on this matter: "In terms of physical abuse, I have never accepted the principle of 'spare the rod and spoil the child.' I will be forever grateful for a father who never laid a hand in anger upon his children. Somehow he had the wonderful talent to let them know what was expected of them and to give them encouragement in achieving it. . . . Children don't need beating. They need love and encouragement. They need fathers to whom they can look with respect rather than fear. Above all, they need example" ("Save the Children," *Ensign*, Nov. 1994, 52).

This chapter and the supporting scriptures below illustrate the consequences—rewards—of righteous decisions and behavior. There are some wonderful examples of Book of Mormon prophets, and the Lord Himself, giving encouragement and positive reinforcement, which are the consequences of righteous behavior *if* a parent is wise and alert to opportunities. When a child performs or reacts in a constructive way, positive reinforcement by a peer or a respected adult reaffirms that particular behavior and helps the child learn what behavior is acceptable and what is not. Positive reinforcement accomplishes three important goals: (1) it instills pride and confidence in the child, (2) it inspires her to take on greater responsibility and enjoy special privileges commensurate with her growth and development, and (3) it encourages her to repeat the same behavior in the future. The examples in the Book of Mormon illustrate methods the Lord and prophet-leaders used to accomplish these three goals of positive reinforcement. Below are some ways that positive reinforcement can be used. We will discuss variations of these further in the following pages.

1. *Offering earned expressions of trust and appreciation.* ("Yes, Becky, you can go to the party tonight because I know I can trust you to remember our curfew guidelines.")

2. *Observing or having others point out the privileges received by those who abide by the family rules.* ("Your big brother cleaned his room early this morning, and now he gets to watch his favorite TV show. Maybe we should hurry and clean yours, too, so you can join him.")

3. *Leisure as an incentive.* ("If you all help get the fruit picked this morning, we can go swimming together this afternoon.")

4. *Verbal rewards for good choices.* ("Thank you, Susan, for choosing to share your toys with your sister.")

5. *Praise for good effort and achievement.* ("Sam, you did it! You remembered to come right home after school today! Good for you.")

Expressions of Appreciation and Trust Instill Confidence and Pride

Sprinkled throughout the Book of Mormon are events when Christ praised a particular prophet or group of people for their righteousness. How encouraging that must have been coming from the Savior Himself! Most of us are too prone to express disappointment, even anger, when our children misbehave. We fail to express appreciation and pleasure at times when they are obedient, cooperative, and helpful. You might find it revealing to check yourself by taking an inventory someday on the number of positive versus negative comments you make to your children. For example, how does this sound as the first words a child hears from you each afternoon: "Billy, how many times do I have to tell you, don't slam the door when you come in!" versus, "Billy, I'm so glad you came home right after school as you promised. Thank you for being obedient"? If his habit of slamming the door must be dealt with, do it as a gentle reminder after you have expressed your appreciation for his obedience. Then when he does close the door properly, acknowledge it in a positive way. Another revealing exercise would be to read the following scriptural examples of praise and appreciation, but substitute your name for the prophet's name and see how it makes you feel. Then you'll understand what your child feels like when you express your appreciation to him. "And when I had spoken these words, the Spirit cried with a loud voice, saying: Hosanna to the Lord, the most high God; for he is God over all the earth, yea, even above all. And blessed art thou, Nephi, [substitute your name] because thou believest in the Son of the most high God; wherefore, thou shalt behold the things which thou hast desired" (1 Nephi 11:6).

In Enos 1:5–10 and 12, the Lord offers positive reinforcement to Enos for his faith, and He makes it clear to Enos why he is blessed. Rather than just saying, "You're such a good girl, Amy," it is always more helpful for children to know exactly what called forth your praise. "Thank you, Amy, for taking care of your baby sister while I fixed dinner. That was so helpful." In the case of Enos, once it was made clear to him just why he was blessed, he felt more confident of his standing with the Lord and was ready to move ahead as the Lord's servant. Once a child understands he does not have to compete with siblings for parental favors, but warrants them through his own behavior, he feels more in control and can bless a sibling rather than being competitive.

> And now, my son [substitute your name], I trust that I shall have great joy in you, because of your steadiness and your faithfulness unto God; for as you have commenced in your youth to look to the Lord your God, even so I hope that you will continue in keeping his commandments; for blessed is he that endureth to the end.
>
> I say unto you, my son, that I have had great joy in thee already, because of thy faithfulness and thy diligence, and thy patience and thy long-suffering among the people of the Zoramites. (Alma 38:2–3)

Again, the Lord expressed His confidence and joy in Alma for his faithfulness, and was specific about what it was that caused Him to feel so.

> Blessed art thou, Alma, [again, substitute your name], and blessed are they who were baptized in the waters of Mormon. Thou art blessed because of thy exceeding faith in the words alone of my servant Abinadi.

> And blessed are they because of their exceeding faith in the words alone which thou hast spoken unto them.
>
> And blessed art thou because thou hast established a church among this people; and they shall be established, and they shall be my people.
>
> Yea, blessed is this people who are willing to bear my name; for in my name shall they be called; and they are mine. (Mosiah 26:15–18)

The Lord gave Alma positive reinforcement because of his faith and courage, and promised him the choicest blessing—eternal life. When children have the courage to stand up against their peers and make righteous decisions on their own, be generous with praise and trust them with a little more decision making in the future: "Mark, I'm so sorry your soccer team decided to practice on Sundays. We're not going to tell you what to do because you know what's right, and you've always made good decisions. We know you'll give this matter some thought and prayer and make the right decision this time too."

"And now, behold, my joy is great, even unto fulness, because of you, and also this generation; yea, and even the Father rejoiceth, and also all the holy angels, because of you and this generation; for none of them are lost" (3 Nephi 27:30). Christ gave His disciples responsibilities, and when they completed the assignment, He praised them and explained why their behavior pleased Him (see 3 Nephi 18:5, 10). Children respond to responsibility much better when they receive recognition for their good efforts and feel that what they did made an important contribution to the family.

The following story will illustrate this principle. Jared was excited to be ordained a deacon at first, and felt important when he was trusted to collect fast offerings for the poor one Sunday each month. But after a few months he began to grow tired of the responsibility and began seeing it as a chore and disruption to his

Sunday afternoons. His dad took him out one cold winter evening to visit some of the widows in the ward and explained to him how the fast offerings Jared gathered went to pay for needed food and heat for the elderly women who no longer could afford those necessities. The following fast Sunday, Jared gladly jumped up from the board game he was playing with his little brother to gather the fast offerings.

Note these good examples of Book of Mormon father-leaders who encouraged their children and followers in righteous behavior:

> And now, these are the words which king Benjamin desired of them; and therefore he said unto them: Ye have spoken the words that I desired; and the covenant which ye have made is a righteous covenant.
>
> And now, because of the covenant which ye have made ye shall be called the children of Christ, his sons, and his daughters; for behold, this day he hath spiritually begotten you; for ye say that your hearts are changed through faith on his name; therefore, ye are born of him and have become his sons and his daughters. (Mosiah 5:6–7)

King Benjamin acknowledged his people's desires to keep their covenants. In Alma 7:6, 17–20, and 26, Alma commends the people of Gideon for their righteousness by using phrases such as: "I trust that ye are not in a state of unbelief," "I trust that ye are not lifted up in the pride of your hearts," "I know that ye believe them," "Because your faith is strong," "Great is my joy," "My desires have been gratified," "I perceive that ye are in the paths of righteousness," "My soul doth exceedingly rejoice because of the exceeding diligence and heed which ye have given unto my word."

Before you send your sixteen-year-old out on a date with the family car, try some of these "trust you" statements. Your son will not want to disappoint you.

Alma's son, Corianton, made poor decisions in the mission field. After chastising and teaching him the importance of repentance, Alma encouraged him and sent him forth again, showing his trust in his son (see Alma 42:31). The Lord showed the same trust and faith in Joseph Smith when He chastened him and then again called him to the work (see D&C 10:3).

Here is an example of positive feedback from father to son as Mormon speaks to his son Moroni through his letters: "An epistle of my father Mormon, written to me, Moroni; and it was written unto me soon after my calling to the ministry. And on this wise did he write unto me, saying: My beloved son, Moroni, I rejoice exceedingly that your Lord Jesus Christ hath been mindful of you, and hath called you to his ministry, and to his holy work" (Moroni 8:2).

While it is a good idea to praise a child face-to-face with an arm around his shoulder, it is also a good idea occasionally to write a loving letter or note of appreciation so he may read and reread it as a strength and reminder to him when you are not there. "But behold my son, I recommend thee unto God, and I trust in Christ that thou wilt be saved" (Moroni 9:22).

What son would not enjoy that kind of recommendation from his father?

Preparing Children for New Responsibilities

Expressions of appreciation and trust prepare children to accept new responsibilities and enjoy special privileges. The following passage from the book of Ether provides a great example of this principle:

> And the Lord said unto him: Because of thy faith thou hast seen that I shall take upon me flesh and blood; and never has man come before me with such exceeding faith as thou hast; for were it not so ye could not have seen my finger. Sawest thou more than this?
>
> And he answered: Nay; Lord, show thyself unto me.

> And the Lord said unto him: Believest thou the words which I shall speak?
>
> And he answered: Yea, Lord, I know that thou speakest the truth, for thou art a God of truth, and canst not lie.
>
> And when he had said these words, behold, the Lord showed himself unto him, and said: Because thou knowest these things ye are redeemed from the fall; therefore ye are brought back into my presence; therefore I show myself unto you.
>
> And never have I showed myself unto man whom I have created, for never has man believed in me as thou hast. Seest thou that ye are created after mine own image? Yea, even all men were created in the beginning after mine own image. (Ether 3:9–13, 15)

The Lord praised the brother of Jared for his faith, took him into His confidence and showed him something no man had seen before. Along with this privilege came increased knowledge (seeing the spirit body of Jehovah), which brought added responsibility. Where "much is given, much is required" (D&C 82:3). I think the brother of Jared felt awed by his experience with the Lord, but also gratified that the Lord trusted him with this added knowledge concerning His nature. Children are more willing, even happy, to accept added responsibility if they are helped to feel good about what they are doing. Children quickly learn that added responsibility is an indication of their growing maturity rather than a job or burden to carry.

If children are allowed to make small decisions on their own and then more important ones later, appropriate to their age and maturity, they grow in experience and confidence and can be trusted with more and more responsibility. A young child might be trusted to hold his small baby brother while you sit next to them. When he shows he can be careful and gentle, he might be allowed to hold the baby for longer periods. As both children mature, the older one may be trusted with the care of his younger sibling at play, first while you are present, then, perhaps in the backyard with you nearby, and eventually, he may be given full charge while Mom and Dad go out for a short evening. Each time you praise him for his tenderness and patience, point out the trust that is developing between the two of them, and the need for the older one to be protective and a good example.

Teenagers struggle with autonomy. In fact, their major job during those teen years is to discover who they are and to prove to their parents and the world that they can make good decisions on their own. They crave freedom. They need to feel in control of their lives; that's what growing up is all about, but at the same time, underneath that bravado, they are just a little scared. They aren't always sure they know what's best, and deep down inside they want someone or something to stop them if they approach the deep end. That makes a parent's job a little more complicated. We have to know the child well enough to know just how much freedom to give while at the same time establishing some boundaries beyond which the child may not go. Our job is to guide them safely through this tumultuous time, gradually adding more and more responsibility and more privileges while teaching them that the freedom they crave is really up to them. When they are obedient and responsible, they prove themselves trustworthy. Once a child understands that principle, he will be hesitant to destroy that trust and lose that freedom.

This concept is illustrated in several other places in the Book of Mormon. In Helaman 10:4–12, for instance, the Lord praises and blesses Nephi for his righteousness and bestows upon him great power and added responsibilities because he has earned them. As you read that section, ask yourself, "Would Nephi ever be tempted to disappoint the Lord after that kind of validation?" I think not. I think Nephi must have been so overwhelmed with the trust and confidence the Lord had in him that he was ready at that point to tackle any assignment given him.

Oh, that we could instill that same sense of privilege and that same kind of determination to succeed in our modern missionaries. If our young men and women are brought up to feel they must earn the trust and confidence of the Lord to go forth at young ages to represent Him, they will be anxious, as Nephi was, to never disappoint the Lord while holding a position of trust.

Long before a child becomes a teenager, a parent has many opportunities to help the child experience the satisfaction of a job well done, a decision well made, a confidence well earned, and prepare him for further positions of trust. Being alert to any conscientious attempts on the part of a child to do his best and then providing him with positive feedback on that effort can help accomplish the intended goal. Even a difficult or unpleasant chore can become a source of personal pride.

Our eight-year-old son David, as well as the other children, hated to clean the chrome kitchen chairs. Cleaning them was hard and tedious work, second only to cleaning toilets and showers. One Saturday David was the last one up to draw his "job card," and the only job left was the dreaded chrome chairs. Grumbling something about it being unfair, he snatched the toothbrush needed for cleaning the crevices between the cushion and frame, some cleanser, a few rags I handed him, and set to work. After an hour or so of digging, scraping, scrubbing, and polishing, he had those chairs sparkling. It was a joy to sit down on them at dinner that night. I told him so in glowing terms, praising his good work before the whole family. He was so pleased with his work and the validation he received for it he asked for the "privilege" of being responsible for cleaning those chairs every Saturday.

Using Melchizedek as an example, Alma explains how freedom, which is personal power, and more responsibility are the rewards for obedience (see Alma 13:3–4, 10, 13–14, 18). Notice how in this next example the Lord first praises Lehi for his righteous behavior, encouraging him, and *then* gives him direction for an added responsibility.

> For behold, it came to pass that the Lord spake unto my father, yea, even in a dream, and said unto him: Blessed art thou Lehi, because of the things which thou hast done; and because thou hast been faithful and declared unto this people the things which I commanded thee, behold, they seek to take away thy life.
>
> And it came to pass that the Lord commanded my father, even in a dream, that he should take his family and depart into the wilderness.
>
> And it came to pass that he was obedient unto the word of the Lord, wherefore he did as the Lord commanded him. (1 Nephi 2:1–3)

In viewing 3 Nephi 28:1–15 we find an example of Jesus speaking to His disciples one by one. He wanted to know their deepest desires. Then He praised them for their choices, especially the three who chose to remain on the earth, and He granted them their desires. He further honored them by allowing them to observe a very sacred ordinance that none other could see or experience. As you read this section in the Book of Mormon, look for at least three good techniques the Lord used that we as parents might try in order to encourage continued good behavior—praise, rewards, and special privileges.

Next, read Jacob 7:5: "And he [Sherem] had hope to shake me from the faith, notwithstanding the many revelations and the many things which I had seen concerning these things; for I truly had seen angels, and they had ministered unto me. And also, I had heard the voice of the Lord speaking unto me in very word, from time to time; wherefore, I could not be shaken."

Because of past positive reinforcement, Jacob could not be shaken from his position of faith in the Lord. The same commitment can be instilled in our children. For example, Amanda's friends tried to persuade her to stay longer at a party than she was supposed to, but because Amanda's parents had previously expressed appreciation for her obedience, she could not be persuaded to disappoint her parents by being disobedient now. They trusted her, and she did not want to break that trust, even if it meant disappointing her friends.

And finally, the ultimate example of obedience and reward is Christ. Because He was obedient and made the sacrifice needed to carry out the Father's plan, He was rewarded with power and responsibility and has now received all that the Father has.

> And after all this, after working many mighty miracles among the children of men, he shall be led, yea, even as Isaiah said, as a sheep before the shearer is dumb, so he opened not his mouth.
>
> Yea, even so he shall be led, crucified, and slain, the flesh becoming subject even unto death, the will of the Son being swallowed up in the will of the Father.
>
> And thus God breaketh the bands of death, having gained the victory over death; giving the son power to make intercession for the children of men. (Mosiah 15:6–7)

Observing Another's Privileges Provides Incentives

Observing the privileges others are enjoying helps children set goals of obedience. While a parent hesitates to compare one child with another, it can be helpful to point out to a child just why and how someone, be it a sibling or respected figure outside the family, enjoys advantages the child desires. For example, if a child shows an interest in a vocation or talent of another, it might be helpful to find books for him to read about that hero's life and how he got to that point. Success always involves hard work and sacrifice somewhere along the way. Adults and children alike can be inspired to greater works as they witness the success of others.

It's not uncommon for a child to complain to a parent, "Why do I have to go to bed at eight when Margaret gets to stay up until ten?" A good response, if it is true, might be, "Margaret is five years older than you are and has proven she can be trusted to stay up later and still get up in the morning cheerfully and get her chores done. When you can do this, we'll know you are ready to stay up later too." That promise of future "blessings" will encourage a younger child to fulfill the requirements.

In the Book of Mormon, prophets often remind their people of blessings their forefathers received by their righteous behavior, pointing out that they, too, could receive such blessings were they willing to pay the price of obedience. Look at Jacob 3 and read verses 5–7. At this point the Lamanites' righteousness exceeds that of the Nephites, and the Lord rewards that righteous behavior. He also makes sure the Nephites understand why the Lamanites are being blessed and why they are not.

In Mosiah 2:41, King Benjamin points out the happy state of those who are righteous, noting that joy comes from righteous living. This not only reinforces the principle for those who are obedient and keeping the commandments, but hopefully points the way for those who haven't yet figured it out.

> And moreover, I would desire that ye should consider on the blessed and happy state of those that keep the commandments of God. For behold, they are blessed in all things, both temporal and spiritual; and if they hold out faithful to the end they are received into heaven, that thereby they may dwell with God in a state of never-ending happiness. O remember, remember that these things are true; for the Lord God hath spoken it.

Now look at Alma 48:17–19 and read how Helaman affirms the goodness and greatness of Moroni, Ammon, the sons of Mosiah, and Alma and his own sons. This not only provides wonderful affirmation for those men, but a lesson to the people about who their role models ought to be.

Promise of Future Blessings Helps Children Obey

Closely related to observed blessings is the promise that if we do likewise, we too shall enjoy such privileges, as in the case of Margaret and her younger sibling previously recounted. The Lord is eager to make covenants with us, promising us all that He has if we keep all of our covenants. Do we believe Him? How can we know for sure? Alma tells us the only way to develop faith is to try His word, exercising only a particle of faith "even to an experiment upon my words" (see Alma 32:27). Only experience with exercising faith and being blessed assures us that the Lord can be trusted to keep His promises. The Church of Jesus Christ was restored after a fourteen-year-old boy read a promise in the scriptures and decided to take the Lord at His word (see Joseph Smith—History 1:11). Was he rewarded for his efforts? Beyond his wildest dreams.

The Book of Mormon is full of covenants made and broken, but never broken by the Savior, only by humans struggling with worldly temptations. Here's a good rule: never make a promise to a child you cannot keep. It is imperative that he learns from experience that your word can be trusted. Notice Nephi's reply when the Spirit asked, "Believest thou that thy father saw the tree of which he hath spoken?" Nephi answered "Yea, thou knowest that I believe all the words of my father" (1 Nephi 11:4–5).

How did Nephi develop such faith in his father's word? We'll discuss this in more detail later, but here let us consider some of the many promises made by the Lord and His prophets and the effect those promises had on the righteousness of the people.

Laman and Lemuel had a question about something their father had taught them, something they couldn't understand. Nephi asked them if they had asked the Lord, reminding them of a promise the Lord made to all His children. This promise established a consequence, or reward, if you will, of a righteous behavior that he desired of his children. "Do ye not remember the things which the Lord hath said?—If ye will not harden your hearts, and ask me in faith, believing that ye shall receive, with diligence in keeping my commandments, surely these things shall be made known unto you" (1 Nephi 15:11).

Laman and Lemuel chose not to accept that promise, so they never received the blessing. Nephi did, and he was rewarded many times for his faith and obedience. Later in the same chapter, Nephi reminded his brothers of another promise, one made over and over again in the Book of Mormon. Again, Laman and Lemuel chose to ignore it, but Nephi did not. "And I [Nephi] said unto them that it [the rod of iron] was the word of God; and whoso would hearken unto the word of God, and would hold fast unto it, they would never perish; neither could the temptations and the fiery darts of the adversary overpower them unto blindness, to lead them away to destruction" (1 Nephi 15:24). Nephi and his family were blessed when they obeyed and followed the Lord's counsel.

> And thus we see that the commandments of God must be fulfilled. And if it so be that the children of men keep the commandments of God he doth nourish them, and strengthen them, and provide means whereby they can accomplish the thing which he has commanded them; wherefore, he did provide means for us while we did sojourn in the wilderness.
>
> And I will also be your light in the wilderness; and I will prepare the way before you, if it so be that ye shall keep my commandments; wherefore, inasmuch as ye shall keep my commandments ye shall be led towards the promised land; and ye shall know that it is by me that ye are led. (1 Nephi 17:3, 13)

Ether 12 contains a great lecture on faith with at least nine separate examples of people who have been rewarded because they kept their covenants with the Lord. As you read this chapter with your children, add your family's name to that list and make up a similar scripture as though it had already happened: "*For it was by faith that the Johnson family followed all the commandments of the Lord and . . .*" (Fill in the rest according to your family's needs.)

Immediate Rewards Inspire More Good Behavior

You probably noticed that most of the promises I selected above were promises of blessings to be enjoyed in the future, some even after this life. Sometimes it suits God's purposes to test His children and their commitment to righteousness. This test works better for older children and adults, but very young children need more immediate results. As you attempt to apply this principle to your own children, keep in mind that very young children do not have the mental capacity to conceptualize rewards very far into the future. They function better when we say, "Help me pick up the toys and we'll have a story," or "If you are still hungry after you finish your sandwich, you can have a cookie." As a child matures, he learns to anticipate and can benefit from longer-range rewards, i.e., "When we finish reading the Book of Mormon together we could take a family trip to Grandma and Grandpa's and share with them all we've learned this year."

I related in an earlier chapter a story about a family that was experiencing a lot of contention in their home. When they decided to follow the counsel of the Brethren to read the scriptures, have family prayer together every day, and family home evening each week, hearts were softened and the atmosphere in the home changed almost immediately; sometimes the Lord blesses us immediately.

In the case of a personal prayer for help or a plea for an answer to a perplexing problem, the Lord often responds immediately and sometimes very dramatically, as in the case of Joseph Smith in the Sacred Grove. The following examples are found in the Book of Mormon:

While Enos describes his prayer as "mighty prayer and supplication . . . all the day long," that is a comparatively short time to wait for an answer as dramatic as this: "And there came a voice unto me, saying: Enos, thy sins are forgiven thee, and thou shalt be blessed" (Enos 1:5).

Nephi's prayers were rewarded almost immediately.

> And it came to pass that I, Nephi, being exceedingly young, nevertheless being large in stature, and also having

> great desires to know of the mysteries of God, wherefore, I did cry unto the Lord; and behold he did visit me, and did soften my heart that I did believe all the words which had been spoken by my father; wherefore, I did not rebel against him like unto my brothers. (1 Nephi 2:16)

> For it came to pass after I had desired to know the things that my father had seen, and believing that the Lord was able to make them known unto me, as I sat pondering in mine heart I was caught away in the Spirit of the Lord, yea, into an exceedingly high mountain, which I never had before seen, and upon which I never had before set my foot. And the Spirit said unto me: Behold, what desirest thou? (1 Nephi 11:1–2)

I admit I've never had the Lord appear to me, or even had an angel sent to me when I've knelt in supplication, but I have on occasion experienced some pretty quick results when they were needed. Once, for instance, I was ready to go to the temple to do some family names I'd researched. I was very excited for my relatives and for myself, but upon a last-minute check of my temple bag, I realized my recommend was missing. Racking my brain to recall where I could have put it, I finally drew a blank. I checked all the pockets of dresses and jackets I might possibly have worn, checked my purse, drawers, jewelry box—every place I could think of. Finally I knelt in prayer and explained to the Lord how important it was for me to go that day, and could He please help me find my recommend? Even before I'd said amen the thought came to my mind: "Check your temple-name card file." I never, never store my recommend in there, but I was desperate and obeyed the prompting. Just as I opened up the file I saw myself putting it in there the week before, along with the name I'd done that day, thinking, I suppose, I'd put it away later. I've had other immediate answers to prayers when they've involved my family history research and have learned from those experiences that this is a righteous activity and that the Lord is ready and willing to help me with it if I am trying my best.

I once heard another mother say she was desperately seeking her young son's missing shoe so the family could get to church on time. She knelt to pray, and while she was on her knees she opened her eyes and spied the shoe under the couch. Pretty quick response, I'd say!

When we're dealing with a whole nation, or even a whole family, waiting for everyone or at least the majority to comply can often take a few days or months, even years, before the Lord can respond. But the lesson is to do our best to respond promptly to good behavior and to teach our children that Heavenly Father also rewards good behavior.

Rewarding Good Behavior and Ignoring Disruptive Behavior

Sometimes we unwittingly reward a child for being disruptive or disobedient by focusing all our attention on him and the behavior. Often a "naughty" child is a discouraged child and only needs to be taught how to get attention in positive ways. If we want behavior to be repeated, we comment on it, focus on it, or reward it in some way. We help the child feel good about what he has done. A wise man once told me, "A child may not always remember what you say, but he will remember how you made him feel." Help a child experience the joy of obedience as Lehi did: "And as I partook of the fruit thereof it filled my soul with exceedingly great joy; wherefore, I began to be desirous that my family should partake of it also; for I knew that it was desirable above all other fruit" (1 Nephi 8:12).

Samuel the Lamanite tells of the blessings given to the Lamanite people because of the good they did. "And now, because of their steadfastness when they do believe in that thing which they do believe, for because of their firmness when they are once enlightened, behold, the Lord shall bless them and prolong their days, notwithstanding their iniquity" (Helaman 15:10).

What a lesson for parents who often see only the bad and forget the good their children have done.

Nine-year-old Tommy had been quiet all through dinner one evening. His mother could see he was troubled. As she tucked him into bed that night she asked him if he could share with her what was troubling him. Big tears formed in Tommy's eyes as he told how he and his friends, while stopping at a nearby store on the way home from school, had each decided to steal a candy bar. Tommy didn't feel good about it, but when his friends urged him, he put a candy bar in his pocket as well. The others ate theirs on the way home. They were so busy laughing and bragging about how clever they had been that nobody noticed how quiet Tommy was and that he wasn't eating his stolen loot. He just could not bring himself to eat it. It was still in his pocket as his jeans lay flung over the chair in his room where he'd left them as he got ready for bed. Tommy's mother looked into his eyes, offered a little prayer in her heart that she might respond appropriately, and asked, "Tommy, what do you intend to do?"

Again the tears welled up as Tommy softly replied, "I want to take it back tomorrow and apologize."

Mother gave Tommy a big hug and whispered, "I am so proud of you, Tommy. Heavenly Father knows we will make some mistakes while we are here, but He is more concerned about what we do about them. I know He is pleased with your decision, and so am I."

What decision do you think Tommy is apt to make next time he is tempted to steal something?

A friend of ours told how his father overlooked his poor judgment and reinforced his righteous behavior. He said he had wrecked the family car and dreaded having to tell his father what he'd done. Finally he got the courage to do it and took his father out to see the damage, humbly apologizing for his carelessness. His father looked at the ugly dent in the car, looked at his son's repentant face, and said, "Son, I don't care so much about the car, I'm just glad you honor the priesthood."

Brent Top and Bruce Chadwick, professors at Brigham Young University, conducted a study on the religiosity of LDS youth and what factors were involved. Amidst all the data collected from their study, they found this common thread: "Numerous young people in the study pled for their parents to be more liberal with praise and generous with forgiveness. The youth acknowledged their mistakes, but were disappointed that their parents directed most of their attention to such misdeeds and neglected their accomplishments" ("Parents Really Matter in Rearing Children," *Church News*, March 6, 1999, 10).

Principle 8
Allow Natural and Logical Consequences to Teach

The family yard sale had been a successful one, and five-year-old Bobby had earned ten dollars from the sale of his own items—just enough to pay for the extra treats and souvenirs he'd want to buy on their approaching family vacation. His older sister Susan had earned some too, and together they anticipated the fun they'd have. Mother cautioned the children to put their vacation money aside in a safe place so it wouldn't get lost and so they wouldn't be tempted to spend it on other things. Susan was careful to do just that, but Bobby was so proud to have some real money in his wallet he carried it around with him everywhere, even taking it out and counting it over and over. Again mother cautioned him about putting it in a safe place, but her words fell on deaf ears. He was sure he could take care of it just fine in his pocket. Occasionally when he went to the store with his mom to do the shopping he'd see some little treat or toy he wanted and think about the money just burning a hole in his wallet. At first he resisted, but gradually his resistance wore down. The temptation was just too much. He never spent much at one time—a quarter there, fifty cents here, a dollar there. I still have plenty, he'd tell himself. Mother always shook her head and frowned when she saw what he was doing. She even tried a few times to remind him of his goal, but finally realized that any further comment on her part would go unheeded. He'd have to learn the hard way.

Then, the night before the trip, when everyone was busy packing, Bobby found himself almost totally broke. The money had gotten away from him after all, and he had only one dollar left. Tearfully he went to his mother and showed her the nearly empty wallet. She resisted all temptations to say "I told you so," and expressed her sincere sympathy, but at this point there was little else she could do. Bobby was sitting on the front steps, his head in hands, mourning over his predicament, when Dad came home from work. After hearing the sad story from Bobby, Dad reached in his wallet and handed over a ten-dollar bill. He enjoyed seeing his little son's face light up as he ran inside to show his sister the money. Susan was indignant, as was Mother, though Mom didn't say anything just then. Later that night after the children were in bed, she expressed her disappointment to her husband. "What could you be thinking ?" she asked. "How can we teach our son to take responsibility for his own actions if he never has consequences?"

"Oh, it's only ten dollars," her husband replied defensively. "No big deal."

But what did Bobby learn from this experience? What did Susan learn? Just how big a deal was it?

Another example comes from a few years ago when two young boys were killed in a tragic accident. They had broken into a construction shed, found the key to a huge piece of equipment, turned it on, and both were crushed in the ensuing accident. In an interview, one of the grieving parents placed all the blame on the owner of the site and the electrical contractor. He was thinking of suing them both for causing the death of his son. A few days later, a sympathetic but clear-thinking observer wrote the following in a letter to the editor: "First of all, I believe the parents need to think again about who is responsible. The two boys violated the law by breaking into someone else's building. They stole a machine after breaking into it to find the key (again, against the law). It is parents' responsibility to teach their kids right from wrong. By their own acts, the victims caused their own deaths. I really believe it is time for all of us to take responsibility for our own actions instead of looking for someone else to blame when it is our own fault."

Don't we see a lot of "passing the buck" these days? It seems like we've all become sue-happy, looking everywhere but in our own backyard for the cause of our problems. Parents rush to their child's defense if a teacher tries to enforce a school rule. Neighbors are at each other's throats if their children don't get along, eager to show support for their own child, even if he was wrong. If we get throat cancer, it's the cigarette makers' fault; if we have an accident while driving drunk, we sue the beer manufacturer; if a woman experiences an unwanted pregnancy, it's the government's fault for not distributing free condoms. Nobody wants to live with the consequences of their behavior.

Often our children would use as an excuse for some misconduct, "But the other kids started it," or "He told me to do it." Second Nephi 7:1 reminds us that in spite of what others do and say, we are responsible for our own actions. "Yea, for thus saith the Lord: Have I put thee away, or have I cast thee off forever? For thus saith the Lord: Where is the bill of your mother's divorcement? To whom have I put thee away, or to which of my creditors have I sold you? Yea, to whom have I sold you? Behold, for your iniquities have ye sold yourselves, and for your transgressions is your mother put away."

Helaman 14:29–31 teaches this same doctrine:

> And this to the intent that whosoever will believe might be saved, and that whosoever will not believe, a righteous judgment might come upon them; and also if they are condemned they bring upon themselves their own condemnation.
>
> And now remember, remember, my brethren, that whosoever perisheth, perisheth unto himself; and whosoever doeth iniquity, doeth it unto himself; for behold, ye are free; ye are permitted to act for yourselves; for behold, God hath given unto you a knowledge and he hath made you free.

> He hath given unto you that ye might know good from evil, and he hath given unto you that ye might choose life or death; and ye can do good and be restored unto that which is good, or have that which is good restored unto you; or ye can do evil, and have that which is evil restored unto you.

And 1 Nephi 10:20 reads, “Therefore remember, O man, for all thy doings thou shalt be brought into judgment.” Help your children understand that they will be accountable for their choices, not only at home, but in the school and community, and that the consequences are not easier to bear because the “sin” was someone else’s idea.

Teaching by allowing consequences to take place is a hard principle for parents to follow. We love our children. We don’t want them to suffer. We’d like them to sail through life always making the right decisions, always being rewarded, and always being happy. But sometimes we mistake indulgence for love. For some the definition of good parenting is giving them more, softening the road, or reining them in so strictly that they are never allowed to make a poor decision, never allowed to fail. Sometimes children in their shortsightedness beg and plead for something we know is not good for them. If you give in to the pleading (for example, their friends are standing around and you don’t want to embarrass them by insisting they come home by ten) even though you know they’ll regret their decision (to stay out until midnight) because they have an early morning paper route, if you decide to let them have their way, do *not* do the paper route for them because you think that’s what a kind, sympathetic parent would do. Don’t we, in our shortsightedness, find ourselves pleading for something the Lord just doesn’t seem to want to give us? Sometimes He does give in because of our persistence, as in the case of Joseph Smith asking for permission to let the 116 pages of translation go with Martin Harris. We all know the outcome of that fiasco (see D&C 3).

We get another example of not being satisfied with what the Lord gives us in Jacob 4:14:

> But behold, the Jews were a stiffnecked people; and they despised the words of plainness, and killed the prophets, and sought for things that they could not understand. Wherefore, because of their blindness, which blindness came by looking beyond the mark, they must needs fall; for God hath taken away his plainness from them, and delivered unto them many things which they cannot understand, because they desired it. And because they desired it God hath done it, that they may stumble.

Jacob explains that the Lord let the Jews have that which they desired so they could experience the consequences of their desires and learn from them. Some children (and adults) have difficulty in accepting counsel and insist on learning from their own mistakes. We must allow them that opportunity as long as it is not illegal. One young adult said it this way: "I know how to be a mother, to cook, to clean, to sew, and how to teach my children. I learned that from my mom. I am grateful for her good example, but I am also grateful that I learned I want my children to be responsible for their actions. One of my brothers is struggling right now in life and my parents give him too much. I think there comes a time when you have to love your children enough to let them go, make their own decisions, and live with the consequences, or they'll never grow up."

A reformed alcoholic told how, as a youngster, he began experimenting with alcohol and would get into trouble with the law. His mother always bailed him out. After years of substance abuse and years of getting "bailed out," he concluded that though his mother had the best of intentions, her protection only prolonged his addiction and interfered with his ultimate repentance. It wasn't until he was allowed to hit rock bottom that he was able to start the climb back up.

This is what Elder Richard G. Scott said to parents concerning consequences: "Parents, don't make the mistake of purposefully intervening to soften or eliminate the natural consequences of your child's deliberate decisions to violate the commandments. Such acts reinforce false principles, open the door for more serious sin, and lessen the likelihood of repentance. . . . True principles are not easy to live until they become an established pattern of life. They will require you to dislodge false ideas" ("The Power of Correct Principles," *Ensign*, May 1993, 34).

The Lord has much to say about consequences. The Book of Mormon is full of accounts of choices made by individuals and the resulting blessings or consequences. The Lord always makes it clear what actions are required, but He never will take away agency to make the decision for us. That's what coming to this earth was all about, after all—learning to use agency wisely.

There are four simple steps to applying the principle of teaching by consequences:

1. Explain the potential consequences of an action.

2. Allow the child to make his decision.

3. Allow him to experience the consequences.

4. Rejoice with the child over a decision well made, or sympathize sincerely when a child is faced with a bitter consequence, but *do not* say "I told you so" or react angrily or withdraw your love.

In Jacob 5, the allegory of the tame and wild olive trees and its message illustrates all four of these steps:

1. Nurture and teach: "I will prune it, and dig about it, and nourish it, that perhaps it may shoot forth young and tender branches" (verse 4).

2. Allow a choice: "Only a part of the tree hath brought forth tame fruit, the other part of the tree hath bought forth wild fruit; behold, I have nourished this tree like unto the others" (verse 25).

3. Allow a consequence experience: "Pluck off the branches that have not brought forth good fruit and cast them into the fire" (verse 26).

4. Sorrow or rejoice with the child: "Perhaps the trees of my vineyard may bring forth again good fruit; and that I may have joy again in the fruit of my vineyard, and perhaps, that I may rejoice exceedingly that I have preserved the roots and the branches of the first fruit. . . . For it grieveth me that I should lose the trees of my vineyard" (verses 60, 66).

A careful study of both chapters 5 and 6 in the book of Jacob reveals that the Lord is a loving and forgiving Father who allowed the consequences to teach but gave His children many opportunities to repent and try again. The following discussion points in the Book of Mormon exemplify these steps as well.

1. Explain the Possible Consequences

First of all, explain to your children, as Lehi did (see 2 Nephi 2:11–23), that there needs to be "opposition in all things"; otherwise "righteousness could not be brought to pass, neither wickedness, neither holiness nor misery, neither good nor bad." The purpose of mortality, the need to have opposition, the need for law and justice all indicate that if the consequences of that law are not felt, there would be no purpose to this life, for no learning would take place.

In explaining the need for the Atonement to his son Corianton, Alma also explained the need for law and consequences (see Alma 42:16–28). Mercy shall not rob justice—there must be some consequences even for those who repent. President Boyd K.

Packer said, "Alma bluntly told his wayward son that 'repentance could not come unto men except there were a punishment.' The punishment may, for the most part, consist of the torment we inflict upon ourselves. It may be the loss of privilege or progress. We are punished by our sins, if not *for* them" ("The Brilliant Morning of Forgiveness," *Ensign*, Nov. 1995, 19).

In Alma 12:13–14 and 31–32, Alma taught Zeezrom the plan of salvation, the need for agency, and the consequences of choices:

> Then if our hearts have been hardened, yea, if we have hardened our hearts against the word, insomuch that it has not been found in us, then will our state be awful, for then we shall be condemned.
>
> For our words will condemn us, yea, all our works will condemn us; we shall not be found spotless; and our thoughts will also condemn us; and in this awful state we shall not dare to look up to our God; and we would fain be glad if we could command the rocks and the mountains to fall upon us to hide us from his presence.
>
> Wherefore, he gave commandments unto men, they having first transgressed the first commandments as to things which were temporal, and becoming as Gods, knowing good from evil, placing themselves in a state to act, or being placed in a state to act according to their wills and pleasures, whether to do evil or to do good—
>
> Therefore God gave unto them commandments, after having made known unto them the plan of redemption, that they should not do evil, the penalty thereof being a second death, which was an everlasting death as to things pertaining unto righteousness; for on such the plan of redemption could have no power, for the works of justice could not be destroyed, according to the supreme goodness of God.

The Book of Mormon provides some cautions when teaching children about agency and consequences. For instance, in Ether 8:20–24, the Lord spells out the consequences for allowing secret oaths and combinations, but He also reminds us that you don't have to describe to young impressionable minds every possible sin they could commit.

Another caution is to not burden a child with a responsibility he is too young to understand, or insist he live with the consequence when he has not been prewarned of the dangers lurking behind his decision. Younger children need more supervision and protection from their own inexperience and limited understanding. We expect more from our children as they mature, as the Lord did the Nephites in Helaman 7:23–24 who knew better:

> For behold, thus saith the Lord: I will not show unto the wicked of my strength, to one more than the other, save it be unto those who repent of their sins, and hearken unto my words. Now therefore, I would that ye should behold, my brethren, that it shall be better for the Lamanites than for you except ye shall repent.
>
> For behold, they are more righteous than you, for they have not sinned against that great knowledge which ye have received; therefore the Lord will be merciful unto them; yea, he will lengthen out their days and increase their seed, even when thou shalt be utterly destroyed except thou shalt repent.

In that same vein, Nephi explained a principle of mercy that can be applied in parenting children too young to know better: "Wherefore, he has given a law; and where there is no law given there is no punishment; and where there is no punishment there is no condemnation; and where there is no condemnation, the mercies of the Holy One of Israel have claim upon them, because of the atonement; for they are delivered by the power of him" (2 Nephi 9:25).

But once we're taught the law, we are accountable. "But wo unto him that has the law given, yea, that has all the commandments of God, like unto us, and that transgresseth them, and that wasteth the days of his probation, for awful is his state!" (2 Nephi 9:27).

We have been taught that children cannot be held accountable before the age of eight (see Moroni 8:5–29). That does not mean you have to wait until a child is eight years old before you start letting her make decisions and experience consequences. A five-year-old can understand that if she does not put her toys away, they won't be available for a while, or a six-year-old can be taught that if he doesn't make his bed in the morning before school, he might be called home to do it. A wise parent will give the child opportunities to make good decisions and have some control over his life while he is young and the decisions are relatively benign. As he matures, the decisions take on more significance, and when he is old enough to be accountable for sin, he'll have some experience and be better prepared to deal with choices wisely.

One more caution: when you've taught the principle and you're sure you've made it clear, it's time to stop talking. Lehi teaching his children spoke gently and kindly and exhorted them to be obedient, but then he stopped talking and let them make their decision. They could obey and enjoy the blessings, or suffer the consequences of those decisions. "And he did exhort them then with all the feeling of a tender parent, that they would hearken to his words. . . . And after he had preached unto them, and also prophesied unto them of many things, he bade them to keep the commandments of the Lord; and he did cease speaking unto them" (1 Nephi 8:37–38).

Sometimes parents talk too much. We keep nagging and threatening, but we never follow through. Children catch on to this very quickly and soon tune out the threats. *Don't make a rule or establish a consequence you aren't willing to follow through on.* Moroni taught us the importance of being consistent when he said to Zerahemnah, "Now I cannot recall the words which I have spoken" (Alma 44:11), even though it meant more death and destruction to both the Lamanites and the Nephites. It is important to be understanding, sympathetic, and patient, but do not assume the guilt for a poor decision made by a child. You are not the enemy. You're on her side. She needs to know that, but she also needs to know that you respect her right to make her own decisions and her right to enjoy or suffer the consequences of those decisions.

Omni wrote of the blessings of obedience and the consequences of disobedience. The Lord is consistent in His promises because He loves His children.

> For the Lord would not suffer, after he had led them out of the land of Jerusalem and kept and preserved them from falling into the hands of their enemies, yea, he would not suffer that the words should not be verified, which he spake unto our fathers, saying that: Inasmuch as ye will not keep my commandments ye shall not prosper in the land.
>
> Wherefore, the Lord did visit them in great judgment; nevertheless, he did spare the righteous that they should not perish, but did deliver them out of the hands of their enemies. (Omni 1:6–7)

We, as parents, love all our children as the Lord loves all of us. It is because of this love that we must be consistent in allowing all our children freedom to make choices and progress. They must be able to trust our word. An excellent example of that is found in 1 Nephi 17:31–38. Nephi is recounting the history of God's dealings with Israel: "According to his word he did destroy them; and according to his word he did lead them; and according to his word he did do all things for them." In other words, the Lord made covenants with the children of Israel, and He followed through on His word.

Plan A and Plan B—We Cannot Choose the Consequences

That there might be no misunderstanding the choices and consequences involved in using our agency, the Lord lays out the options for His children very clearly. I prefer to call these Plan A and Plan B. Plan A represents His blessings to us when we are obedient, while Plan B represents the alternative—disobedience—which brings with it suffering, destruction, and withdrawal of the Spirit and divine support. The most succinct statement supporting this is found in 2 Nephi 4:4: "For the Lord God hath said that: Inasmuch as ye shall keep my commandments ye shall prosper in the land [Plan A]; and inasmuch as ye will not keep my commandments ye shall be cut off from my presence [Plan B]."

Other, more lengthy examples are found in 2 Nephi 1:7–12, with a succinct summary in verse 20; Jarom 1:9–10; Mosiah 26:21–28; Alma 44; most of the book of Helaman; Ether 2:8–9, 12; 9:28–34; 13:20–21; 14:1, 21–25; 15:1–3, 19, 32–33.

In this last reference, Coriantumr chose Plan B. The following presents the outcome of his decision. Ether 15:13 and 19 reveal the heartache and suffering that took place, both in the king's heart and the hearts of those who followed his bad example:

> He began to repent of the evil which he had done; he began to remember the words which had been spoken by the mouth of all the prophets, and he saw them that they were fulfilled thus far, every whit; and his soul mourned and refused to be comforted. (Ether 15:3)

> But behold, the Spirit of the Lord had ceased striving with them, and Satan had full power over the hearts of the people; for they were given up unto the hardness of their hearts, and the blindness of their minds that they might be destroyed; wherefore they went again to battle. (Ether 15:19)

Coriantumr's experience is a good reminder to all of us that while we have the agency to chose our actions, we do not choose the consequences. The Savior has made it possible for us to repent, but the consequences are already in play and cannot be recalled. An example might be found in the experience a friend related to me.

Her father was extremely demanding and short-tempered, even to the point of being physically abusive. Expressions of love and appreciation were rare. As a result, the children made poor choices in their anxiety to get out of the home as quickly as possible. Heartache followed, and lives were ruined as patterns of abuse were set. Later, much to his credit, the father repented and changed his ways, but he had to live with the pain of the debris left behind and the relationships destroyed by his actions. Such damage may never be repaired in this life—and definitely not without Christ's healing powers.

There are certain eternal laws that even the Lord is bound by, and the law determines the consequences. We can teach our children the laws of the land as well as the rules that govern our households by using the laws of nature as an object lesson. When you throw something in the air, it comes down. Once children understand the consistency of the laws of nature, they are ready to understand the consistency of choices and consequences and can thus transfer that understanding to the laws of the land and the laws of the Lord, as well as to the rules of your home.

2. Allow the Decision

After you're sure you've taught your children gospel values and God's laws and consequences, you still have to allow the child to make his or her own decision. Here is a possible scenario: "Mom, Dad, our baseball team just won the city-wide championship and we are going on to play in the state tournament. The problem is, that play-off is scheduled for a Sunday afternoon. As you know, we've never had to play on Sunday before and this is only going to be a one-time thing. This is big for our team. We've never been eligible to play in the state games before and the team really depends on me. What should I do?"

"Son, you know how we feel about playing sports on the Sabbath. You also know what the Lord has said about keeping the Sabbath day holy. We understand this is a hard decision for you, but since you've asked our opinion, we have to be honest. As important as that game seems to you right now, isn't your relationship with your Heavenly Father more important? We understand you don't want to let your teammates down, but do you want to let your Heavenly Father down? You've made commitments to Him too. Think about it, pray about it, and do what your heart tells you. We'll still love you, whatever you decide."

Allow the decision.

3. Allow the Consequences

In your study of the Book of Mormon, you may have noticed that the Lord uses a variety of consequences. In an attempt to understand and follow His parenting example, I have categorized them into the following: (1) long-range consequences, i.e., eternal judgment; (2) immediate retribution, i.e., withdrawal of the Spirit or loss of support; (3) allowing the wicked to punish the wicked; (4) natural versus logical consequences.

Hopefully the following discussion of these four types of consequences will help clarify the possibilities. Once you get a handle on how the Lord uses them, you might want to point them out to your children—both in the scriptures and how you will use them as a family. Most children haven't had enough experience with life to recognize how consequences always follow—especially if they're the long-range/eternal variety, or even if they involve the immediate withdrawal of the Spirit.

It will take work to explain how these types of consequences are to be emulated in family life, as it is more difficult for children to understand logical consequences than it is for them to appreciate natural consequences. For instance, the connection between the act (playing in the street) and the natural consequences of that act (getting run over by a car) are often much easier to understand than the act (playing in the street) and the logical consequences of that act (having to stay in the house).

Suppose your teenage son says to you, "But, Dad, it will be so fun to just go party with the guys after the game. I can handle myself—what could be the harm?" Your parenting alarm goes off in six different directions on that one, but your boy just doesn't hear any of them. If you haven't already had a discussion with your children about consequences and how the Lord uses them, you might want to take this opportunity with your son to turn to some of the following scriptures which illustrate natural and logical consequences.

Long-Range Consequences: The Judgment

In Nephi 15:32–36, Nephi interpreted the tree of life vision wherein the consequences of wickedness are made clear and definite. The fate of those who choose to serve the devil rather than the Lord is also very clear:

> And that great pit, which hath been digged for them by that great and abominable church, which was founded by the devil and his children, that he might lead away the souls of men down to hell—yea, that great pit which hath been digged for the destruction of men shall be filled by those who digged it, unto their utter destruction, saith the Lamb of God; not the destruction of the soul, save it be the casting of it into that hell which hath no end.
>
> For behold, this is according to the captivity of the devil, and also according to the justice of God, upon all those who will work wickedness and abomination before him. (1 Nephi 14:3–4)

Immediate Retribution—Loss of the Spirit /Withdrawal of Support

For some, the consequences of a judgment day in the future are too far removed to be taken seriously, and the rewards of the world just too predominant to resist. For a young child, the threat of no dessert after dinner is not as important as having the cookie right now, or saving money in the bank for college not as appealing as going to the movies today. Young children unable to conceptualize the future will want instant gratification. In this case a more immediate reward or consequence may be required as you strive to teach them about long-term consequences of today's decisions.

Striking Korihor dumb was a good example of the Lord serving an immediate consequence as He honored Korihor's demand to have an immediate sign: "Except ye show me a sign, I will not believe" (see Alma 30:47–50). However, most often in the Book of Mormon, the Lord used a withdrawal of the Spirit, which left the hard-hearted to fend for themselves and eventually destroy each other. Samuel the Lamanite prophesied that the destruction of the Nephites would be a result of this consequence, for the Lord had warned, "Except they repent I will take away my word from them, and I will withdraw my Spirit from them" (Helaman 13:8).

Our children need to understand that the loss of the Spirit can result in even greater consequences. It is sometimes small and undetectable like a rust spot or a tiny sapling, but if allowed to continue, rust will corrode a thing until it is irreparable, or the sapling weed will grow to a mighty oak that cannot be removed but with great difficulty. We can die spiritually an inch at a time, hardly detectable, until we have totally lost our way. Alma is making this point with his son Helaman when he tells the story of the Liahona, sent to their fathers to guide them. There were certain conditions attached, like faith and diligence in following the gospel, and when those conditions were not met, the Liahona stopped working for them. "Nevertheless, because those miracles were worked by small means it did show unto them marvelous works. They were slothful, and forgot to exercise their faith and diligence and then those marvelous works ceased, and they did not progress in their journey. Therefore, they tarried in the wilderness, or did not travel a direct course, and were afflicted with hunger and thirst, because of their transgressions" (Alma 37:41–42).

Then Alma goes on to use the Liahona experience as an analogy (he calls it a "type" and a "shadow") for his son, as well as for parents today to follow and teach their children. Shopping or recreating on Sunday just this once, going along with the crowd to see an inappropriate movie just this one time, smoking just one cigarette, taking just one drink, taking just a peek at that pornographic site on the Internet, taking prayer and scripture study too casually—these are all little things that Satan uses to carefully lead us away from the Spirit as though with a silken thread. That wonderful Spirit that would warn and guide us away from danger is silenced as we gradually become hardened and deaf to its whisper.

Other examples of the gradual withdrawal of the Lord's Spirit and His support in battle are abundant throughout the Book of Mormon (see 1 Nephi 11:36; 17:31–38; 2 Nephi 6:15; 15:15; Mosiah 1:13; 2:36–39; 11:23–25; 17:15–19; Alma 16:9–10; 3 Nephi 9:1–2, 10–12; 16; Mormon 1:13–14, 17; Ether 10:11; 11; Mormon 3:11–15; Moroni 8:25–29).

Let the Wicked Punish the Wicked

In 1 Nephi 22:13–14 we read: "And the blood of that great and abominable church, which is the whore of all the earth, shall turn upon their own heads; for they shall war among themselves, and the sword of their own hands shall fall upon their own heads, and they shall be drunken with their own blood."

Sometimes the Lord accomplishes His purposes by allowing the wicked to punish the wicked. They are either humbled or destroy each other. Though we do not want our children to destroy each other, from time to time they need a perspective change. When our children were small they would often fight and quarrel with one another over what seemed an unending array of petty grievances. David wouldn't move away from the TV so others could see, Terri was sitting where Becky wanted to sit, Mandy knocked down Andy's block tower, Jonathan threw sand on Becky, etc., etc. The offended child would always come running to me to arbitrate, and I was the least qualified as I hadn't witnessed the offense (if there truly was one) and did not know who the true perpetrator was.

I tried many approaches to settling the argument because, like most, I did not want the spirit of contention in our home (or car). But none worked until I realized that most of the time the grievance was insignificant; it was my attention the children really sought.

After reading the scriptures above, I decided to try a new approach. We spent some time in family home evening helping the children learn to settle their differences peacefully through some role play. We taught them that the spirit of peace would leave our home whenever we fought and quarreled with one another, and in our family prayers we asked that we might do our part to have that spirit of peace by being patient and forgiving with one another. We also tried to give our children enough love and attention and positive feedback when they were playing and working happily that they didn't need to seek it in adverse ways. Finally we took a lesson from the Lord and let our naughty fighting children work out their differences between themselves until they learned that fighting is not fun if the parents aren't going to get involved.

Yes, it was hard at first because I continued to feel it was my duty as the adult to intervene. If I was sure no one was going to get seriously injured, I would leave the room when it started so I was not available to them—even if it meant I had to lock myself in the bathroom. Once they discovered that tattling and teasing one another only brought pain and isolation on themselves and no payoff from me, the bickering stopped and they learned to work out their own differences.

Natural vs. Logical Consequences

Perhaps it would be well to take a moment here and distinguish between "natural" and "logical" consequences. The Lord uses both kinds, and we as parents will find there will be occasions when we must choose between one or the other. If the natural consequence is life threatening or just too damaging to the child for the parent to allow, a logical consequence may do just as well. For instance, the natural consequence for a young child playing in the street might be death or being severely maimed. A wise parent would not leave that decision to the child. Instead, a logical consequence could sound like this: "Since I cannot depend upon you to stay in the yard to play, you must play in the house or in the fenced backyard."

In Alma 46:35, Moroni gave the Amalickiahites, his prisoners of war, a choice to either enter into a covenant of peace or be destroyed. He had to cut off the wicked from the righteous to save the righteous. Some chose not to accept the offer and so suffered the promised consequence. As parents, we can give an errant child a choice involving logical consequences. If a child can't decide to get along peaceably with the other children, she will have to spend some time alone so the rest can enjoy peace among themselves. Another example might be a child who insists on disrupting the dinner hour with rude behavior or remarks. Sometimes a quiet time-out in a bedroom alone will help the child get in control of himself and rethink his approach to others.

Since it is an eternal law that the Spirit cannot dwell with wickedness, spiritual death is a natural consequence, but separating the wicked physically from the righteous to protect the righteous is an example of a logical consequence. A good example is found in 2 Nephi 5:20–25 when the Lord cut the seed of Laman and Lemuel off from His presence and marked them that they might be easily recognized by the seed of Nephi and remain separate as long as they persisted in their wickedness.

Can you think of other instances that might require logical consequences? In their book, *I Don't Have to Make Everything All Better,* Joy and Gary Lundberg suggest that a child who has broken a family rule might be made to experience an "ordeal" of some kind to help them remember the rule. As an example they relate the story of a teenage boy caught reading some pornographic literature. His father was disappointed in his son's choice and said to him something like, "Since you seem to enjoy surrounding yourself with garbage, I have arranged for you to spend the day cleaning up the garbage at the park. Here is a bag. When you have filled it completely, you may come home" (Las Vegas: Riverpark Publishing Co., 1995, 132–3).

What do you suppose that young man will think of the next time he is tempted to pollute his mind with pornography? When explaining consequences to a child, a parent must be sure they themselves are willing to live with those consequences. Here is an example: Bobby got a new bike for his birthday. It was a very expensive bike, and his parents explained to him that he would be responsible for taking care of it. He must not leave it outside overnight, and he must not leave it parked in the driveway or street where it could get hit by a car. They told him if the bike was destroyed or stolen, it would not be replaced unless Bobby himself earned the money for another. In addition, if one of his parents had to take care of the bike, he would no longer have access to it.

At first Bobby was very careful and always put his bike away in a safe place in the garage when he wasn't riding it. Then one late afternoon he got careless and forgot. Hurrying in to dinner, he left his bike parked right in the driveway. When Dad came home that night after dark, he barely saw the bike in time to avoid hitting it. Dad had a decision to make. He could either pull the bike into the back of the garage where it was normally kept and say nothing, he could give Bobby a warning and another chance, or he could give the bike away, thus ensuring Bobby would learn to be more responsible in the future. Perhaps, he reasoned, the lesson would be impressed upon his young son more emphatically if he did the latter—and Bobby might take better care of a bike he had earned and paid for himself. But he wasn't positive that Bobby needed that lesson in this instance.

Dad realized his first priority was in helping Bobby learn a valuable lesson, but he also felt he had personally invested too much in the bike to just give it away. Uttering a little prayer for guidance and to calm his anger, he decided to put the bike away, lock it up, and go in and tell Bobby what he had done and why. After expressing his love and his disappointment, he let Bobby help decide how long the bike should be locked up. Taking away privileges or blessings is an example of a logical consequence. It can be effective while still leaving room for repentance.

4. Rejoice or Sorrow with the Child over the Decision Made

The Lord as well as His prophet-fathers found joy in the successes of their children and they sorrowed when the children failed. Doing so is not only a natural response, but reinforces the lesson for the child, and reminds us of the boundaries we must respect in letting our children use their agency. We cannot hold ourselves overly responsible for their choices.

The author of this poem is unknown, but I think it sums up perfectly the principle of agency and consequences. We teach our children as best we can, but we cannot live their lives for them.

FROM PARENT TO CHILD

I gave you life . . . but I cannot live it for you.
I can teach you things . . . but I cannot make you learn.
I can give you direction . . . but I cannot be there to lead you.
I can allow you freedom . . . but I cannot account for it.
I can take you to church . . . but I cannot make you believe.
I can teach you right from wrong . . . but I cannot always decide for you.
I can buy you beautiful clothes . . . but I cannot make you beautiful inside.
I can offer you advice . . . but I cannot take it for you.
I can give you love . . . but I cannot force it upon you.
I can teach you to share . . . but I cannot make you unselfish.
I can teach you respect . . . but I cannot force you to show honor.
I can advise you about friends . . . but I cannot choose them for you.
I can advise you about chastity . . . but I cannot make you pure.
I can tell you about the facts of life . . . but I cannot build your reputation.
I can warn you about the evil influence of drugs . . . but I cannot say no for you.
I can tell you about lofty goals . . . but I cannot achieve them for you.
I can teach you about kindness . . . but I cannot force you to be gracious.
I can warn you about sins . . . but I cannot make your morals.
I can love you as a child of God . . . but I cannot make your place in God's family.
I can pray for you . . . but I cannot make you walk with God.
I can teach you about Jesus . . . but I cannot make Jesus your Lord.
I can tell you how to live . . . but I cannot give you eternal life.

—Author unknown

Principle 9
Correct Children with Love

Samuel the Lamanite, speaking to the Nephites, told them that the Lord had chastened them, not out of anger or revenge, but out of love. "Yea, wo unto this people who are called the people of Nephi except they shall repent, when they shall see all these signs and wonders which shall be showed unto them; for behold, they have been a chosen people of the Lord; yea, the people of Nephi hath he loved, and also hath he chastened them; yea, in the days of their iniquities hath he chastened them because he loveth them" (Helaman 15:3).

Despite this example, it seems many still discipline their children in anger. Anger is the great destroyer of families and family relationships. Often, words spoken in harshness can never be taken back. Bruised hearts are difficult to mend. And in this day and age, we hear more and more accounts of physical abuse, even death, dealt to small children because of angry outbursts and fits of parental rage. Of course children try our patience, but so what! We were all children once, and surely we remember the times we were hurt when someone verbally abused us or we saw anger between family members. One of the lessons we came to earth to learn is patience. As children move from a stage of innocence to accountability, they must learn self-control, discipline, and sociability the same as you and I did, and in that learning, they, too, must try their wings. If we cannot learn to control our emotions, to temper our anger, to dig deeper for patience in this life, to sacrifice for others, we are not yet fit for any kingdom of glory in the hereafter.

Of her home experiences one young student said:

> My dad was raised in a strict boarding school without the benefit of a warm and loving parental relationship. As a result he does not know how to parent. He is very severe with us and tries to control us though fear. He becomes angry so easily that as children we were all terrified of him if we did the least thing wrong. We avoided having any interaction with him when he came home from work because we knew he would get mad about something. He forced us to have family home evening, but no matter what we did, it would always end up being unpleasant for everyone because he always got angry about something before we were through. Every one of my brothers and sisters left home as soon as they were able to do so. My sister ran away from home and got married when she was only sixteen. The marriage has not been a happy one, but she felt it was the only way she could get away from our father's controlling [approach] and anger.

It is true that children need firmness—rules and structure—but that must be coupled with love and kindness. The experience of this family is tragic.

President Ezra Taft Benson admonished Church members: "Your homes should be havens of peace and joy for your family. Surely no child should fear his own father—especially a priesthood father. A father's duty is to make his home a place of happiness and joy. . . . The powerful effect of a righteous father setting an example, disciplining and training, nurturing and loving is vital to the spiritual welfare of his children" ("To the Fathers in Israel," *Ensign*, Nov. 1987, 50).

President Gordon B. Hinckley provided this counsel:

> I do not hesitate to say that no man who is a professed follower of Christ and no man who is a professed member

> of this Church, can engage in abuse of children without offending God who is their Father and repudiating the teachings of the Savior and his prophets. It was Jesus himself who declared: "Whoso shall offend one of these little ones . . . it were better for him that a millstone were hanged about his neck, and that he were drowned in the depth of the sea" (Matt. 18:6).
>
> "Bring up your children in the love and fear of the Lord; study their dispositions and their temperaments, and deal with them accordingly, never allowing yourself to correct them in the heat of passion; teach them to love you rather than to fear you." (Gordon B. Hinckley, "The Environment of Our Homes," *Ensign*, June 1985, 3)

[He then quoted President Brigham Young:] The Lord, through Joseph Smith, said: "No power or influence can or ought to be maintained by virtue of the priesthood, only by persuasion, by long-suffering, by gentleness and meekness, and by love unfeigned; . . . Reproving betimes with sharpness, when moved upon by the Holy Ghost [and only then, I think]; and then showing forth afterwards an increase of love toward him whom thou hast reproved, lest he esteem thee to be his enemy; That he may know that thy faithfulness be stronger than the cords of death" (D&C 121:41, 43–44).

In contrast with the story about the boarding-school father, listen to this young adult's experience:

> My parents weren't perfect, but we always knew they loved and supported us, even when we made mistakes. They were generous in expressing that love openly to us and to one another. They have always kissed one another in front of their children and let us know that it was a natural part of a healthy relationship to show affection. If we were embarrassed by it, they said at least we knew they loved one another and

we never had to worry about them leaving each other. What a comforting thing for a child to know. As a result, we also felt comfortable expressing love to one another.

When my oldest sister was in high school, I remember she made a point to say that she loved each one of us before she went to bed. At first I thought it was kind of weird of her to make such a point of it, but I found that I loved it. There was a time when it seemed we had no money even for food or clothing, and yet we were preserved and kept safe through it all. Staying together as a family was the most important thing, and one of the only things we could control.

Perhaps some of the best counsel to fathers came from President Joseph F. Smith:

> Fathers, if you wish your children to be taught in the principles of the gospel, . . . if you wish them to be obedient to and united with you, love them! And prove to them that you do love them by your every word or act to them. . . . When you speak or talk to them, do it not in anger; do it not harshly, in a condemning spirit. Speak to them kindly; get down and weep with them, if necessary, and get them to shed tears with you if possible. Soften their hearts; get them to feel tenderly towards you. Use no lash and no violence, but . . . approach them with reason, with persuasion and love unfeigned. With this means, if you cannot gain your boys and your girls . . . there will be no means left in the world by which you can win them to yourselves." (Quoted by Ezra Taft Benson, "Great Things Required of Their Fathers," *Ensign*, May 1981, 34)

Elder F. Enzio Busche gave this personal example of how such an approach might work:

One day when circumstances made it necessary for me to be at home at an unusual time, I witnessed from another room how our eleven-year-old son, just returning from school, was directing ugly words towards his younger sister. They were words that offended me—words that I had never thought our son would use. My first natural reaction in my anger was to get up and go after him. Fortunately, I had to walk across the room and open a door before I could reach him, and I remember in those few seconds I fervently prayed to my Heavenly Father to help me to handle the situation. Peace came over me. I was no longer angry.

Our son, being shocked to see me home, was filled with fear when I approached him. To my surprise I heard myself saying, "Welcome home, son!" and I extended my hand as a greeting. And then in a formal style I invited him to sit close to me in the living room for a personal talk. I heard myself expressing my love for him. I talked with him about the battle that every one of us has to fight each day within ourselves.

As I expressed my confidence in him, he broke into tears, confessing his unworthiness and condemning himself beyond measure. Now it was my role to put his transgression in the proper perspective and to comfort him. A wonderful spirit came over us, and we ended up crying together, hugging each other in love and finally in joy. What could have been a disastrous confrontation between father and son became, through the help from the powers above, one of the most beautiful experiences of our relationship that we both have never forgotten. ("Love Is the Power That Will Cure the Family," *Ensign*, May 1982, 70)

Sometimes, because of our love for our children and because we are their mentors, it is necessary to chastise or correct them as

Elder Busche did in the example above. If we always keep in mind the pure purpose of our reprimands, we will be just and loving.

When we develop a loving relationship with our children, they are more apt to accept our discipline and our values and are more likely to respond to our requests in positive ways. I once asked a young man I respected why he felt compelled to always be obedient to his parents' wishes when some of those his age were defiant and rebellious. He answered it was because he couldn't bear the thought of disappointing his parents or causing them concern in any way. He was not obedient out of fear, but out of his love and respect for them.

The Lord also found it necessary to chastise His children on numerous occasions as did great prophet-fathers in the Book of Mormon. The following scriptures show how these prophets used love to influence their people. We too would do well to remember that our purpose as parents is to teach with a spirit of love rather than contention. The Lord is not sympathetic to contention: "For verily, verily I say unto you, he that hath the spirit of contention is not of me, but is of the devil, who is the father of contention, and he stirreth up the hearts of men to contend with anger, one with another. Behold, this is not my doctrine, to stir up the hearts of men with anger, one against another; but this is my doctrine, that such things should be done away" (3 Nephi 11:29–30).

The Lord chastised Lehi for murmuring and complaining, yet demonstrated compassion by providing him and his family with the Liahona as a guide (see 1 Nephi 16:25–28, 29).

Despite repeated divine rebukes that temporarily humbled Laman and Lemuel, the Lord was quick to accept their repentance on the occasions when it did come: "And it came to pass that the Lord was with us, yea, even the voice of the Lord came and did speak many words unto them, and did chasten them exceedingly; and after they were chastened by the voice of the Lord they did turn away their anger, and did repent of their sins, insomuch that the Lord did bless us again with food, that we did not perish" (1 Nephi 16:39).

Sometimes it is hard for parents to recover their relationship with a child once it has fractured. Perhaps that's why we are admonished never to correct children in anger but to do so in a calm, loving, and patient way. Then the children have a chance to repent. Perhaps the old advice to give yourself a few minutes to calm down (the old "count to ten" advice, or a quick prayer) before you teach will save you and your children a lot of heartache.

In 2 Nephi 10, Jacob describes how the Lord chastised the Jews for their hard hearts, but then He explained how they would be gathered again and blessed in the last days. The Lord does not hold grudges when a person repents. He also extends His trust and confidence in His children again.

An example is found in Ether 2:14–16. The Lord chastened the brother of Jared for not staying in contact with Him through prayer, but then He forgave him and had him go back to his leadership of the Jaredites. What a reassurance to us that the Lord expects us to live His commandments, but when we are remorseful, He is quick to forgive and encourages us to continue in our stewardships.

In the following scriptural examples of fathers chastising their children, note the tone and approach they use. Their love and concern for their children envelops the reprimand.

> And he did exhort them then with all the feeling of a tender parent, that they would hearken to his words, that perhaps the Lord would be merciful to them, and not cast them off; yea, my father did preach unto them. (1 Nephi 8:37)

> O that ye would awake; awake from a deep sleep, yea, even from the sleep of hell, and shake off the awful chains by which ye are bound, which are the chains which bind the children of men, that they are carried away captive down to the eternal gulf of misery and woe. (2 Nephi 1:13)

> Wherefore we labored diligently among our people, that we might *persuade* them to come unto Christ, and partake of the goodness of God, that they might enter into his rest. (Jacob 1:7, emphasis added)

This is our responsibility—to persuade our children to come unto Christ through our example of loving them as our Heavenly Father and Savior do.

Children's Needs

Principle 10
Listen! Listen! Listen!

A wise old owl sat in an oak.
The more he heard, the less he spoke.
The less he spoke, the more he heard.
Why can't we be like that wise old bird?

One wise father said, "I learned more about my son during a half hour of listening than I had learned during several years of lecturing" (Ted Hindmarsh, "A Listening Ear," *Ensign*, Sep. 1994, 44). The counsel to listen applies to all of our relationships, but especially to that with our children. The Book of Mormon has several good examples of the importance of listening. In Mosiah 5:1, for instance, King Benjamin set a good example in finding out what his followers thought about his remarks: "And now, it came to pass that when King Benjamin had thus spoken to his people, he sent among them, desiring to know of his people if they believed the words which he had spoken unto them."

King Benjamin had many good reasons to listen to his people. But an additional benefit was to gain increased love and respect from his people and more influence over them. Sister Michaelene P. Grassli, former Primary general president, said, "If we would listen more, we could discover how to be successful with [our children]. They are more likely to listen to us when they know they are listened to and understood. Listen with your heart" ("Teaching Our Children," *Ensign*, Apr. 1994, 62).

Along these lines, Elder H. Burke Peterson suggested:

> In the home, the father has a primary obligation to stay close to family members and administer to their needs. Not only through his observations but also in personal interviews the father evaluates his family's needs. I know several fathers who have a personal interview with each of their children on a weekly basis. A time when a father really listens can be a memorable and not soon forgotten experience for both. This would be a time when the father would not monopolize the conversation, but rather would lead out with a simple well-chosen question or two and then sit back and listen. There is nothing that can take the place of a listening father. His ears and heart must both be in tune. There is no substitute. ("The Father's Duty to Foster the Welfare of His Family," *Ensign*, Nov. 1977, 87)

I know of another listening father and how his willingness to hear his son out and not pass judgment worked out well for both of them. This son was having a hard time in the Missionary Training Center and was pretty sure he wasn't cut out to be a missionary. He called his father to tell him he was coming home. The father asked him just to stay long enough for the two of them to get together for lunch and talk about it. After getting special permission from the MTC president, father and son went out to lunch where they could be alone and talk. Instead of chastising his son and preaching to him about how important it was for him to serve a mission, the father calmly asked his son to tell him all that he was feeling; then he just listened to his son. Afterward, without demonstrating any anger or disappointment at what he was hearing, the father handed his son a paper napkin and asked him to write down all the reasons he felt he should come home, and alongside that list, to put the reasons he should stay. The son complied while the father patiently and quietly waited. The young elder completed his list, looked at it, and said, "I think I'd better stay." The father smiled, gave his son a hug and a father's blessing, and they parted. The young elder returned to the MTC and completed a very successful mission, becoming a mission leader. He kept that napkin on his dresser the entire two years he served so that whenever he became discouraged, he could simply look at the napkin and remember his purpose. But most importantly, he also knew that his father loved him, trusted him, and cared about his feelings.

Elder Marvin J. Ashton tells us that "listening is more than being quiet. Listening is much more than silence. Listening requires undivided attention. The time to listen is when someone needs to be heard. The time to deal with a person with a problem is when he has the problem. The time to listen is the time when our interest and love are vital to the one who seeks our ear, our heart, our help, and our empathy" ("Family Communications," *Ensign*, May 1976, 53).

Sometimes parents tell me they'd love to listen to their teenagers, but they can't get them to talk. I've had that frustrating experience myself on occasion. Some children are just more private about their feelings than others, and we have to accept that, but there may be other reasons as well. Elder Ashton suggests, "We should all increase our ability to ask comfortable questions, and then listen—intently, naturally. Listening is a tied-in part of loving" (ibid.).

In Alma 20:8–16, there is an excellent example of what *not* to do. King Lamoni's father made demands on his son. He asked superficial questions and became angry without really listening and trying to understand what was going on in his son's mind and heart. Put yourself and your child in this account to see if this scene sounds a little familiar:

> And it came to pass that as Ammon and Lamoni were journeying thither, they met the father of Lamoni, who was king over all the land.

And behold, the father of Lamoni said unto him: Why did ye not come to the feast on that great day when I made a feast unto my sons, and unto my people? [Why didn't you come to our family reunion?]

And he also said: Whither art thou going with this Nephite, who is one of the children of a liar? [Then without waiting for an answer, he went on, attacking his son's friend.]

And it came to pass that Lamoni rehearsed unto him whither he was going, for he feared to offend him.

And he also told him all the cause of his tarrying in his own kingdom, that he did not go unto his father to the feast which he had prepared.

And now when Lamoni had rehearsed unto him all these things, behold, to his astonishment, his father was angry with him [his father had already made up his mind and wasn't even listening to Lamoni's explanation], and said: Lamoni, thou art going to deliver these Nephites, who are sons of a liar. Behold, he robbed our fathers; and now his children are also come amongst us that they may, by their cunning and their lyings, deceive us, that they again may rob us of our property.

Now the father of Lamoni commanded him that he should slay Ammon with the sword. And he also commanded him that he should not go to the land of Middoni, but that he should return with him to the land of Ishmael. [Notice that this was a commandment, not a request.]

But Lamoni said unto him: I will not slay Ammon, neither will I return to the land of Ishmael, but I go to the land of

> Middoni that I may release the brethren of Ammon, for I know that they are just men and holy prophets of the true God.
>
> Now when his father had heard these words, he was angry with him, and he drew his sword that he might smite him to the earth.

LDS marriage and family counselor Larry Langlois has taught that we often put up barriers to listening, usually without knowing it. Some of the barriers he suggested might include:

1. *Being judgmental.* The fastest way to stop a person from talking is to jump in and criticize or make a judgment about what they have said without letting them finish. For example, what if your young daughter comes home from school and says, "The kids at school just don't like me. I don't have any friends." Suppose you jump in and say, "Well it's your own fault. You're just too shy. Why don't you speak up and talk to people and let them know you want to be friends?" How do you think such a response would make her feel about sharing her concerns with you next time?

2. *Confusing understanding with agreement.* Understanding what someone says doesn't mean that you agree. Whether you agree is not the issue in the listening process. For example: Your son or daughter comes home from school and says: "The kids at school just don't like me. I don't have any friends." You jump in and say, "That's not true. You have lots of friends," instead of waiting to hear more or asking, "What makes you feel that way?"

3. *Confusing listening with discussing.* Listening is a one-way process. It requires a speaker and a hearer. Sometimes children, like adults, don't want a discussion; they just want to vent their feelings and are asking only for a listening ear.

4. *Confusing listening with problem solving.* To listen is to understand, not to solve the problem. Helping find solutions might be a next step, but it is not part of the listening process and may even interfere. Parents shouldn't be too quick to try to solve

their children's problems. Let them talk about the problem and come to their own solutions, if possible. Some careful guidance might help like, "What do you think you can do about that?"

5. *Indulging in the need to correct errors.* When people are expressing strong feelings they often exaggerate. "I've got a hundred zits on my face. I am so ugly!" You might be tempted to say, "You're not ugly!" Your daughter may *feel* ugly; therefore, telling her that her feelings aren't factual doesn't help.

6. *Blocking a message we really don't want to hear.* As with Lamoni and his father, when the listener has made up his or her mind about something, they block out any other view no matter how much sense it makes. Maybe out of fear we close our minds and refuse to consider any other point of view (see "When Couples Don't Listen to Each Other," *Ensign*, Sep. 1989, 16).

It has been my experience that sometimes children say things they don't really believe just to get our reaction. They may be developing some ideas of their own, and, like politicians, they raise a "trial balloon" to see what we think. When we refuse to even listen to them, we almost force them to defend a position they don't really believe in. For instance, I have a friend whose daughter, a high school senior, told her mother she and her boyfriend wanted to get married. The mother felt the daughter was way too young for such a step and was scared to death her daughter might be serious. She was wise enough to know that if she opposed the idea too vehemently she might drive them together, so she controlled her natural impulse to oppose the idea and listened. When the daughter, shocked that she wasn't getting a return argument, finally asked what her mother thought of the idea, the mother was able to say, calmly, that she felt they were too young and they might want to consider waiting a year or two. She brought out some challenges she thought they might not have considered, but concluded with, "I trust you to make the right decision, and we'll do all we can to support you." The daughter thought it over for several days, then announced they'd changed their minds. The wedding was off. Had the parents vehemently opposed the boyfriend and the marriage, perhaps forcing the daughter to defend herself and her boyfriend, the outcome could have been quite different.

I would add one more obstacle to the mix: time. Many times the problem is that we just don't spend enough time together. A child doesn't share his innermost feelings on demand or by appointment. Spending time together in a comfortable, relaxed situation will naturally encourage talking and sharing. Sharon Larsen, former second counselor in the Young Women general presidency, gave the following account from her childhood:

> I used to farm with my dad. I didn't always enjoy it, but when lunchtime came we'd sit in the shade of the tall poplar trees, eat our lunch, and talk. My dad didn't use this as a golden teaching moment to lay down the law and straighten out his daughter. We just talked—about anything and everything.
>
> This was the time I could ask questions. I felt so safe I could even ask questions that might provoke him. I remember asking him, "Why did you embarrass me in front of my friends last week when I had stayed out too late and you came and got me?" . . .
>
> He wasn't being arbitrary. There were certain standards of behavior I was expected to live. He said, "Having you out late worried me. Above all, I want you safe." I realized his love for me was stronger than his desire to sleep or the inconvenience of getting dressed and driving down the road looking for me.
>
> Whether it is a hayfield or other casual places, those times together can fill the reservoir for other times that may not be as idyllic and serene. Relationships stay intact with this kind of investment—in spite of hard doctrine and correction—or maybe because of it.

> Love is *listening* when they are ready to talk—midnight, 6 A.M. on their way to seminary, or when you're busy with your urgencies. . . . I remember, when I was about sixteen years old, overhearing Mom talking to Dad. She was concerned about some choices I was making. I was not guilty of any sin more serious than the immaturity of youth, but Mom was worried. What Dad said seared into my heart. "Don't worry," he said to Mom. "I trust Sharon, and I know she'll do the right thing." Those hours in the hayfield paid off then and there. From that moment on I was bound to those loving, trusting parents. ("Fear Not: For They That Be with Us Are More," *Ensign*, Nov. 2001, 67–68)

Sister Larsen had a wonderful relationship with her father because he was willing to listen to her.

The following young man had a similar relationship with his mother. "My mom was a great listener. I could talk to her about anything, even my deepest and most personal concerns. I needed a listening ear then, and now, as a newly married man. I find this freedom I felt at home to speak from my heart has made it easy for me to share intimate feelings and thoughts with my wife."

Check yourself the next time you have an opportunity to listen to one of your children and see if you are putting up any barriers. If children run into these communication barriers enough times, they learn to stop sharing anything meaningful.

The scriptures provide some help in this area. James 1:19 says, "Let every man be swift to hear, slow to speak, slow to wrath." Ecclesiastes 3:1, 7 adds, "To every thing there is a season, and a time to every purpose under the heaven. . . . [There is] a time to keep silence, and a time to speak."

Missionaries are taught to find out what investigators think about a particular principle they have taught. It's an important step in teaching and learning. As a missionary myself later in life, I found this to be one of the most difficult steps to remember. I wanted to just barrel through the discussions and cram all the knowledge I could into their heads without stopping to find out if they believed what I was saying. When I became aware of the problem, I also became aware of doing the same thing with my children at home. I learned that parents, as well as missionaries, would do well to stop lecturing long enough to find out what is going on in the minds of their children. It's even better to listen first, before attempting to teach anything.

Unfortunately Lamoni's father did not do that. It was only after Ammon fought with the king to save him from killing his own son, and overpowered him, that the father was forced to listen. In Alma 20:26–27, as he listened to Ammon's pure motives in behalf of his son's welfare, the king's heart softened and he was ready to listen and learn from what this Nephite and his son had to say.

> And when he saw that Ammon had no desire to destroy him, and when he also saw the great love he had for his son Lamoni, he was astonished exceedingly, and said: Because this is all that thou hast desired, that I would release thy brethren, and suffer that my son Lamoni should retain his kingdom, behold, I will grant unto you that my son may retain his kingdom from this time and forever; and I will govern him no more—
>
> And I will also grant unto thee that thy brethren may be cast out of prison, and thou and thy brethren may come unto me, in my kingdom; for I shall greatly desire to see thee. For the king was greatly astonished at the words which he had spoken, and also at the words which had been spoken by his son Lamoni, therefore he was desirous to learn them.

My husband and I had a similar experience with our teenage son. While out on a date one night he missed the agreed-upon curfew, and as the minutes and then hours went by, we began to get very concerned. Many emotions escalated the tension as we waited angrily for the sound of the key in the lock to tell us he was home safely. Finally he was standing in front of us, and all that tension was released on him in a tirade of angry words. What could he have been thinking? Where on earth had he been? Did he understand the consequences for breaking our family rule? We asked all the questions, and we didn't even wait for an answer; we were so sure there couldn't be one sufficient to justify his behavior. We were expressing all our feelings but didn't allow him equal time.

Finally he walked off to bed looking a little discouraged. The next morning, we were calm enough to really listen to his explanation. Our son told us that when he took his date home, they heard fighting and yelling coming from inside her house and she began to cry. Our son listened patiently while she described some of the difficulties her parents were having with their relationship and how hard life was for her and her brothers and sisters. She wanted to know if there really were parents in the world who actually cared about their children and enjoyed them.

After some time she grew quiet, and our son told her that such families do exist. He began telling her about our family and how much we loved each other and how patient and understanding his parents were! Finally, when it was quiet inside the house and it appeared everyone had gone to bed, she thanked him for waiting with her and for listening. Then he came home—only to listen to his own parents vent their emotions without first taking the time to listen to him. What a poor example we were that night. We've tried not to make that mistake again.

In Alma 60, we find an exchange of letters between Moroni and Pahoran, a good example of how jumping to conclusions and misjudging others is often the result of not listening to the other person's side of the issue first. If Pahoran had not been humble and aware of Moroni's situation, their relationship might have been permanently damaged. Children's actions are often misconstrued and their innocent attempts seen as mischief or deliberate disobedience by parents who misjudge and jump to conclusions as did Moroni.

One final benefit of listening is that it allows our children to become better problem solvers. Ether 2:23–25 gives us a good "how to teach" scripture, but it also illustrates the principle of listening. The Lord asked the brother of Jared to work out the problem of lighting the barges himself. Then the Lord listened and considered his request.

Sometimes children actually know the solution to their problems but don't trust their own instincts. We can help them develop self-confidence by encouraging them to think the issue through and come up with a workable solution themselves. If we are too quick to think for them and tell them what should be done, they lose a good learning opportunity. At other times when children come to us with a problem, what they really want is a sounding board while they talk it out. What they don't want is for us to tell them what to do. Be wise and not so quick to solve their problems for them. Encourage them to figure it out while you help them to think it through. A good example is found in Ether. Jared and his brother held a family council to inquire after the thoughts of their people:

> And the brother of Jared began to be old, and saw that he must soon go down to the grave; wherefore he said unto Jared: Let us gather together our people that we may number them, that we may know of them what they will desire of us before we go down to our graves.
>
> And it came to pass that they did number their people; and after that they had numbered them, they did desire of them the things which they would that they should do before they went down to their graves. (Ether 6:19, 21)

What a wonderful idea! That's part of what should happen in all family councils. Many times my husband asked our children at a family home evening session what we could do to be better parents to our children. They always had some profound ideas to help our family make better decisions and build a better spirit in our home. Try it!

Principle 11
Children Need a Sanctuary

Children need to feel loved and valued even when they don't measure up to your expectations. They need to feel connected to parents no matter what else they do. They must have a place where they will always feel safe and loved—a sanctuary from the world. This principle requires a nurturing, loving leader in the home, a parent who is not afraid to give guidance and direction, but who also has a soft heart and can extend mercy and patience when mistakes are made.

Remember that the home we create is meant to be a training ground, an apprenticeship, for the celestial kingdom. We aren't perfect at this point in our lives—parenthood makes that obvious—but we want to learn. Children come to us innocent; they must feel free to experiment, to learn for themselves what we already know. To paraphrase Elder Jeffrey R. Holland, "The [home] is not a monastery for perfect people; "sometimes it is a hospital where we nurse and take care of those we love" ("He Hath Filled the Hungry with Good Things," *Ensign*, Nov. 1997, 66).

When a child leaves our home, she will be buffeted by worldly influences. She will be bruised on occasion, and her worth will be challenged by others. Her peers may be cruel about her braces, thick glasses, poor complexion, or lack of social grace because that's all they see at this point. But when a son or daughter comes home and finds love, acceptance, and encouragement, he or she can recover the strength and courage to go forth again and again until that confidence is restored and becomes a permanent part of his or her character.

A young college-age friend of ours described her home life where her mother always had something fun for her and her friends to look forward to after school. Sometimes it was just as simple as an "apple" party, consisting of sliced, peeled apples in a pie tin with cinnamon and sugar on them. She said her mother had a special way of making simple things fun. Her mother always took time to sit with her a few minutes to ask about her school day. If she'd had an exciting event to share, she knew her mother would be excited too. If she'd had a bruising day, she knew she could come home to be healed. For her, home really was a sanctuary.

Elder Marvin J. Ashton said, "Home should be an anchor, a port in a storm, a refuge, a happy place in which to dwell. . . . Home should be where life's greatest lessons are taught and learned. Home can be the center of one's earthly faith where love and mutual responsibility are appropriately blended" (*Ye Are My Friends* [Salt Lake City: Deseret Book], 1982, 44).

President Monson reminds us:

> True love can alter human lives and change human nature. If a child is treated commensurate with his potential, if he is trusted and accorded respect, his character will rise to a level consistent with the confidence those around show him. This truth was stated so beautifully on the stage in My Fair Lady. Eliza Doolittle, the flower girl, [explains it to another character]: "You see, really and truly, apart from the things anyone can pick up [the dressing, and the proper way of speaking, and so on], the difference between a lady and a flower girl is not how she behaves, but how she's treated. I shall always be a flower girl to Professor Higgins, because he always treats me as a flower girl, and always will; but I know I can be a lady to you, because you always treat me as a lady, and always will" (Adapted from *Pygmalion*, in *The Complete Plays of Bernard Shaw,* 260). Eliza Doolittle was but expressing the profound truth that when we treat people merely as they are, they will remain as they are. When we

> treat them as if they were what they should be, they will become what they should be (Adapted from a quotation by Johann Wolfgang Von Goethe). (Thomas S. Monson, "With Hand and Heart" *Ensign*, Dec. 1971, 131)

Treating a child in such a manner requires parents who understand a child's possibilities, see a child as Father in Heaven sees him—more precious and valuable than jewels or gold.

Our earthly home should be an extension of our heavenly home, for we are all spirit beings trying to adjust to a mortal, worldly environment. An infant arrives with a spiritual innocence but needs to be nourished spiritually if he is to flourish. That can't happen in a home filled with contention, criticism, and anger.

Our homes are to be sacred places, comparable to chapels and blessed by the Spirit of the Lord. Elder Dean Larson expressed it this way: "It would be well if each day we could 'go home to church.' There should be no other place where the Spirit of the Lord is more welcome and more easily accessible than in our own homes" ("Winding up Your Spiritual Clocks," *Ensign*, Nov. 1989, 63).

We have that precious opportunity every time we gather our children about us in gospel study, family prayer, scripture reading, and at family home evenings where we express appreciation and affection, teach gospel principles, laugh and relax with one another, and participate in emotionally bonding activities.

Providing a sanctuary for your child means providing a safe place for her to grow—a place where physical needs are met, yes, but also a place where she'll be protected both emotionally and spiritually until she is mature enough to face the world. It means providing support and backup when wobbly legs are learning to stand and giving guidance when the way is unclear. It means unselfishly making parental sacrifices where needed for the best interests of the child. A sanctuary is a place full of people he can count on, people he can trust, people who will nurture and comfort him in times of discouragement and provide encouragement for a brighter day. A sanctuary is a place where a child can practice failing and succeeding and, with careful planning on the part of the parents, experience more success than failure. A sanctuary is a place where children make mistakes, are forgiven, and always feel loved. The Book of Mormon is full of examples of these requirements.

Prepare a Place and a Plan

The Lord showed His love for us by preparing an earth for us to live on and learn the lessons we needed to learn. And He has mansions prepared for us when we finish our sojourn on this earth. He prepared a choice land for the Nephites, a land of promise for them after they left Jerusalem. "And inasmuch as ye shall keep my commandments, ye shall prosper, and shall be led to a land of promise; yea, even a land which I have prepared for you; yea, a land which is choice above all other lands" (1 Nephi 2:20).

When a couple first learns of a new offspring, they begin preparing a place for that child—a nursery or special corner of a bedroom. They provide warmth, food, and comfort, and all they can to furnish a pleasant, peaceful environment for their child to live in—a sanctuary. Why? Because we love our children and because we are commanded to "provide for their physical and spiritual needs" ("The Family: A Proclamation to the World"), and "[Parents] will not suffer [their] children that they go hungry, or naked" (Mosiah 4:14).

Part of providing a sanctuary for children is providing a plan. A good leader has a good plan. The Lord had a plan that called for Lehi's family to have a scriptural record to take with them, and wives for Lehi's sons (see 1 Nephi 3:1–4; 7:1–2). It was apparent that this move was to be permanent. The Lord knows the end from the beginning and He showed His plan to Lehi and Nephi. Jerusalem was not a safe place to reside. The Lord's plan encompasses all of us, as Alma told Zeezrom (see Alma 12). The purpose of the plan is for us to gain happiness in this world and eternal life in the world to come (see D&C 59:23). Our sojourn in mortality might be compared with the sojourn of the children of Israel.

> Yea, do ye suppose that they would have been led out of bondage, if the Lord had not commanded Moses that he should lead them out of bondage? [Provided a leader.]
>
> But ye know that the Egyptians were drowned in the Red Sea, who were the armies of Pharaoh. [Provided protection.] And ye also know that they were fed with manna in the wilderness. [Provided food.]
>
> Yea, and ye also know that Moses, by his word according to the power of God which was in him, smote the rock, and there came forth water, that the children of Israel might quench their thirst. [Provided water.] (1 Nephi 17:24, 27–29)

Just as the Lord provided Moses to lead His children out of Egypt, He provides leaders for His children when they come to mortality. Parents are to be the leaders in the homes to which these special spirits come. Parents are there to teach, guide, protect, nurture, and provide for their children as they prepare for adulthood. Parents must counsel with each other to develop their own family plan so as to be in harmony with the divine plan. Parents can set marriage and family goals together and then outline the essential steps necessary to achieve them.

Providing a Sanctuary Often Requires Parental Sacrifices

"And he cometh into the world that he may save all men if they will hearken unto his voice; for behold, he suffereth the pains of all men, yea, the pains of every living creature, both men, women, and children, who belong to the family of Adam" (2 Nephi 9:21).

Our Father in Heaven sacrificed His Only Begotten Son in our behalf. Christ gave us His life—the ultimate offering upon the altar. Though parents aren't often asked to give their lives, parenthood demands many sacrifices daily.

> And he shall go forth, suffering pains and afflictions and temptations of every kind; and this that the word might be fulfilled which saith he will take upon him the pains and the sicknesses of his people.
>
> And he will take upon him death, that he may loose the bands of death which bind his people; and he will take upon him their infirmities, that his bowels may be filled with mercy, according to the flesh, that he may know according to the flesh how to succor his people according to their infirmities. (Alma 7:11–12)

As parents, we often think we love our children enough to give our lives for them, but isn't it harder to *live* with them sometimes, sacrificing time and self in less dramatic ways? Quiet heroes don't always receive the applause of the world, but they make men and women out of boys and girls.

To truly "walk with a child" from infancy through the teen years, we must put ourselves in their place, see the world through their eyes, and "come down among them" as Christ did with us. The Lord was not only willing to die for us, which He did, but He first suffered the pains of living among us, teaching and ministering and setting the example. Can a parent really know a child and his needs without spending time with him? There are no shortcuts here.

One young man said, "My mom is one of the most unselfish people I know. She is her children's number-one fan. She attended every sporting event, Mutual activity, or anything else her kids were involved in. If you were feeling down or upset, she was a great person to tell because you knew she could keep a secret and you knew she would hear you out, even if she thought you were wrong."

How does one truly become a parent? Biological ties are not sufficient. Father, mother, son, and daughter are titles that must be earned through meaningful hours of serving, giving, and investing in family members.

In 3 Nephi 17:7–8, Jesus asked, "Have ye any that are sick among you? Bring them hither. Have ye any that are lame, or blind, or halt, or maimed, or leprous, or that are withered, or that are deaf, or that are afflicted in any manner? Bring them hither and I will heal them, for I have compassion upon you; my bowels are filled with mercy." At this point, Christ had been teaching for hours. He must have been tired Himself and ready to rest, but when He saw they desired He stay longer and minister to them, He stayed. A loving father and mother will be willing to sacrifice time and energy for their children when they see the children really need them. The need may even come at an inconvenient time—it usually does—but what an important message the child receives: you are more important to me than my own comfort.

A young mother said:

> It takes an enormous amount of time and energy to be a good parent. It is easier to let my children fall asleep in front of the television while I pick up the house and then put them to bed than it is to read the scriptures to them, have prayer and stories, and tuck them in. But they look forward to this evening ritual, and I know this investment, even when I'm too tired to move, will pay eternal dividends." (Sharon G. Larsen, "Fear Not: For They That Be with Us Are More," *Ensign*, Nov. 2001, 68)

Of course, very young children, the ones who require the greatest investment of time, aren't very likely to appreciate their parents' sacrifices in their behalf, but that day will come as they mature and are given opportunities to make sacrifices of their own in behalf of their family members.

A five-year study by Brigham Young University faculty members Bruce Chadwick and Brent Top revealed three main influences on the moral and character development of children: peer influences, private religious behaviors, and family relationships. They found that family connectedness, defined as an emotional bond between child and other family members, grows out of (1) love and support of parents and other family members, (2) establishing rules, and (3) personal expression—freedom to be themselves.

"Family connectedness requires time, especially one-on-one time," Chadwick said. "A hug, an arm around the shoulder, [and] kind and loving words will help keep parents and teens connected. Raising teenagers is a time-intensive endeavor, and even though parents are busy, they should support their teens in school, church, and similar activities" ("Parents Really Matter in Rearing Children," *Church News*, March 6, 1999, 10).

The Elements of a Sanctuary

Sanctuary–A Place of Safety

Lehi explained to his family that the Lord preserved this new land to which they sailed as a place for the righteous. Lehi prophesied: "There shall none come into this land save they shall be brought by the hand of the Lord. . . . And behold, it is wisdom that this land should be kept as yet from the knowledge of other nations; for behold, many nations would overrun the land, that there would be no place for an inheritance" (2 Nephi 1:6, 8).

The Nephites were warned by the Lord to remove themselves from the Lamanites in order to establish a land of peace (see 2 Nephi 5:5). Nephi, as their protector and priest, was concerned about their physical as well as spiritual welfare:

> And I, Nephi, did take the sword of Laban, and after the manner of it did make many swords, lest by any means the people who were now called Lamanites should come upon us and destroy us; for I knew their hatred towards me and my children and those who were called my people.
>
> And I did teach my people to build buildings, and to work in all manner of wood, and of iron, and of copper, and of brass, and of steel, and of gold, and of silver, and of precious ores, which were in great abundance.

> And I, Nephi, did build a temple. (2 Nephi 5:14–16)

Alma talks about enemies of a different kind:

> For what shepherd is there among you having many sheep doth not watch over them, that the wolves enter not and devour the flock? And behold, if a wolf enter his flock doth he not drive him out? Yea, and at the last, if he can, he will destroy him.
>
> And now I say unto you that the good shepherd doth call after you; and if you will hearken unto his voice he will bring you into his fold, and ye are his sheep; and he commandeth you that ye suffer no ravenous wolf to enter among you, that ye may not be destroyed. (Alma 5:59–60)

Part of the parents' role is to protect their young from physical and spiritual enemies until the children are old enough and strong enough to protect themselves. There are wolves in our midst that threaten children and their welfare. Sometimes these wolves come dressed as an entertaining movie or magazine. They creep into our homes through the Internet or television. Even if you are watching a fairly benign program, the trailers for upcoming programming can assault innocent eyes and minds. Parents must be alert in order to keep the wolves at their door out of their homes, protecting and preparing their children to recognize and successfully fight those wolves when they leave the safety of home. Children must be armed with faith and testimony and confidence in the principles of the gospel, knowing that home is always a sanctuary of peace and harmony.

Part of arming our children to deal with the world is to be honest about it and not to shelter them in such a way that their innocence is a disadvantage later. Alma told Helaman to teach the people about the dangers of secret combinations but without revealing methods, lest the Nephites be caught up in the web:

> And now, my son, I command you that ye retain all their oaths and their covenants, and their agreements in their secret abominations; yea, and all their signs and their wonders ye shall keep from this people, that they know them not, lest peradventure they should fall into darkness also and be destroyed.
>
> Therefore ye shall keep these secret plans of their oaths and their covenants from this people, and only their wickedness and their murders and their abominations shall ye make known unto them; and ye shall teach them to abhor such wickedness and abominations and murders; and ye shall also teach them that these people were destroyed on account of their wickedness and abominations and their murders. (Alma 37:27, 29)

Similarly, Moroni wanted his people to be alert to the insidious evils about them that they might not be taken unawares:

> And now I, Moroni, do not write the manner of their oaths and combinations, for it hath been made known unto me that they are had among all people, and they are had among the Lamanites.
>
> And they have caused the destruction of this people of whom I am now speaking, and also the destruction of the people of Nephi.
>
> Wherefore, O ye Gentiles, it is wisdom in God that these things should be shown unto you, that thereby ye may repent of your sins, and suffer not that these murderous combinations shall get above you, which are built up to get power and gain—and the work, yea, even the work of destruction come upon you, yea, even the sword of the justice of the Eternal God shall fall upon you.

> Wherefore, the Lord commandeth you, when ye shall see these things come among you that ye shall awake to a sense of your awful situation, because of this secret combination which shall be among you. (Ether 8: 20–21, 23–24)

This is good advice for parents too. While we don't want innocent children to stumble into wickedness because they are too naive to know what it is, we must carefully prepare them for life outside our home without whetting their curiosity for evil. Pornography is a prime example in our day. Our children should know there is such a thing, but we want to prevent their access to it in our home while we prepare them for the temptations and dangers they could possibly face outside the home.

Similarly, many parents were concerned, and rightly so, when sex education was introduced as a mandatory class in the elementary schools. The problem, of course, is not that children shouldn't be taught about the natural functions of the body and the miracle of procreation, but that they would be instructed in this information apart from moral values or implications. The result was that the children were taught the mechanics of sexual reproduction in a way that triggered curiosity, but there was no context of marriage or being responsible as adults for children that might be conceived. Too much factual information without the maturity and moral foundation to handle it can be a dangerous thing. At that age, with immoral music shouting out the need to shed inhibitions, these students were faced with the social pressure to experiment outside the classroom with this new, exciting knowledge.

The Lord warned the Nephites about interacting with their wicked cousins and put a mark on Laman and Lemuel so that their seed might be easily recognized. "And this was done that their seed might be distinguished from the seed of their brethren, that thereby the Lord God might preserve his people, that they might not mix and believe in incorrect traditions which would prove their destruction" (Alma 3:8).

Too often among our children's associates, the wicked are indistinguishable from the decent and righteous. It would be well for parents to know their children's friends and their families and something of their standards and values. When our neighbor's children were in their teens, she and her husband encouraged them to bring their friends to their home to watch videos or play games, or to just "hang out," as teens are inclined to do. She told me they became friends with their friends, went out of their way to make them feel comfortable in their home, took the time to chat with them about their goals and challenges and, on occasion, gave advice when it seemed appropriate. They made it a point to know the other parents and invited them to their home as well so they would be comfortable knowing what kind of environment their children were in when they were at their friends' homes. This approach must have worked pretty well. Even when their youngest son went on his mission, his friends still came over to visit and enjoy my neighbor's company and treats they'd come to enjoy.

As we liken the scriptures unto ourselves, the Book of Mormon gives us clues as to how to fight the battle with Satan and his agents. There are additional helps found in the strategies necessary against the king-men, Amalickiahites, and Lamanites in Alma 49:4–5 and Alma 51–52.

A Sanctuary Is a Place of Guidance and Support

The Lord did not place us on the earth only to leave us defenseless. When He gave a commandment to the Nephites, He supported and assisted them in accomplishing what He required of them (see 1 Nephi 3:7; 17:3, 5, 13). This required continual revelation on a large- and small-scale basis. We continue to receive direction through scripture, prophetic counsel, and personal revelation through the Holy Ghost. Lehi's dream speaks of the iron rod, or the word of God (see 1 Nephi 15:24).

The Lord gave us the scriptures as a guidebook to refer to. Parents, too, need rules or guidelines for their children to use as a standard when they leave home and confront the real world.

Family rules help children internalize what is expected of them. Such guidelines might be as simple and direct as "How to clean a room," "Family dating rules," "Steps to apologize," or "How to say no and mean it." As a child grows in maturity, the guidelines can be less direct and more principle-based, such as "Do unto others . . ." or "Be honest in all thy dealings," or "Return with honor." As with the scriptures, having rules in written form can prevent confusion and free a child from any fear that he won't get it right.

The Lord also gave us the avenue of prayer. We can communicate with Him any time we need His help. On countless occasions in the Book of Mormon record, we have an account of His answering petitions. Parenting, though a difficult assignment, is made easier when we remember that our children are His children too. He has a vested interest in them and will help us parent them if we will seek His help. Perhaps the classic example of a parent's prayer being answered comes from the account of Alma the Elder praying for his wayward son in Mosiah 27.

Mosiah, like so many missionary parents, trusted the Lord to care for his son as he sent him out into the mission field (see Alma 19:23). We pray for our children daily as we send them off to school or out with friends for the evening—outside the protection of our homes. Sometimes, especially when our children are wayward and won't take counsel, praying may be our only recourse. While parents must allow children to experience the consequences of their choices, they can give support, teach a child how to cope with challenges, and let a child know he is loved, as we find illustrated in Mosiah 24:12–15.

> And Alma and his people did not raise their voices to the Lord their God [because they were forbidden to do so], but did pour out their hearts to him; and he did know the thoughts of their hearts.
>
> And it came to pass that the voice of the Lord came to them in their afflictions, saying: Lift up your heads and be of good comfort, for I know of the covenant which ye have

> made unto me; and I will covenant with my people and deliver them out of bondage.
>
> And I will also ease the burdens which are put upon your shoulders, that even you cannot feel them upon your backs, even while you are in bondage; and this will I do that ye may stand as witnesses for me hereafter, and that ye may know of a surety that I, the Lord God, do visit my people in their afflictions.
>
> And now it came to pass that the burdens which were laid upon Alma and his brethren were made light; yea, the Lord did strengthen them that they could bear up their burdens with ease, and they did submit cheerfully and with patience to all the will of the Lord.

Another application of this scripture has to do with parental suffering. I recall a desperate phone call I received from a good friend whose children were causing her and her husband great pain and suffering because of their lifestyle choices. Through tears she told me, "I didn't know parenthood could be so hard. I'm not sure we can cope with this much longer, and we don't know what to do. Why does it have to be so hard?"

When we allow our children agency, and when we have done our best to teach our children only to have it thrown back in our faces, parenting *is* hard. It is hard to sit by and watch our flesh and blood make decisions that not only cause disruption and loss of peace and tranquility in our home, but which we know will cause them pain in the future when they face the consequences. We may find it hard to be as cheerful as Alma's people were, but if we are faithful, and continue in long-suffering and patience, we can turn our burdens over to the Lord, who also loves our children. He will bless us with a sense of peace that we have done all we can do and thus take away the "burden" of parenthood.

Elder Eyring made a point that serves as both a warning and a comfort:

> Even in service to God, you will not be consciously praying always. So why does the Master exhort us to "pray always"? I am not wise enough to know all of His purposes in giving us a covenant to always remember Him and in warning us to pray always lest we be overcome. But I know one. It is because He knows perfectly the powerful forces that influence us [and our children] and also what it means to be human. . . .
>
> Time has taught me. As the forces around us increase in intensity, whatever spiritual strength was once sufficient will not be enough. And whatever growth in spiritual strength we once thought was possible, greater growth will be made available to us. Both the need for spiritual strength and the opportunity to acquire it will increase at rates which we underestimate at our peril. ("Always," *Ensign*, Oct. 1999, 12)

One of the most beautiful examples of a father praying for his children is found in 3 Nephi 19:20–33 when the Savior prayed three times for His disciples and those who believed in Him. We also find this awe-filled observation in 3 Nephi 17:17. "And no tongue can speak, neither can there be written by any man, neither can the hearts of men conceive so great and marvelous things as we both saw and heard Jesus speak; and no one can conceive of the joy which filled our souls at the time we heard him pray for us unto the Father."

Support your children with your prayers, and in turn your Father will support your parenthood by answering those prayers. The above examples show that the Lord will sustain His faithful followers. If we do what He asks of us, we need not fear that we'll be stuck out on a limb alone. It is important that children know that their parents and family will always love them and encourage them, even if it seems that the world is against them, and it is important they know that God will always support them. Joseph Smith withstood a multitude of lies and venomous threats from disbelievers and evildoers because his family believed his story, supported his efforts, and because he knew that God had called him to a great work. As we give our children guidance, we should not neglect to seek it from our Father in Heaven.

A Sanctuary Is a Place of Nurture and Comfort

A child needs to be nurtured physically and emotionally. Studies have shown that infants being cared for in an orphanage often die of an ailment known as marasmus. This condition develops not simply from a lack of nutrition but from emotional neglect—a lack of touch, cuddling, and emotional nurturing (see *The American Heritage Stedman's Medical Dictionary,* [Boston: Houghton Mifflin], 2002). The Book of Mormon shows us that our Father in Heaven is a nurturing Father who cares about His children's emotional needs and comfort, and tends to their hurts. Nephi foresaw that during Christ's mortal ministry, He would nurture and care for Nephi's posterity.

> And he spake unto me again, saying: Look! And I looked, and I beheld the Lamb of God going forth among the children of men. And I beheld multitudes of people who were sick, and who were afflicted with all manner of diseases, and with devils and unclean spirits; and the angel spake and showed all these things unto me. And they were healed by the power of the Lamb of God; and the devils and the unclean spirits were cast out. (1 Nephi 11:31)

> Surely he has borne our griefs, and carried our sorrows; yet we did esteem him stricken, smitten of God, and afflicted.

> But he was wounded for our transgressions, he was bruised for our iniquities; the chastisement of our peace was upon him; and with his stripes we are healed.

> All we, like sheep, have gone astray; we have turned every one to his own way; and the Lord hath laid on him the iniquities of us all. (Mosiah 14:4–6)

To a lesser degree, all parents experience the emotions their children experience—their joys and their disappointments. Right or wrong, having six children and a husband I love very much, I often feel I am eight different people, for each one of them is a part of me, and I feel what they feel. How much more intense is the Lord's sorrow and joy over His children.

Children need to be nourished just as the elements in our physical landscape, such as the flowers and trees. Read Alma 32:37–40, 43, and substitute the word *child* or *relationship* for *tree.*

Another way of nurturing is to give comfort. A child needs a place where he can go to be comforted and to feel the support of his parents.

In Ether 12:25–26, the Lord comforted Moroni in his concern and promised to support him as a loving father comforts a child and gives support:

> Thou hast also made our words powerful and great, even that we cannot write them; wherefore, when we write we behold our weakness, and stumble because of the placing of our words; and I fear lest the Gentiles shall mock at our words. [Moroni had a concern.]

> And when I had said this, the Lord spake unto me, saying: Fools mock, but they shall mourn; and my grace is sufficient for the meek, that they shall take no advantage of your weakness. [The Lord offered support and comfort.]

Because of the Lord's support, Moroni was confident in his mission. We can nurture confidence in our children much as the following young woman's parents did: "They were always quick to say 'I love you' and reaffirm their feelings towards me. This validating communication gave me confidence and faith to believe that I could do anything with the Lord's help. Through obedience, the Spirit was constantly in our home, and I felt safe and accepted."

A child must feel safe and accepted at home, even when he makes mistakes. A misbehaving child is a discouraged child, and if no hope is offered, the discouragement that leads to misbehavior will continue. Similar to our own situations when we err, the Lord offers us hope through repentance and the opportunity to try again. "And behold how great the covenants of the Lord, and how great his condescensions unto the children of men; and because of his greatness, and his grace and mercy, he has promised unto us that our seed shall not utterly be destroyed, according to the flesh, but that he would preserve them; and in future generations they shall become a righteous branch unto the house of Israel" (2 Nephi 9:53).

In addition to teaching our children they can make mistakes and repent, priesthood blessings, given by a worthy father at home, can be another source of comfort and hope. (See examples of blessings found in 2 Nephi 1:28; 2 Nephi 4:5; and Alma 17:18.)

A Sanctuary Is a Place Where a Child Can Practice Success

A wise parent or leader looks ahead and prepares ways for children to be successful. When we give a child a task to perform, we need to be sure he is capable of performing that task and of having a successful experience. That may take some planning and preparation on our part, but it will be worth the effort to build our child's trust and confidence in us and in his own abilities. For instance, as our children mature and are given added responsibilities, we initially go through the steps with them, ensuring they understand what is expected of them. Then, as they practice a skill, they become more confident, and finally feel the joy of success.

When our children were young, we gave them simple chores to do not only because we needed their help but, more importantly, we wanted them to feel they had a role or function in the family and were a necessary and integral part. We also wanted them to enjoy a feeling of accomplishment and pride in a job well done.

After much trial and error I finally figured out a pattern that seemed to work for our children. As they each became old enough to make their bed, I showed them how by letting them help me. A three-year-old is eager to help with the most mundane of chores! After a few practices I'd let my child tackle the job alone, with my supervision, making corrections or suggestions where necessary, but basically remaining positive lest he become discouraged. Maybe the bed didn't come out as smoothly as it would have had an adult done it, but I made sure the child got plenty of praise for his efforts. Sometimes I had to bite my tongue and look the other way, but I tried not to remake it.

As our children took on more complex chores like cleaning the bathroom, after letting them help me a few times, I gradually moved out of the picture until I was playing the supporting role and they were taking the lead. Finally I was able to remove myself altogether, but I left a chart tacked to the inside of the door that listed all the necessary steps in cleaning a bathroom. If they forgot from one week to the next what "cleaning the bathroom" meant, they could consult the chart, checking off the steps and being confident that they had done a good job. Making a bed or cleaning a bathroom are simple tasks, but children gain confidence in themselves when they learn how to do something well.

Sociality can be practiced at home, too, with role-playing during family home evening, and discussions and demonstrations around the dinner table. When our children were old enough to date, we took comfort in the knowledge that we had taught them proper table etiquette, how to present themselves at the door, how to answer the phone and take messages, how to carry on an appropriate conversation with the opposite sex, and how to introduce themselves to their date's parents. We'd practiced all those things ahead of time.

The Lord never gave one of his children an assignment without first preparing the way for success. We are all familiar with Nephi's declaration in 1 Nephi 3:7 and how that assignment turned out. There are other examples as well—1 Nephi 7:5; 9:3, 5–6; 22:20; 2 Nephi 9:10, to name a few.

In Alma 8:20–21 the Lord gave Alma the difficult task of preaching to the wicked people of Ammonihah. The Lord let Alma try to do it on his own, but when he was unsuccessful, the Lord stepped in and helped by preparing a companion to aid him in the task. With Amulek's help, Alma was successful.

A Sanctuary Is a Place of Refuge Even for Difficult Children

I found a little children's book by Rick Walton called *Will You Still Love Me?* (Salt Lake City, UT: Deseret Book, 1992). I like to read it to my grandchildren. I wish I'd had it when my own children were little. All children (and adults) need to know they will be loved and valued by somebody no matter what happens to them.

In Principle 1, we explored many scriptures about the importance of teaching children family values and even *how* to do that. Many of you are already consistently doing those things. Even so, despite all that effort, there will be some children who, for one reason or another, choose a different path for a time, seemingly unable to resist the voices outside the home that beckon and call them to dangerous ports. Agency dictates they have that right and must be given the opportunity to set their sails, but those decisions need not be final unless we make them so. It may not always be the case, but sometimes a confused child is testing us in just how far she can go before you stop loving her. Some children just have to know the depth of the water, the height of the sky, how valued they are. And the answer must be as deep, as high, and as much as it takes. We must never give up hope—never—and never permanently lock doors and hearts against a wayward child.

President Monson tells the following story:

> Let us look in on a family with a lad named Jack. Throughout Jack's early life, he and his father had many serious arguments. One day, when Jack was seventeen, they had a particularly violent quarrel. Jack said to his father, "This is the straw that breaks the camel's back. I'm leaving

home, and I will never return!" So declaring, he went to his room and packed a bag. His mother begged him to stay, but he was too angry to listen. He left her crying at the doorway.

Leaving the yard, Jack was about to pass through the gate when he heard his father call to him: "Jack, I know that a large share of the blame for your leaving rests with me. For this I am truly sorry. I want you to know that if you should ever wish to return home, you'll always be welcome. And I'll try to be a better father to you. I want you to know that I'll always love you." Jack said nothing, but went to the bus station and bought a ticket to a distant point. As he sat on the bus watching the miles go by, he thought about the words of his father. He realized how much love it had required for his father to do what he had done. Dad had apologized. He had invited him back and had left the words ringing in the summer air, "I love you."

It was then that Jack understood that the next move was up to him. He knew that the only way he could ever find peace with himself was to demonstrate to his father the same kind of maturity, goodness, and love that Dad had shown toward him. Jack got off the bus, bought a return ticket to home, and went back.

He arrived shortly after midnight, entered the house, and turned on the light. There in the rocking chair sat his father, his head bowed. As the father looked up and saw Jack, he rose from the chair, and they rushed into each other's arms. Jack often said, "Those last years that I was home were among the happiest of my life."

Here was a boy who overnight became a man. Here was a father who, suppressing passion and pride, reached out to rescue his son before he became one of the vast "lost battalion" resulting from fractured families and shattered

> homes. Love was the binding band, the healing balm. Love—so often felt, so seldom expressed. ("Heavenly Homes, Forever Families," *Ensign*, Oct. 1991, 5)

"Nevertheless, ye shall not cast him out of your synagogues, or your places of worship, for unto such shall ye continue to minister; for ye know not but what they will return and repent, and come unto me, with full purpose of heart, and I shall heal them; and ye shall be the means of bringing salvation unto them" (3 Nephi 18:32).

Sister Sharon Larsen expressed this idea in a conference talk:

> One of the greatest tests for parents and leaders is to love the one who seems to be unlovable. This is tough duty. It stretches the heartstrings and wrenches the soul. When heartbroken parents pray for help, the help often comes in the form of angel aunts or uncles, grandmas or grandpas, good friends, and leaders surrounding our loved one. They can reinforce our very message that may put our child on the track we've been praying for. ("Fear Not: For They That Be with Us Are More," *Ensign*, Nov. 2001, 68)

The Lord does not give up on His children, and He allows time for their change and repentance. The Book of Mormon is replete with examples of love, mercy, charity, and forgiveness as the Lord waits upon His wayward, stiff-necked children to turn from a wicked course to Him. Such turning, however, does not eliminate the consequences of their past behavior. The Lord allowed the children of Israel to suffer the consequences of their refusal to accept Him, but He still loved them and promised mercy if they would turn back: "For a small moment have I forsaken thee, but with great mercies will I gather thee. In a little wrath I hid my face from thee for a moment, but with everlasting kindness will I have mercy on thee, saith the Lord thy Redeemer" (3 Nephi 22:7–8).

In disciplining children, sometimes parents must withdraw while their children experience the consequence of their actions:

> But remember the iniquity of king Noah and his priests; and I myself was caught in a snare, and did many things which were abominable in the sight of the Lord, which caused me sore repentance;
>
> Nevertheless, after much tribulation, the Lord did hear my cries, and did answer my prayers, and has made me an instrument in his hands in bringing so many of you to a knowledge of his truth. (Mosiah 23:9–10)

Alma repented of his actions as a priest of King Noah. After allowing Alma to experience the anguish of his wickedness, the Lord forgave him and he became a righteous servant. We can't know exactly what Alma meant by "much tribulation," but we might assume he went through the agony of repentance before his forgiveness was complete.

Sometimes the discipline necessary to help a child might take the form of a natural consequence or a logical one. A temporary separation is sometimes necessary to help a child learn obedience by having to think about the consequence of his actions. The Lord used this means many times (see 1 Nephi 10:3, 14; 13:30–33; 13–20; 2 Nephi 6:11; 25:16–17; and Jacob 5–6). For a younger child, this may be a time-out. With an adult child, and especially if you have younger impressionable children still at home, to invite that errant child to find another place to live until he feels ready to respect the peace and sanctity of your home may be the only option. Make sure he understands your door and arms will always be open to him. That puts the responsibility and consequences for his actions on him, where it belongs, rather than on you.

Regardless of the direction such a child goes, we are required to forgive the trespasses of others, and we must assume that "neighbor" includes our children too. Sometimes we forget that complete forgiveness means we also forget and don't continue to bring up past mistakes. "And ye shall also forgive one another your trespasses; for verily I say unto you, he that forgiveth not his neighbor's trespasses when he says that he repents, the same hath brought himself under condemnation" (Mosiah 26:31). For more examples of God's compassion for His children, and His endless capacity to forgive, read following passages: 2 Nephi 9:26; Jacob 6:4; Mosiah 7:33; 8:20–21; 23:9–10; 26:31; Alma 5:33–38; 3 Nephi 17:5–6; Ether 9:35; Ether 11:8.

In addition to the Lord as an example, we find great examples of loving, persistently forgiving, prayerful parent-leaders who never gave up on their children. Lehi and Sariah grieved over the hard-heartedness of their two oldest sons, but they never stopped trying (see 1 Nephi 18:17–20) even to their dying day (see 2 Nephi 2:30).

Alma continued in mighty prayer over his wayward sons (see Mosiah 27), and Mormon repented of his oath to forsake serving as a military leader over his wicked people (see Mormon 5:1). Like Mormon, sometimes out of frustration we threaten to cut off or disown a child in some way because of his behavior. In quiet moments, after we've had time to cool down and think it over, we often regret such words. It is important that parents have courage to repent and apologize to their children before the die is cast, "lest he esteem thee to be his enemy" (D&C 121:43).

"My mom and I are very different," said one young student. "Our personalities often clash, but there is no question she is the mother I needed. She has taught me about unlimited love. No matter how much of a brat I was in my teen years, she never turned her back on me. It was a comfort to know that she would always be there for me when I decided I needed her."

A Sanctuary Is a Place to Share Joy and Sorrow

In his dream, when Lehi partook of the fruit, his first thought was to share this great joy with his family, and he began at once to look for them (see 1 Nephi 8:12–15). When we love others as we love ourselves, we naturally want to share every good and joyful thing with them so that they too might experience the same joy. As children experience success or sorrow in their lives outside home and family, where do they first go to share the news? To the people who love them most—hopefully home to Mom and Dad.

When King Lamoni was converted, his first thought was for his own father. He wanted to share his newfound joy with him. Unfortunately, his father wasn't open to listening until his life was threatened. Hopefully your children will find ready listeners as they rush in the door with exciting and stimulating news, and that you will reciprocate and share that which is exciting to you with them.

One young man wrote, "The most important teaching my parents gave me was transmitted in their testimonies. They loved the gospel and wanted us to love it too. When I heard my parents' testimonies growing up, I was sure that the Church was true. The principles they taught made sense and I respected what they said because I was sure of their love for Jesus Christ." Do your best to make your home a sanctuary where your children know their sorrows will be heard and comfort will be offered, a place where every member feels free to express that which brings them happiness and joy, and a place where they can be warmed by the fire of your testimony.

Principle 12
Be Trustworthy, Dependable, Consistent, and Fair

Trustworthy and Dependable

Isaiah declared his faith in the Lord: "I will trust, and not be afraid" (Isaiah 12:2). Barbara Smith, a previous president of the general Relief Society added, "Trust is to human relationships what faith is to gospel living. It is the beginning place, the foundation upon which more can be built. Where trust is, love can flourish" ("A Safe Place for Marriages and Family," *Ensign*, Nov. 1981, 83–84). According to Dr. Carlfred Broderick, the "really rewarding . . . experiences in life are to be found in trusting and lasting relationships. Security and stability, integrity and inner peace, certainty of another person's commitment—these are profoundly satisfying things" (*Couples* [New York: Simon and Schuster], 1979, 158–59). His book focuses on couple interaction and the marriage relationship, but the need for trust holds true for any deeply personal relationship, including that of parent and child. According to Erik Erikson's hierarchy of human needs, one of the essential building blocks of a child's development, the one upon which all other blocks are built, is trust (*Childhood and Society* [New York: Meredith Press], 1964). To progress well emotionally in life, a child must develop trust in his parents and his environment so that he can be free to love and learn. How is such trust developed?

Trust develops when a child's physical and emotional needs are met consistently by loving, nurturing parents as they first respond with food when he's hungry, new diapers when he's wet, cuddling and soothing when he's distraught or lonely, and stimulation when he's bored. Later, trust will be fostered in more complex ways, such as when you are being truthful and honest, practicing your own sermons, and fulfilling promises. Trust is developed through experience, much as faith in God is learned through personal experiences with Him. When your actions and speech say to a child, "I love you, and your comfort, safety, and happiness are my primary concerns," then trust is most likely to develop. If you are consistent, dependable, fair, and trustworthy, your child will absorb that message.

If we want to be a positive influence on our children, they must trust us. A child who first learns to trust parents whom she can see will have an easier time transferring that trust to a loving Heavenly Father whom she can't see. Oh, that all children could feel and express the trust this young person has when she says, "I think there isn't a thing I could ask advice about from my dad and not believe whatever he said was absolutely the truth and the right thing to do. I love him and trust him because I have learned that he wants only what's best for me."

Our Heavenly Father has a plan for us. Earlier, we discussed that plan and the importance of every family having a plan too. He helps us in applying the principles of the plan through scriptural examples, the teachings of living prophets, conference addresses, and the writings of living prophets, as well as our own personal revelation. We can know what He expects of us and what we may gain in return for our obedience. He is not a capricious Father and is "no respecter of persons." The plan and the requirements of obedience are the same for all His children. If we obey the principles He has given us, we can expect the blessings, for "he will fulfill all his promises which he shall make unto you" (Alma 37:17). It's that clear. It's that simple. We can trust Him and we can trust His direction, for He has no other agenda except our personal welfare and happiness. He told us that, "this is my work and my glory, to bring to pass the immortality and eternal life of man" (Moses 1:39). To believe this statement is to have faith in Him.

Isn't that your goal, too, for your children? If parents can convince their children, as the young woman quoted earlier was convinced, that our only purpose is to help them live full, happy lives and achieve their highest potential, they will want to be obedient because they love us and trust us.

It is evident from Nephi's account in the first part of the Book of Mormon that Lehi frequently taught his children. Those who were teachable and soft of heart learned to trust in his words as did Nephi: "Yea, thou knowest that I believe all the words of my father" (1 Nephi 11:5). Nephi was able to transfer that same trust to the Lord. It was that confidence in God that allowed him to follow the Lord's direction to secure the brass plates. It was this trust that caused him to be "led by the Spirit, not knowing beforehand the things which [he] should do" (1 Nephi 4:6).

A child needs to know that he can go to his father or mother with a question or concern and be received patiently and kindly. He must not feel brushed aside, ridiculed, or chastised for his queries. Nephi had a few questions that required answers. He was not afraid to ask. "And it came to pass that I, Nephi, being exceedingly young, nevertheless being large in stature, and also having great desires to know of the mysteries of God, wherefore, I did cry unto the Lord; and behold he did visit me, and did soften my heart that I did believe all the words which had been spoken by my father; wherefore, I did not rebel against him like unto my brothers" (1 Nephi 2:16).

And again, seeking answers and desiring to know for himself the things his father had seen and "believing that the Lord was able to make them known unto me" (1 Nephi 11:1), Nephi went to the Lord and was blessed with a vision of his own.

Does your child have that kind of faith in you? Have you shown him by your past reactions and examples that he can trust you with the things of his soul, or that you will follow through with what you have promised? Listen to the testimonies of those who had experience with the Lord and know Him to be trustworthy and totally dependable. "And it came to pass that according to his word he did destroy them; and according to his word he did lead them; and according to his word he did do all things for them;

and there was not any thing done save it were by his word" (1 Nephi 17:31).

In 1 Nephi 22:8–22, Nephi, with full confidence, lists a number of things the Lord will and will not do. Never does he use a wishy-washy "maybe, could be, or perhaps." How can he be so sure? Because he had experience with the Lord. He knew, as Omni did, that "[the Lord] would not suffer that [His] words should not be verified" (Omni 1:6).

Another example comes from Enos. Enos heard the Lord say, "I will visit thy brethren according to their diligence in keeping my commandments. . . . And after I, Enos, heard these words, my faith began to be unshaken in the Lord" (Enos 1:10–11). King Benjamin also spoke with confidence and from experience when he declared, "And he has promised you that if ye would keep his commandments ye should prosper in the land; and he never doth vary from that which he hath said" (Mosiah 2:22).

Alma adds this testimony: "For he will fulfil all his promises which he shall make unto you" (Alma 37:17). "The decrees of God are unalterable" (Alma 41:8). "And thus we see how merciful and just are all the dealings of the Lord, to the fulfilling of all his words unto the children of men; yea, we can behold that his words are verified" (Alma 50:19). "But behold, we trust in our God who has given us victory over those lands" (Alma 58:33).

There are many powerful testimonies of the dependability and trustworthiness of the Lord in the following scriptures: 3 Nephi 27:18; Ether 3:11–12; 3:25–26; 12:6–22, 30–31; Helaman 8; and 3 Nephi 29, especially verses 1, 3, 8. These are excellent examples of dependability and trustworthiness.

In a passage above, Nephi exhorted his brothers to trust in the Lord by reviewing the history of God's dealings with the Israelites. In time, your children will also have a "history" of your dealings with them and will react to your counsel according to what experience has taught them. If you have taught them that you mean what you say and you speak only the truth, they will respond differently than if you have threatened but not followed through "according to your word."

A Parent Must Be Consistent and Fair

In the same article quoted earlier, President Barbara Smith said, "When children are treated fairly, there is no cause for jealousy because there is no partiality" (ibid.). Have you ever heard your children react to what they perceive to be an injustice with statements like these?

"Why is it always *my* fault?"

"You never let me be first!"

"She always gets her own way. You spoil her!"

"Why can't I go too? You let Molly go."

"Everybody else gets to stay up late, why can't I?"

"When I was her age, you didn't let me do that!"

Children are quick to notice any discrepancies, or perceived discrepancies, in justice. To them black is black and white is white. If parenting were only as simple as that. But before I discuss the need for discrepancies, let's begin with the need to be consistent and fair as illustrated by the Lord's example.

The Lord said that He is no respecter of persons. In 1 Nephi 17:32–35, 38, Nephi reasoned with his brothers that the Lord would not have allowed the Israelites to destroy the inhabitants of Canaan had those inhabitants been righteous.

> And after they had crossed the river Jordan he did make them mighty unto the driving out of the children of the land, yea, unto the scattering them to destruction.
>
> And now, do ye suppose that the children of this land, who were in the land of promise, who were driven out by our fathers, do you suppose that they were righteous? Behold, I say unto you, Nay.
>
> Do ye suppose that our fathers would have been more choice than they if they had been righteous? I say unto you, Nay.

> Behold, the Lord esteemeth all flesh in one; he that is righteous is favored of God.
>
> And he leadeth away the righteous into precious lands, and the wicked he destroyeth, and curseth the land unto them for their sakes.

The Lord does not punish some and exalt others simply at His own whim, but covers all His children with the same blanket of love and justice: be righteous and be blessed, be wicked and be damned. The choice is ours. If parents wish to be trusted by their children, they will follow that firm example and treat each child fairly by allowing the consequences of their choices to do the disciplining. The Lord always keeps His word, and His punishments are meted out justly according to His promises.

The Lord is a model of consistency—a twin concept to fairness. "For he is the same yesterday, to-day, and forever; and the way is prepared for all men from the foundation of the world, if it so be that they repent and come unto him" (1 Nephi 10:18).

Being consistent means we can always trust His promises when we do what He asks of us. Consistency on the part of a parent frees a child to act without any doubts on his part about the outcome and increases the child's trust in his parents. He also knows that the parental promises pertain to all the children alike.

Other passages attesting to the Lord's fairness and consistency can be found in 2 Nephi 2:11–16, 19, 22–23; 28; 29:1; Mosiah 27:30; 3 Nephi 17:8; and Moroni 8:18. There are also several references in the Book of Mormon that have to do with God's laws. Here's one example: "And the law is given unto men. And by the law no flesh is justified; or, by the law men are cut off. Yea, by the temporal law they were cut off; and also, by the spiritual law they perish from that which is good, and become miserable forever" (2 Nephi 2:5–7).

Now for the tricky part. It is important to have family rules and to be consistent and fair, but a parent must also help a child understand that rules need to be adjusted for age, maturity, and occasional circumstances. Sometimes you simply don't know all the facts, yet you're expected to be the arbitrator and judge. In those instances, consequences are often the best teacher. If two children in the adjoining room are fighting over the same toy and both claim to have had it first, you can either let them "fight" it out and discover that the pain isn't worth the cost (natural consequences), or you can remove the toy until they can figure out that it's better to take turns than do without it (logical consequences), or you can talk to them about taking turns and enlist their cooperation. One thing you might not want to do is always insist the older child give in to the younger one—not unless you're trying to raise a little monster nobody can get along with. Other scenarios might require you to sympathize and explain, "I know you'd like to do all the things Molly does, but she is sixteen and you're only twelve. You have that experience to look forward to," or, "I know that Jared doesn't help as much as you do, but he's younger and can't do all the things you can. We ask him to do what we think he can handle, and when he's your age we'll expect more from him too."

If you have three children, unless they're triplets, they aren't likely to be the same age and at the same level of maturation. To treat them fairly you have to treat them differently. The Lord explained the law and gave all the opportunity to obey according to their understanding. "Wherefore, he has given a law; and where there is no law given there is no punishment; and where there is no punishment there is no condemnation. . . . For the atonement satisfieth the demands of his justice upon all those who have not the law given to them (2 Nephi 9:25–26; see also Alma 29:4–5; 30:8–11).

The Lord is consistent in His love for all His children (see 2 Nephi 11:5; 3 Nephi 16:1–5). From His perspective it is consistent to judge children under the age of eight differently than children eight and older.

> Little children cannot repent; wherefore, it is awful wickedness to deny the pure mercies of God unto them, for

> they are all alive in him because of his mercy. (Moroni 8:19)

> For behold that all little children are alive in Christ, and also all they that are without the law. For the power of redemption cometh on all them that have no law; wherefore, he that is not condemned, or he that is under no condemnation, cannot repent; and unto such baptism availeth nothing. (Moroni 8:22)

As parents, we would not think of expecting the same thing from an innocent baby as we do from our more mature children. To be fair, everyone must be judged on his level of understanding and ability. The Lord teaches us the principle and its application. And as Barbara Smith suggested, if you give each of your children the love and attention each one needs, they'll find there is no need for jealousy and competition—the twin outcomes of insecurity and self-doubt.

Principle 13
Involve the Children and Get a Commitment

Children are more likely to follow a rule if they have been involved in its formation and when they make a physical or verbal commitment to obey its provisions. We learned this only after years of trial and error. Eventually we took a tip from the Book of Mormon and came up with a workable program.

Twice a year, at the beginning and again at the end of the school year, our family would devote a family home evening to reviewing and, in some cases, restructuring our family rules. My husband and I were already pretty much in agreement on our expectations and goals for our family, but as our children matured and seasons changed the external environment, we felt it necessary to spell things out in greater detail. We involved the children in this process because we desired and needed their input and cooperation. We had finally learned that children and adults alike respond more favorably to rules they've had a part in formulating. Such rules might include issues such as appropriate bedtimes, curfew times for older children, television privileges, division of household tasks and responsibilities, study expectations and use of time after school, use of the family car, etc. We also reviewed expectations that never changed: Sabbath day observance and activities, table manners, dating behavior, etc. At the end of those planning sessions, I typed up the agreed-upon rules and posted them in a prominent place should they need an occasional review. (And, in spite of all the preplanning we did, it was necessary, on occasion, to review them.)

We didn't ask our children to swear on the Bible or take an oath to obey the rules, but we made sure that we all agreed that the rules were fair and equitable and that we were committed to living them. We'd had other parents tell us that their children had to put their signature on the agreement. It works either way. (See "Physical Signs of Commitment" later in this chapter). After we'd reviewed our rules, in the months to follow, whenever someone had a question about a desired activity, or whenever a rule was broken, we would ask that child, "Well, what is the rule we all decided upon about that issue?" In cases of memory lapse we'd refer them to the posted rules. Sometimes just repeating a rule out loud was sufficient to make the decision easier.

The Lord uses a similar technique. We were in attendance at the grand council in the premortal life, were given choices to make, and we made them. Latter-day Saints are a covenant-making people; we understand the blessings and consequences of covenants, and we must make choices. Elder Bruce R. McConkie explained: "In the gospel sense, a covenant is a binding and solemn compact, agreement, contract, or mutual promise between God and a single person or a group of chosen persons" (*Mormon Doctrine* [Salt Lake City, Utah: Bookcraft], 1966, 166–67). Elder McConkie lists several covenants a devoted Latter-day Saint makes in the course of a lifetime: baptismal covenants (renewed weekly through the sacrament), temple covenants and the "new and everlasting covenant of marriage," tithing, Sabbath observance, Word of Wisdom, etc. While we don't sign our names to a document as we do in the legal world, each covenant is accompanied by an outward manifestation—an ordinance—which becomes our "signature" or agreement that we will honor the provisions of the covenant.

Verbal Commitments

A wise parent makes it clear to their child that with liberty and freedom come responsibility. We need commitments from our children as Mosiah achieved with the Nephites:

> Therefore they relinquished their desires for a king, and became exceedingly anxious that every man should have an equal chance throughout all the land; yea, and every man expressed a willingness to answer for his own sins.
>
> Therefore, it came to pass that they assembled themselves together in bodies throughout the land, to cast in their voices concerning who should be their judges, to judge them according to the law which had been given them; and they were exceedingly rejoiced because of the liberty which had been granted unto them. (Mosiah 29:38–39)

When parents discuss family rules with their children and receive a commitment from them, the children are more willing to obey and govern themselves, as we learn from King Mosiah's example.

> Now it came to pass that in the first year of the reign of the judges over the people of Nephi, from this time forward, king Mosiah having gone the way of all the earth, having warred a good warfare, walking uprightly before God, leaving none to reign in his stead; nevertheless he had established laws, and they were acknowledged by the people; therefore they were obliged to abide by the laws which he had made. (Alma 1:1)

In Alma chapter 5, Alma reviewed basic gospel principles with the people of Zarahemla and persisted in asking a few questions to obtain a commitment from them that they would repent and change from time to time. One of the better-known verses in this series of probing questions is, "If ye have experienced a change of heart, and if ye have felt to sing the song of redeeming love, I would ask, can ye feel so now?" (v. 26). Then he asked more questions that required each to make a personal evaluation of their spiritual standing. A parent might use a similar technique when a child refuses to perform his particular assigned household task (such as taking out the garbage) by asking, "What is our rule about household jobs?" "Is it a fair rule?" "Is it fair for the rest of us to have to live with the garbage cluttering up and smelling up the kitchen because you don't feel like doing your part?"

In the past, the missionary program utilized what was called "the commitment pattern," which is: (1) Prepare (build relationships of trust), (2) Invite (teach the principles and help those you teach to recognize the Spirit), (3) Follow up (obtain a commitment), and (4) Find out (resolve concerns). Ammon used this process in teaching King Lamoni (Alma 17–19), and it is a helpful pattern for parents to follow with children. Depending on the situation, the third and fourth steps can be reversed.

1. *Build relationships of trust.*

> Now they wept because of the fear of being slain. Now when Ammon saw this his heart was swollen within him with joy; for, said he, I will show forth my power unto these my fellow-servants, or the power which is in me, in restoring these flocks unto the king, that I may win the hearts of these my fellow-servants, that I may lead them to believe in my words. (Alma 17:29)

2. *Teach principles and help children recognize the Spirit.*

> Now Ammon being wise, yet harmless, he said unto Lamoni: Wilt thou hearken unto my words, if I tell thee by what power I do these things? And this is the thing that I desire of thee.
>
> And the king answered him, and said: Yea, I will believe all thy words. And thus he was caught with guile.
>
> And Ammon began to speak unto him with boldness, and said unto him: Believest thou that there is a God?
> And he answered, and said unto him: I do not know what that meaneth.

> And then Ammon said: Believest thou that there is a Great Spirit?
>
> And he said, Yea.
>
> And Ammon said: This is God. (Alma 18:22–28)

3. *Ask find-out questions.*

> And Ammon said unto him again: Believest thou that this Great Spirit, who is God, created all things which are in heaven and in the earth?
>
> And he said: Yea, I believe that he created all things which are in the earth; but I do not know the heavens. (Alma 18:28–29)

And Ammon continued to teach and find out, and teach and find out, and resolve concerns as he answered first King Lamoni's questions and then the queen's in Alma 18–19.

4. *Follow up with a commitment.*

> And it came to pass that when Ammon arose he also administered unto them, and also did all the servants of Lamoni; and they did all declare unto the people the selfsame thing—that their hearts had been changed; that they had no more desire to do evil. (Alma 19:33)
>
> And it came to pass that there were many that did believe in their words; and as many as did believe *were baptized*; and they became a righteous people, and they did establish a church among them (Alma 19:35, emphasis added). [Baptism then, as it is now, is an outward sign of an internal commitment.]

We can use the same method with our children. Rather than saying, "Take out the garbage," as a command, perhaps we could say, "Will you take out the garbage now?" (or "before you go to bed," etc.). Rather than saying, "Let's all try to keep the family rules we've just agreed upon," perhaps a statement like this will be more helpful: "Will you commit to keep these family rules we've just reviewed?"

Helaman was faced with whether to continue fleeing from the mighty Lamanite armies who were pursuing them, or to stop, turn, face them, and fight. His soldiers consisted of two thousand stripling warriors who were not only very young but had little or no training or experience in combat. Unlike the opposing leader, Ammoron, who climbed to the top leadership rung through cunning, treachery, and murder, and who cared nothing for the lives of his men, Helaman loved his young men as his own sons, caring only for their welfare and success. He did not order them to face what might have been certain death for them, but rather he put it to them to decide. "Therefore what say ye, my sons, will ye go against them to battle?" (Alma 56:44). They, then, having made the decision themselves, gave it their all, being fully committed to the cause which had now become their own.

Physical Signs of Commitment

Writing down your name or signing an agreement is a way of strengthening a commitment and letting others know you are taking the agreement seriously, and they and you will be held accountable. "And now, king Benjamin thought it was expedient, after having finished speaking to the people, that he should take the names of all those who had entered into a covenant with God to keep his commandments" (Mosiah 6:1).

Burying swords was a physical, outward sign of the commitment the Anti-Nephi-Lehies made to never fight again. Baptism and temple endowments are another example.

Children can be helped to keep their resolves in a similar way. A friend of mine told me that for family home evening one night they talked about sins and repentance and asked everyone to write down their "sins" on a piece of paper and throw them away in the wastebasket. Wouldn't that be an effective activity for a family home evening?

In the example below, the Nephites participated in an outward sign of the deep commitment they made to the Lord.

> Behold, whosoever will maintain this title upon the land, let them come forth in the strength of the Lord, and enter into a covenant that they will maintain their rights, and their religion, that the Lord God may bless them.
>
> And it came to pass that when Moroni had proclaimed these words, behold, the people came running together with their armor girded about their loins, rending their garments in token, or as a covenant, that they would not forsake the Lord their God; or, in other words, if they should transgress the commandments of God, or fall into transgression, and be ashamed to take upon them the name of Christ, the Lord should rend them even as they had rent their garments.
>
> Now this was the covenant which they made, and they cast their garments at the feet of Moroni, saying: We covenant with our God, that we shall be destroyed, even as our brethren in the land northward, if we shall fall into transgression; yea, he may cast us at the feet of our enemies, even as we have cast our garments at thy feet to be trodden under foot, if we shall fall into transgression. (Alma 46:20–22)

Reminders of One's Commitment

Children often need a visual reminder of their commitments—like the popular CTR ring, a picture of Jesus in their room, a scripture or statement taped on the mirror, or a favorite temple picture. Many families have designed a family creed or mission statement and illustrated it on a banner they display as a reminder to all family members. "And it came to pass also, that he caused the title of liberty to be hoisted upon every tower which was in all the land, which was possessed by the Nephites; and thus Moroni planted the standard of liberty among the Nephites" (Alma 46:36).

The Lord recognized the need for His children to be reminded weekly of their commitments as He asked baptized members of the Church to partake of the sacrament each Sunday:

> And this shall ye do in remembrance of my body, which I have shown unto you. And it shall be a testimony unto the Father that ye do always remember me. And if ye do always remember me ye shall have my Spirit to be with you.
>
> And when the disciples had done this, Jesus said unto them: Blessed are ye for this thing which ye have done, for this is fulfilling my commandments, and this doth witness unto the Father that ye are willing to do that which I have commanded you.
>
> And this shall ye always do to those who repent and are baptized in my name; and ye shall do it in remembrance of my blood, which I have shed for you, that ye may witness unto the Father that ye do always remember me. And if ye do always remember me ye shall have my Spirit to be with you. (3 Nephi 18:7, 10–11; see also Moroni 4:1–3; 5:1–2)

A daily or weekly reminder helps children (and adults) stay on track. It is important that families "meet together oft"—at mealtimes, prayer time, during family scripture study, and through weekly family home evenings—to strengthen and support one another and recommit to uphold the family values and goals.

Fight the Good Fight

Principle 14
We Are at War

My husband and I occasionally conduct marriage and parenting seminars. In one California stake, after several sessions together, we separated the men and women, and I spoke on the topic, "Mom, Could You Use a Little Help?"

My plan was to talk to the mothers about some of the resources women often overlook when struggling with parenting little ones—a sense of humor, your spouse, the children themselves, and most importantly, the Lord. I started out with a little humorous anecdote and spent time illustrating the principle that "crisis plus time" equals humor, pointing out that raising young children can be a delightful experience if you can see a little humor in some of the situations that arise. During a break in my presentation, one mother approached me and said, "Sister Brinley, if you'll take a good look at the mothers in your class, you'll see they are, like me, most likely dealing with teenagers rather than preschoolers, and we need some serious help! We fight against every temptation there is here in California—drugs, alcohol, peer pressure, premarital sex, too much leisure time, gangs, and horrible movies and videos. We are at war with Satan over the very souls of our children! These issues are not very humorous and never will be."

She was right. I really hadn't taken a good look at my audience. I was teaching principles, not people. When she left me to join the others for a snack, I found a secluded place and prayed as hard as I could for direction in the last part of the session. When the women came back into the room I turned to an often overlooked resource—the Book of Mormon.

The Lord taught me that day just how serious the present war against Satan is and how to fight back. That's when I discovered why the Book of Mormon authors included the war chapters in Alma: we are at war!

It is just as this woman said and as parents everywhere are learning—we are fighting a battle with Satan over the very souls of our children. Just as the strength and future of the Church lies in the testimonies of our youth, so Satan also knows that if he can win them to his side when they are young and impressionable, he can prevail in their lives. It was just as true in A.D. 3 as it is now. Listen to this account:

> And there was also a cause of much sorrow among the Lamanites; for behold, they had many children who did grow up and began to wax strong in years, that they became for themselves, and were led away by some who were Zoramites, by their lyings and their flattering words, to join those Gadianton robbers.
>
> And thus were the Lamanites afflicted also, and began to decrease as to their faith and righteousness, because of the wickedness of the rising generation. (3 Nephi 1:29–30)

What is the meaning of the phrase "they became for themselves"? I think it means they wanted to make their own decisions just like our teenagers do today. I think it means teenagers were struggling with their autonomy just as they are today, and if we haven't armed our children for the battles before they reach that vulnerable age, they too can be "led away." How can we fight this war? What weapons do we have? What strategies must we know?

The Book of Mormon is full of battles between the Lamanites and Nephites. As we read and ponder these accounts and do as Nephi counseled—"liken the scriptures unto ourselves"—we are taught how to win battles, what techniques Satan uses, and what we must do to prevail over his nefarious schemes. We learn as the

Nephites did that we can never conquer our enemies without the help of the Lord. The Book of Mormon gives us some "battle strategies" and shows us how we can better prepare ourselves and our children to face and win this spiritually deadly war.

In Alma 43 we find the Zoramites, Amalekites, and Lamanites joined together to contend with the Nephites. Zerahemnah, the most blood-thirsty of all the leaders, was appointed chief captain. "For behold, his designs [Zerahemnah's] were to stir up the Lamanites to anger against the Nephites; this he did that he might usurp great power over them, and also that he might gain power over the Nephites by bringing them into bondage" (Alma 43:8).

One of Satan's familiar tactics is to stir up contention between family members, especially between parents and their children. Often power struggles develop not only between parent and child, but between parent and parent. The Lord counsels us against allowing contention in our families. "And ye will not suffer your children . . . that they transgress the laws of God, and fight and quarrel one with another, and serve the devil. . . . But ye will teach them to walk in the ways of truth and soberness; ye will teach them to love one another, and to serve one another" (Mosiah 4:14–15).

Nevertheless, contentions outside the home will arise. The Nephites hated war, but they were forced to confront their adversaries when their own homes, families, and way of life were threatened. "And now the design of the Nephites was to support their lands, and their houses, and their wives, and their children, that they might preserve them from the hands of their enemies; and also that they might preserve their rights and their privileges, yea, and also their liberty, that they might worship God according to their desires" (Alma 43:9).

The Nephites only wanted the freedom to rear their families in love and peace. Parents today want the same blessings of spiritual protection for their children and peace at home. The Nephites were striving to keep themselves and their children free from the bondage of the Lamanite intruders. We want to keep our children free from the bondage of intruders like pornography, drugs, alcohol, tobacco, and perverted media presentations. The Nephites didn't want war; we don't want war. But when our liberty and peace is threatened, we must fight with all our might, using all the weapons in our arsenal (see Alma 48:14, followed by Alma 48:10).

"And it came to pass that he [twenty-five-year-old Moroni] met the Lamanites in the borders of Jershon, and his people were armed with swords, and with cimeters, and all manner of weapons of war" (Alma 43:18). It is the responsibility of every parent to arm their children with every righteous weapon at their disposal before their offspring head out the door. President Boyd K. Packer called such protective gear "the shield of faith" or "the armor of God." An analogy of this armor is found in 2 Nephi 1:23, where Lehi pleads with his sons to "put on the armor of righteousness."

The armor that protects children is forged with faith, prayer, and a knowledge of who they are and their importance to God—this independence allows them to function away from your home in confidence, with experience in decision making, and in ways that help them recognize and resist temptation. Children learn these battle tactics at home, in family home evenings where they are taught through role-play, family scripture study, parental instruction and example, and in studying articles in Church magazines. Though all of this can be reinforced by Primary, seminary, Young Men and Young Women meetings, priest quorums and missionary service, preparing children to face the world is primarily the parents' job. President Packer taught:

> The ministry of the prophets and apostles leads [us] ever and always to the home and the family. That shield of faith is not produced in a factory, but at home in a cottage industry. . . .
>
> Lest parents and children be "tossed to and fro," and misled by "cunning craftiness" of men who "lie in wait to deceive" (Eph. 4:14), our Father's plan requires that, like the generation of life itself, the shield of faith is to be made and

> fitted in the family. No two can be exactly alike. Each must be handcrafted to individual specifications.
>
> The plan designed by the Father contemplates that man and woman, husband and wife working together, fit each child individually with a shield of faith made to buckle on so firmly that it can neither be pulled off nor penetrated by those fiery darts. ("The Shield of Faith," *Ensign*, May 1995, 8)

Seeing that the Nephites were armed did not totally discourage the Lamanites; they just looked for another way to approach them. Satan may be thwarted temporarily, but he'll look for weak spots elsewhere.

> Behold, now it came to pass that [the Lamanites] durst not come against the Nephites in the borders of Jershon; therefore they departed out of the land of Antionum into the wilderness, and took their journey round about in the wilderness, away by the head of the river Sidon, that they might come into the land of Manti and take possession of the land; for they did not suppose that the armies of Moroni would know whither they had gone. (Alma 43:22)

Note Moroni's response: "But it came to pass, as soon as they had departed into the wilderness Moroni sent spies into the wilderness to watch their camp; and Moroni, also, knowing of the prophecies of Alma, sent certain men unto him, desiring him that he should inquire of the Lord whither the armies of the Nephites should go to defend themselves against the Lamanites" (Alma 43:23).

Moroni sent men unto Alma desiring of him to inquire of the Lord where the armies of the Nephites should go to defeat the enemy. What a great parenting principle: ask the Lord to reveal your weaknesses so that you may eliminate them. What weaknesses might Satan find in the protective walls of your home and family?

A weak relationship due to a lack of time spent together? Failure to teach consistently? Failure to agree as parents on your disciplinary methods? Failure to support each other in parenting decisions? Competition between spouses for a child's attention? If there are weaknesses to be found, rest assured, Satan will exploit them. But the Lord is also aware of your weaknesses, as well as your strengths, and He can assist you if you honestly seek inspiration.

"Moroni knew the intention of the Lamanites, that it was their intention to destroy their brethren, or to subject them and bring them into bondage" (Alma 43:29). What are Satan's intentions for today's children? To destroy them through the destruction of the family, of course. Knowing the adversary's goal is very helpful for us, for knowledge is half the battle. If you know the intention of the enemy and his battle plan, you can be better prepared defensively. Every parent must know the enemy and his tactics. Believe that Satan *does* exist. Don't be naive about this! And don't let children be naive about it either. Even though we don't see him, we see his efforts through wicked men.

And who is our captain—our Moroni? Who are the watchmen? The Lord's living prophets warn us as to how we might prepare and protect ourselves and confront the enemy. Our task is to listen and apply their counsel. At every general conference, they remind us to strengthen our families through the following actions:

1. Daily family prayer
2. Reading the scriptures together as a family
3. Consistent weekly family home evening(see "Letter to the Members of the Church," First Presidency, February 27, 1999).

Yet despite their urgent pleadings and warnings, one study revealed that only about half of those who are active Church members follow this counsel (see Brent Top and Bruce Chadwick, *Rearing Righteous Youth of Zion* [Salt Lake City, UT: Bookcraft], 1998).

What else can we learn from the war chapters?

> And as the Lamanites had passed the hill Riplah, and came into the valley, and began to cross the river Sidon, the army which was concealed on the south of the hill, which was led by a man whose name was Lehi, and he led his army forth and encircled the Lamanites about on the east in their rear.
>
> While on the other hand, there was now and then a man fell among the Nephites, by their swords and the loss of blood, they being shielded from the more vital parts of the body, or the more vital parts of the body being shielded from the strokes of the Lamanites, by their breastplates, and their armshields, and their head-plates; and thus the Nephites did carry on the work of death among the Lamanites. (Alma 43:35, 38)

What do we learn from these verses? To cover all of our bases, surround the enemy, and protect our "spiritual vital parts." What are the vital parts of our children? Where and when are your children most vulnerable? It is imperative that parents know their children's strengths, weaknesses, and what temptations are most likely to appeal to them. You must know their friends, their concerns, their needs.

> Now in this case the Lamanites did fight exceedingly; yea, never had the Lamanites been known to fight with such exceedingly great strength and courage, no, not even from the beginning.
>
> And they [the Lamanites] were inspired by the Zoramites and the Amalekites, who were their chief captains and leaders, and by Zerahemnah, who was their chief captain, or their chief leader and commander; yea, they did fight like dragons, and many of the Nephites were slain by their hands, yea, for they did smite in two many of their head-plates, and they did pierce many of their breastplates, and

> they did smite off many of their arms; and thus the Lamanites did smite in their fierce anger. (Alma 43:43–44)

Know that a cornered enemy fights back with even greater determination. Temporary victories may be won or lost. But be prepared for every situation. It may appear at times that Satan has won as you watch a wayward child make choices contrary to what you taught them, but we must never give up teaching and working with our children. Continue the fight with love, patience, faith, and prayer, and if it becomes necessary to remove the offender from the family for the protection of innocent siblings, always keep the door and your heart open.

> Nevertheless, the Nephites were inspired by a better cause, for they were not fighting for monarchy nor power but they were fighting for their homes and their liberties, and their wives and their children, and their all, yea, for their rights of worship and their church.
>
> Therefore for this cause were the Nephites contending with the Lamanites, to defend themselves, and their families, and their lands, their country, and their rights, and their religion. (Alma 43:45, 47)

We, too, are fighting for a better cause. The Lord is on our side, and if we teach our children principles of righteousness and doctrine while they are in our homes, they will be well equipped to fight the battles they must fight when they leave the protection and safety of home.

What a simple message: God is on our side; prepare your children for the world outside your home using the weapons you have been given—the Holy Ghost, teaching moments, setting a good example of righteousness, and following His prophets. In the end, they that be with us are more than they that be with them (see 2 Kings 6:16).

Principle 15
Grandparenting—Another Chance

Now that we've discussed some of the most important principles of parenting, let us not forget that the fight is not over—lost or won—when our own children have left home and begun their own families. Many parents, seeing their children leave the nest, experience feelings of regret, even panic, as they see their teaching opportunities diminish. Numerous questions bombard them. How did they grow up so fast? Have we prepared them for life? What more should we have taught them? Maybe the intentions of the parents were good, but other demands seemed more crucial at the time, until suddenly the children were gone. Though we may not be able to greatly influence the consequences of our early parenting, there is always repentance and new wisdom that we can apply today—with our own adult children and with our children's children.

President Hinckley, in a BYU devotional, addressed the important role that grandparents play in the lives of their posterity. He compared families to a great chain of generations and admonished us not to be the weak link in our family chain. He recalled an experience he had at the dedication of the Columbus Ohio Temple. There he was, accompanied by his wife, daughter, granddaughter, and great-grandchildren. Sitting in the celestial room of the temple, he thought about his great-grandfather, his grandfather, and his own father:

> These three good men represent the three generations of my forebears who have been faithful in the Church. . . .

> [Then] while seated in the temple, I looked down at my daughter, at her daughter, who is my grandchild, and at her children, my great-grandchildren. I suddenly realized that I stood right in the middle of these seven generations—three before me and three after me.
>
> In that sacred and hallowed house, there passed through my mind a sense of the tremendous obligation that was mine to pass on all that I had received as an inheritance from my forebears to the generations who have now come after me. ("Keep the Chain Unbroken," *Speeches*, Nov. 30, 1999, BYU University Press)

In that sacred precinct, President Hinckley vowed to himself to never become a weak link in the generational chain.

As they set out on their missions, Helaman entreated his sons Nephi and Lehi to remember their forefathers' (after whom they were named) good examples as patterns to follow. To feel connected and to be part of a family chain, children need to know something of their background and heritage. If they feel such a connection, they will be more likely to make proper choices, honor the family name, and follow the example of a grandparent or great-grandparent in being a part of something good. Leaving a respectable name for your posterity is far more valuable an inheritance than money or property. As a teenager goes out the door to spend an evening with friends, a simple "remember who you are"—in homes where one's heritage has been valued—can remind him of his ancestors and strengthen his resolve to make good decisions and avoid peer pressure to do otherwise.

> Behold, my sons, I desire that ye should remember to keep the commandments of God; and I would that ye should declare unto the people these words. Behold, I have given unto you the names of our first parents who came out of the land of Jerusalem; and this I have done that when you remember your names ye may remember them; and when

> ye remember them ye may remember their works; and when ye remember their works ye may know how that it is said, and also written, that they were good.
>
> Therefore, my sons, I would that ye should do that which is good, that it may be said of you, and also written, even as it has been said and written of them. (Helaman 5:6–7)

Elder Stephen B. Oveson of the Seventy expressed his gratitude for the legacy his grandparents left him:

> Although he died when I was just a boy, my grandfather has always been one of my heroes. I have studied his journal, which recounts over and over again his willingness to answer the calls that came to him throughout his lifetime. . . .
>
> Whether we descend from generations in the Church or are the first link in the generational chain, we have a responsibility to convey to our posterity a heritage of faith, manifest through our daily actions. . . . We need to begin today to build a more exemplary life so that those dearest to us will "see [our] good works, and glorify [our] Father which is in heaven" (Matt. 5:16).
>
> What are we doing to ensure that [our] legacy is being passed to our beloved children and to our grandchildren? ("Our Legacy," *Ensign*, Nov. 1999, 29–30)

Elder Joseph B. Wirthlin shared this insight:

> Grandparents, too, can help. When I'm at a family gathering, I try to spend time, when appropriate, to have a one-on-one discussion with some of our grandchildren. I sit with them and ask them a few questions: "How are you doing?" "How is school?"

> Then I ask them how they feel about the true Church, which means so much to me. I try to discover the depth of their faith and testimony. If I perceive areas of uncertainty, I'll ask them, "Would you accept a goal from your granddad?"
>
> Then I'll suggest they read the scriptures daily and recommend they kneel down every morning and night and pray with their father and mother and have personal prayers. I admonish them to go to their sacrament meetings. I admonish them always to keep themselves pure and clean, always attend their meetings, and finally, among other things, always strive to be sensitive to the whisperings of the Lord.
>
> Now one time after a talk with Joseph, our eight-year-old grandson, he looked into my eyes and asked this pointed question: "May I go now, Granddad?" He ran from my arms and I thought, "Did I do any good?" Apparently I did, because the next day he said, "Thanks for the little talk we had."
>
> If we approach them with love rather than reproach, we will find that the faith of our grandchildren will increase as a result of the influence and testimony of someone who loves the Savior and His divine Church. ("Shall He Find Faith on the Earth," *Ensign*, Nov. 2002, 82–83)

As grandparents we have wonderful opportunities to be an influence in the lives of our grandchildren in several ways: through example as we live our lives, written testimonies in the journals we write, taking advantage of teaching moments when we are together, personal letters and e-mails if we are at a distance, traditions, overnight stays, and prayers when we are together. All of these actions take time, of course, and you must stay involved as a grandparent. We find several examples of these generational contacts in the Book of Mormon.

> *Teaching moments:* Lehi called his grandchildren together, and taught and blessed them (see 2 Nephi 4:3–10).
>
> *Righteous traditions:* In Mosiah 10:12 and 17, there is an example of how unrighteous traditions propagated by unrighteous parents and grandparents destroyed a whole nation.
>
> *Prayer:* Nephi prayed continually for his posterity and bore testimony to them one final time before his death (2 Nephi 33). Mormon prayed for his son and his posterity's welfare as he transferred the responsibility of the records to Moroni for our benefit (see Words of Mormon 1:2).
>
> *Journals and personal letters:* Nephi took great pains to keep a record for future generations that they might benefit from his wisdom and experiences (see 2 Nephi 25:21–23, 26–27).

Prophets have asked us to record for our posterity the events of our lives including thoughts, testimony, and faith-promoting experiences. These are a few good reasons to keep a journal that will bless our children and our children's children, thus reaching across the generations to future posterity even after we ourselves have gone (see also 2 Nephi 25:8; 26–28 (entire chapters); Jacob 1:1–4; 4:1–3; Mosiah 1:3–4; Moroni 10). In fact, the Book of Mormon itself is a journal written and preserved "to show unto the remnant of the House of Israel what great things the Lord hath done for their fathers; and that they may know the covenants of the Lord, that they are not cast off forever—And also to the convincing of the Jew and Gentile that Jesus is the Christ, the Eternal God, manifesting himself unto all nations" (title page).

Elder Neal A. Maxwell recommended we ask ourselves a few questions: "Parents and grandparents, please scrutinize your schedules and priorities in order to ensure that life's prime relationships get more prime time!" ("Take Especial Care of Your Families," *Ensign*, May 1994, 90).

Elder Henry B. Eyring reminds us that the time to be good parents and good grandparents is now. However, all is not lost if we made mistakes in the past. There is always repentance, opportunities to change past relationships, and new little ones we can help raise more effectively:

> Even should we be forgiven at some later time, the Lord cannot restore the good effects our repentance today might have had on those we love and are to serve. That is particularly poignant for the parents of young children. In those tender years there are chances for shaping and lifting spirits which may never come again. But even the grandfather who may have missed chances with his own children might, by choosing to repent today, do for grandchildren what he once could have done for their parents. ("Do Not Delay," *Ensign*, Nov. 1999, 34)

Parenting is an awesome responsibility. I don't suppose there is a parent in the Church, or in the world, actually, who feels they've done the job perfectly. Many eat their hearts out mourning over the struggles and mistakes their children make, and wonder if they could have done something more. Maybe that just comes with the territory. I don't know how to eliminate that entirely, but I do know this: whatever your experience is or has been, the Lord is on your side. He wants you to succeed. These children are His children and He loves them and knows them far better than we ever could. You couldn't ask for a better partner than Him.

Conclusion

The scriptures and other helps the Lord has given us are proof of His love and interest in our parenting success. I hope my attempt to illuminate some of the essential parenting principles found in the Book of Mormon is helpful, but I'll be the first to admit the principles I discovered are not exclusive. It is my hope this will only be a beginning for your own search of the scriptures as a parenting guide.

Whatever happens, do not be discouraged long-term, do not give up or lose hope. We may stumble. Our children may stumble. There may be some anguish and pain involved. But if we are humble, righteous, prayerful, and give this magnificent, sacred calling everything we've got, we will succeed—especially if that includes heeding the word of the Lord, for "the words of Christ will tell you all things what ye should do" (2 Nephi 32:3). As you read, I know the Lord will inspire you with ideas concerning your particular concerns for your children.

Maybe you need a little more lightheartedness in your home, more laughter. Perhaps you need more family recreation or just more family time together. Maybe more talking. Maybe less talking and more doing. Maybe you'll find your family's vulnerable spot is lack of structure, or maybe it's too much structure. Maybe you just need to relax and enjoy each other more. Enjoy the different stages of your life and your children's lives. When you are on your knees asking for help, stop a minute in your pleading and relate to your Father in Heaven one happy moment you experienced that day—one bright spot your child created in your life. I think the Lord would like that.

Remember that there are many who will inspire you; foremost among them will be the Book of Mormon—a parental guide worthy of the description "a marvelous work and a wonder" (2 Nephi 25:17). If we read and heed the parenting principles within, we will be blessed. Our children will be blessed. And we will know joy.

APPENDIX A
Hands-On Teaching Ideas

In Principle 1 we talk about the importance of teaching and discuss the issues of why, when, what, and how to do so. Over the years I've collected many hands-on ideas for what and how, but did not feel that the introductory sections on those topics was an appropriate place to include brainstorming for hands-on application. I include them here as that—brainstorming ideas you can use or adapt for you family's individual needs.

Teach them to love and serve one another:

In a family home evening, discuss the scriptures given in Principle 1 (What to Teach), and tell them the story of the girl who paid for her friend to go to the youth activity; then ask the children if they would be willing to participate in an experiment. Ask them to choose a person—it could be a family member or an acquaintance they don't know very well at school or in the neighborhood—and to think of little acts of kindness and/or service they can do for that person, at least once each day. Ask them to be ready to report in family home evening the following week. At that time, to stimulate their thinking, ask questions like, "How do you feel about that person when you see them now? How has your response to them changed? How has their response to you changed?"

Teach them to be grateful:

Teaching children to be grateful involves three components: helping them recognize blessings, reminding them occasionally of the importance of their blessings, and setting the example yourself by expressing gratitude frequently.

It might be wise at this point, however, to remind ourselves of the importance of timing. An angry, hurting heart may be too hardened to acknowledge any blessings. This was the case of Alma the Younger in Alma 10:5–6, 22–23. When a child is angry, hurt, and suffering, it is probably not the time to start reminding him to count his blessings. As Gary and Joy Lundberg point out in chapter three of their book, *I Don't Have to Make Everything All Better* (Las Vegas: Riverpark Publishing Co., 1995), that becomes a time to listen, to "walk with the child" in his misery until he knows you understand. Arguing with a child about why he is wrong to feel the way he does is not effective. Once a child realizes that someone really understands their pain, they are ready to resolve the issue and move on. Then, and only then, will a child be open to listening to a litany of things about which they ought to be happy. Sometimes children—and adults, such as in the instance of my reading glasses—don't recognize a blessing when they see it. We take so much for granted, forgetting to express gratitude for the many unsolicited blessings of daily life.

Some of our best family home evenings have been when we've given each child a piece of paper and asked them to write one thing they really like about each of their brothers and sisters and why they are grateful that child is part of our family. Each child, in turn, takes a seat in front of the family while all share the positive things that they've written.

Another evening you might direct the children to say why they are thankful for the Savior, the gospel, their Sunday School teacher, a Scoutmaster or a Young Women instructor. The scriptures on gratitude found in Principle 1 (What to Teach) might also inspire one to express appreciation for grandparents and ancestors who have made crucial sacrifices for our and future generations by accepting the gospel.

This is not a bad idea in relation to spouses. We recently heard of a couple who, before retiring for the night, exchange with each other the phrase, "Today I loved you because ______." They then recall a specific incident that has taken place earlier in the day. This is now a nightly tradition for them. If every couple did something like this, surely there would be far fewer divorces in our society.

Mosiah taught his people that gratitude is best expressed by the service we render in return for the blessings we receive. Is that not true of our children as well? How much more meaningful is a "thank you" to a mother when it is accompanied by willing and cheerful assistance from both her children and spouse. "Thank you for the great dinner; see you later" doesn't mean half so much as, "Thank you for a great dinner; let me do the dishes." We don't often see a child connecting the two concepts unless she has been taught the connection by example and perhaps discourse. Parents will be sadly disappointed if they say nothing to their children and yet think they will learn to express gratitude on their own.

Mosiah 2:20–21 is an instructive scripture and helps children think of how they might express gratitude and be of service themselves. Fathers can be a great help in this situation because children will more quickly learn from Dad's example—especially if he involves them in his service for Mom with something like, "Honey, that was a great dinner. Come on kids, let's show Mom how much we enjoyed it by clearing the table and doing the dishes."

We can help children recognize blessings and generate feelings of gratitude if we are grateful. Children need to hear us express appreciation in our family prayer for specific blessings we enjoy every day, not just when we've made it through a crisis (see 2 Nephi 4:16–35; Alma 49:28).

Teach them that agency and responsibility go together:

Parents must allow their children to use their agency but also to experience the consequences, even when you are sure the child's decision is a mistake. Note the difference between a *mistake* and a *sin*. It's a mistake to go to school without a jacket in freezing weather. It's a mistake to go to school without some kind of breakfast. It's a mistake to neglect homework a time or two. It's a mistake to dress and behave in a fashion that identifies you with the drug culture even though you may or may not be taking drugs. And it's a mistake to drop out of high school before graduation. While all of these are choices many young people make and which lead to disastrous consequences, it can also be a mistake for parents to become so irate over the affront to their values or teachings that the parent-child relationship is shattered and the child is driven even further into a lifestyle from which he may never return. It is at such times that mistakes often turn into sins. Do your best to ensure that your child understands your feelings and knows the possible consequences, but also help her to know that you empathize with the temptations and challenges she faces every day, that you trust her and love her, and that your home is a haven of safety for her even when she makes mistakes. Let your home be a safe place of learning, not a battleground.

Your child may have a difficult time understanding the link between obedience and agency because they seem to contradict each other. In 2 Nephi 2:26–29, Nephi clearly explains how giving up our will to the Lord actually frees us from bondage. We may feel very virtuous and comfortable giving of our material goods and even occasionally our time in acts of service, but we are not truly righteous if we don't submit our wills to God. Elder Neal A. Maxwell made this observation:

> The many other things we give to God, however nice that may be of us, are actually things He has already given us, and He has loaned them to us. But when we begin to submit ourselves by letting our wills be swallowed up in God's will, then we are really giving something to Him. . . . It is the only possession we have that we can give, and there is no lessening of our agency as a result. Instead, what we see is a flowering of our talents and more and more surges of joy. Submission to Him is the only form of submission that is completely safe. ("Insights from My Life," *Ensign*, Aug. 2000, 9)

Explain frequently to your children that bondage comes not from rules but from making the wrong choices. Help them understand that once they have made a decision and acted upon it, they are no longer free to choose the consequences and may forfeit further freedom, and that they are accountable. When advising a child on a particular decision, as far as you can and as clearly as you can, explain what the consequences of such decisions might be and what they might mean to the child. This is best done when you are not angry, but as a matter of instruction regarding civil law or God's law. Plead with a child, if necessary, to consider their options carefully before acting.

An example of this principle might be if your child decides to come home late for dinner. The consequences might be that he will have to go without dinner that night. Let's say your family has decided on the rule that all jobs must be done before a child is free to play. Now suppose one of the children, knowing of the family rule, fritters away time set aside to complete a family chore when a friend invites him to go to an afternoon movie. He has lost his freedom to choose whether or not to go to the movie. The consequences are that he must miss the movie and stay home to do chores. A much more serious example might involve immorality. Many in today's world seem to be confused about just when the decision to have a baby is made. They call it "The Right to Choose." Of course a person is free to decide whether or not to have sexual relations, but after the act is committed and pregnancy results, the decision to decide whether one is a mother or not is moot.

Agency and its wise use is an important part of the entire Book of Mormon message. The book is full of excellent examples. The following scriptures deal with examples of agency and would be useful to parents attempting to teach their children how agency works, how it can be a blessing or a curse depending on how it is used, and how responsibility relates to it. In a family home evening session, you might read one of scriptures below, for instance, then ask the children what they think it means and how they might relate that to themselves.

Jacob 4:14	"And because they desired it God hath done it, that they may stumble."
Mosiah 3:19	"The natural man is an enemy to God . . . unless he yields to the enticings of the Holy Spirit, and putteth off the natural man."
Mosiah 11:2	"And he did walk after the desires of his own heart . . . and did cause his people to sin."
Alma 3:26–27	"Reap the rewards according to their works. . . . For every man receiveth wages of him whom he listeth to obey."
Alma 5:39–40	"And now if ye are not the sheep of the good shepherd, of what fold are ye? . . . whatsoever is good cometh from God, and whatsoever is evil cometh from the devil."

Alma 10: 6	"I did harden my heart, for I was called many times and I would not hear."
Alma 22: 16	"Bow down before God . . . repent of all thy sins . . . then shalt thou receive the hope which thou desirest."
Alma 29:4–5	"He granteth unto men according to their desire . . . whether he desireth good or evil, life or death, joy or remorse of conscience."
Alma 42:27–28	"Whosoever will not come the same is not compelled to come; . . . If he has desired to do evil . . . evil shall be done unto him."
Alma 47	Amalickiah lies, deceives, and uses others to accomplish his selfish motives, and then he turns on them and destroys them just as Satan lies to deceives us.
Helaman 14:29	"If they are condemned they bring upon themselves their own condemnation."
3 Nephi 11:33–34	"And whoso believeth in me, and is baptized, the same shall be saved."
3 Nephi 26:4	"And all nations and tongues shall stand before God, to be judged of their works, whether they be good or whether they be evil."
3 Nephi 27:17	"And he that endureth not unto the end, the same is he that is also hewn down and cast into the fire."
Mormon 3:18–19	"[Ye] shall be judged according to your works."
Mormon 6:21–22	"Then ye must stand before the judgment seat of Christ to be judged according to your works."
Ether 2:23	A lesson in making decisions and problem solving.
Ether 10	An entire chapter dealing with men who had opportunities to provide righteous leadership. Some did, others chose wickedness.

Moroni 7:13, 17	"Everything which inviteth and enticeth to do good, and to love God, and to serve him, is inspired of God. . . . Whatsoever thing persuadeth men to do evil, and believe not in Christ, and deny him, and serve not God, then ye may know with a perfect knowledge it is of the devil."

Teach tolerance:

Often we are frightened and intolerant of people and ideas we don't understand. After discussing the scriptures and examples suggested in this section during a family home evening, you might invite an unfamiliar family to your home—a family of a different race or culture or religion—or attend a cultural function different from your own. You might want to prepare the children ahead of time for some of the obvious differences they will encounter like color, cultural traditions, dress/food restrictions, etc., and answer any questions they might have then. Remind them that these people are your brothers and sisters and you expect that they will be treated with respect. Let the children help make preparations for the event—planning activities, food, etc., so they'll feel a part of the event. When the family arrives, if they feel comfortable, ask them to tell something of their background, traditions, and culture. Later, or appropriately in context, point out to your children similarities that you see on which a basis for friendship may be established.

We once had a young woman in our ward who was blind and a bit autistic. The children were a little afraid of her because she was different, and they avoided speaking to her. My husband talked to our children about this young woman's challenges, and he had them try to eat and dress themselves while blindfolded. He even took them down the street and told them to try to find their way to our house. We hoped to build our children's empathy and respect for others. Then we invited her and her parents over for a family home evening dinner. This sister was very gifted at the piano—she could play anything after only hearing it once. She agreed to play for us that night. It was a memorable evening, and the best part was that our children were no longer afraid of her and were more comfortable speaking to her whenever the opportunity presented itself. Our hope is that this lesson carried over as our children faced other opportunities to learn to understand and empathize with others who were different.

Teach the value of the scriptures:

Share with your children the story of Lehi asking his boys to make a very dangerous journey back to Jerusalem for the brass plates. He was told of the importance of this mission by the Lord (see 1 Nephi 3:2–4). This was a clear indication to him and to us of the value of scripture. Read with your children the references made by father-leaders to children-followers, again illustrating their value and importance. What would have happened, for example, had the Nephites not had the plates? (see 1 Nephi 15:24; 2 Nephi 4:1–2; 11:2; 12–24; Mosiah 1:2–5; Alma 37:9)

Help your children discover the Book of Mormon messages for our day—a warning (see 2 Nephi 33:2), a promise (see 2 Nephi 25:8), a hope (see Enos 1:13, 16; Ether 8:25–26), and a testimony of its truthfulness (see Moroni 10:3–7). Share your testimony of their value in your life.

It has been said that those who do not learn from history are doomed to repeat it. We see in our day the same mistakes being made that we find in the Book of Mormon. Prosperity leads to pride, pride leads to destruction. The hope is that we will rear a generation that will break this cycle of pride and destruction and avoid the same pattern of failure in the days ahead. We must continually be on guard to avoid the arrogance that leads to class distinctions so prevalent in the Book of Mormon. We must ask ourselves frequently how we're doing in this modern era of labor-saving gadgets and devices. Are we doing any better than the Nephites? Help your children to understand the simple stories of the text and to liken the scriptures unto themselves in order to experience the power that comes into the lives of those who read the scriptures and hearken unto their words.

Teach the value of prayer:

Share with your children your own testimony of prayer and how it has blessed you. As they leave your home, send them off with the sound of your prayers for them resounding in their ears and hearts. "Never let a day go by without holding family prayer and family scripture study," said L. Tom Perry. "Put this, the Lord's program, to the test; and see if it does not bless your home with greater peace, hope, love, and faith. I promise you that daily family prayer and scripture study will build within the walls of your home a security and bonding that will enrich your lives and prepare your families to meet the challenges of today and the eternities to come" ("Back to Gospel Basics," *Ensign*, May 1993, 92).

Teach the wisdom of obedience:

Tell your children the story of the Anti-Nephi-Lehies and the covenant they made with the Lord to never raise weapons again, even to an enemy (see Alma 23–24). Then tell about their sons, the two thousand stripling warriors, and read the following scriptures:

> And they were all young men, and they were exceedingly valiant for courage, and also for strength and activity; but behold, this was not

> all—they were men who were true at all times in whatsoever thing they were entrusted.
>
> Yea, they were men of truth and soberness, for they had been taught to keep the commandments of God and to walk uprightly before him. (Alma 53:20–21)
>
> Yea, and they did obey and observe to perform every word of command with exactness; yea, and even according to their faith it was done unto them; and I did remember the words which they said unto me that their mothers had taught them. (Alma 57:21)
> But behold, they have received many wounds; nevertheless they stand fast in that liberty wherewith God has made them free; and they are strict to remember the Lord their God from day to day; yea, they do observe to keep his statutes, and his judgments, and his commandments continually; and their faith is strong in the prophecies concerning that which is to come. (Alma 58:40) [Wouldn't you love to have that written somewhere of your children?]

As you read this section of the Book of Mormon with your children, point out to them that just as the sons of Helaman were called upon to fight the Lamanites in their day, that they, too, are engaged in a battle. They are fighting the adversary and his angels of darkness, and they need the help of the Lord to win. Help them to see that without His counsel we are all in danger, both mortal and spiritual. Safety is found in being obedient to God and His chosen leaders. Read Ether 6:17 with your children. "And they were taught to walk humbly before the Lord; and they were also taught from on high." Explain that "walking in humility" means they were obedient. The Lord asks all of us to be humble and obedient.

Sometimes children don't understand why they have to be home by midnight or why they can't watch a particular movie. By the world's standards, our demands often seem unreasonable and irrational to them because of their peers' influence. At that stage of their lives they don't have the foresight to see the dangers, and besides, don't all youth think they're invincible? When you get such an argument from one of your children, read with them 1 Nephi 9:5–6: "Wherefore, the Lord hath commanded me to make these plates for a wise purpose in him, which purpose I know not. But the Lord knoweth all things from the beginning; wherefore, he prepareth a way to accomplish all his works among the children of men; for behold, he hath all power unto the fulfilling of all his words. And thus it is. Amen."

Nephi was commanded to make plates of gold and to make an account of his ministry. You might also turn to 1 Nephi 19:1–7; Jacob 7:27; Words of

Mormon 1:7; Alma 37:2, 12, 14, 18. These prophets didn't appreciate the value of keeping a journal and especially of keeping a second one. Perhaps they wondered if this request was unreasonable and irrational, but they were diligent out of obedience to the Lord, for they knew there was "a wise purpose," even if they didn't understand it. Now, of course, two millennia later, the Lord's reasons are obvious. If they had not been obedient, we would not have access to these scriptural guidelines.

Here's a good story to end your lesson:

> A man was about to board a train. The night was dark and stormy and he was worried. He saw the conductor walking about the front of the train and he asked, "Excuse me, but aren't you a little worried to be taking this train out on such a dark night?"
>
> "Oh," was the response, "I'm not going to be traveling in the dark."
>
> "But I thought we were leaving in a few minutes."
>
> "We are, but, you see the light in front of the engine? I will always be traveling in that light."

Like this man, the sons of Helaman, and other prophets of the Book of Mormon, we can travel in the light. If we are obedient to the counsel of the Lord, the Holy Ghost will light the way for us one step at a time. In hindsight, we will be able to see the value of His inspiration to us at crucial times in our lives.

Teach the doctrine:

Perhaps in your own family, when you see children making decisions that lead them away from the Spirit and gospel values, you might patiently review gospel principles with them as Alma did with his son. This way there can be no misunderstanding what is expected of them and the consequences of disobedience.

Perhaps the most important thing to teach your children about doctrine is that the gospel is eternal—never changing. The philosophies of men sway in popularity like a pendulum on a clock, but the Lord's laws are constant. Chastity will never be outdated. Honesty is an eternal principle. If a particular precept is new to you, ask the Lord if it is right before you teach it to your children. Teach them that "cursed is he that putteth his trust in man, or maketh flesh his arm, or shall hearken unto the precepts of men, save their precepts shall be given by the power of the Holy Ghost" (2 Nephi 28:31).

Teach the joy and value of work:

Share with your children the following experience expressed by a young university student about this subject.

> My grandpa was a farmer and my grandma was in a serious car accident when my dad was quite young, so my dad and his brothers and sister were expected to take on a great deal of responsibility both on the farm and in the home. There was much work to be done and they all learned the importance of hard work at a very young age. Now, as a father with a family of his own, Dad taught us the importance of hard work. He always tells us kids to do a job so that it can't be done better. He doesn't get angry when we don't do things perfectly, but patiently shows us how we could do the job better, if needed. As a result I know how to work hard and I enjoy work because doing a good job makes me feel good about myself.
>
> My parents also instilled in me a very good and rigorous work ethic. From daily chores around the house to Saturday projects in the yard, my parents taught me to work. I had a paper route at age eleven and have been working constantly ever since. Now that I'm married, I'm grateful my wife and I have both been brought up knowing how to work.

Some children do come to the point in their maturity when they see their weaknesses and, reflecting back on their childhood, wish they had been taught to work at home while they were young. Note the following comments:

> My parents did not expect enough from us. For instance, I was not a very good worker. Our house was often full of neighborhood kids and things got quite messy. Instead of teaching us to be responsible and pick up as soon as we were done, my parents just left the mess there without saying anything but then got angry three days later when we had not picked it up. But they'd still just do it themselves. We had two chores every Saturday and a night of dishwashing every week, but that was about it. Our rooms did not need to be cleaned, even though it was encouraged. In my own family I want my children to really understand the importance of work and to do it a lot.
>
> My parents have often said, "If we are guilty of anything, it is loving you too much." Loving too much is not a sin or a fault if it means spending time together and giving support, but it can become a fault if

> it means doing everything for your children, not requiring anything of them, and giving them everything they want. I was spoiled rotten. I have not been pushed by my parents to work as hard as I could. I do not put the blame on them completely, because I am a brat, but I would like to instill in my children a little bit more of a work ethic.
>
> My mother basically did my Eagle Project for me. I received a car upon turning sixteen. My sisters also got cars soon after getting their driver's licenses. We were never pressured very hard to get jobs. This kind of parenting has fostered a theme of ingratitude in my life that I hate about myself. I still feel sometimes that my parents owe me something. I am still far more dependent on them than I should be. My younger sister is infinitely worse. I hope that I will have the patience and love necessary to teach my children the importance and satisfaction of work.

If you are sharing these accounts with your children in a family home evening setting where there is opportunity to share ideas, you might ask them to express how they feel when they have accomplished a task, been of service, or reached a goal. By way of contrast you might ask them if they have ever felt discouraged, frustrated, or useless when they can't achieve a goal, finish a task, or help someone in need. Ask them what they think self-esteem is, or self-confidence, and for ideas on how one can get it.

Teaching children to appreciate and enjoy their ability to work and accomplish goals, even when those goals are very hard—especially when they are hard—is a lesson that will serve them all the days of their lives.

APPENDIX B
Additional Resources for Parents

The following resources are organized according to the principles taught within each chapter; they chronologically and directly correlate with the subsections within each principle.

ADDITIONAL RESOURCES CORRELATING WITH PRINCIPLE 1: WHY AND WHEN TO TEACH

Please see the following for additional reading on:

When to teach:

Tom Sehaefer, "Parents Must Lay Faith's Foundation," *Deseret News*, Oct. 19, 2002, 3.

L. Tom Perry, "Teach Them the Word of God with All Diligence," *Ensign*, May 1999, 6.

M. Russell Ballard, "Like a Flame Unquenchable," *Ensign*, May 1999, 85.

Patricia P. Pinegar, "Peace, Hope, and Direction," *Ensign*, Nov. 1999, 67.

Neal A. Maxwell, "Lord, Increase Our Faith," *Ensign*, May 1994, 117.

Boyd K. Packer, "Teach the Children," *Ensign*, Feb. 2000, 10.

Boyd K. Packer, "Children," *Ensign*, May 2002, 7.

L. Tom Perry, "Called of God," *Ensign*, Nov. 2002, 7.

R. Scott Lloyd, "Special Visitor Attends Stake Conference," *Church News*, Nov. 16, 2002, 3.

Colleen K. Menlove, "A Voice of Gladness for Our Children," *Ensign*, Nov. 2002, 13.

Scriptures relating to teaching:

D&C 93:40–43 "But I have commanded you to bring up your children in light and truth."

Moses 5:12 "They made all things known unto their sons and daughters."

Proverbs 22:6 "Train up a child in the way he should go."

D&C 68:25 "Inasmuch as parents have children . . . that teach them not to understand the doctrine . . . the sin be upon the heads of the parents."

ADDITIONAL RESOURCES CORRELATING WITH PRINCIPLE 1: WHAT TO TEACH

Please see the following for additional reading on:

Teaching children to love and serve one another:

Merrill J. Bateman, "Because He First Loved Us," *BYU Speeches*, April 1998, University Press.
Dallin H. Oaks, "Give Thanks in All Things," *Ensign*, May 2003, 95–98.
Steven R. Snow, "Gratitude," *Ensign*, Nov. 2001, 43–44.
Joseph B. Wirthlin, "Live in Thanksgiving Daily," *Ensign*, Sep. 2001, 6–13.
Gordon B. Hinckley, *Standing for Something* [New York: Times Books], 2000, 101.

Teaching the use of agency:

Henry B. Eyring, "A Life Founded in Light and Truth," *Ensign*, July 2001, 6–13.
James M. Paramore, "Hold On!" *Ensign*, Feb. 2002, 64–65.
Robert S. Wood, "On the Responsible Self," *Ensign*, Mar. 2002, 27–31.
William R. Bradford, "Righteousness," *Ensign*, Nov. 1999, 85.
Richard G. Scott, "He Lives," *Ensign*, Nov. 1999, 87.
Boyd K. Packer, "Atonement, Agency, Accountability," *Ensign*, May 1988, 69.

Teaching tolerance:

M. Russell Ballard, "Doctrine of Inclusion," *Ensign*, Nov. 2001, 35–38.

Teaching the value of prayer:

Henry B. Eyring, "Prayer," *Ensign*, Nov. 2001, 15–17.
John B. Dickson, "Draw Near Unto Me: The Privilege and Power of Prayer," *Ensign*, Feb. 2001, 18–22.
H. Kent Rappleye, "No Substitute for Family Prayer," *Ensign*, Feb. 2001, 24–29.
Henry B. Eyring, "Always," *Ensign*, Oct. 1999, 7.

Teaching the value of obedience:

H. Ross Workman, "Beware of Murmuring," *Ensign*, Nov. 2001, 85–86.
Henry B. Eyring, "Finding Safety in Counsel," *Ensign*, May 1997, 24.
James E. Faust, "Obedience: The Path to Freedom," *Ensign*, May 1999, 45.
Boyd K. Packer, "Spiritual Crocodiles," *Ensign*, May 1976, 30.

Teaching the doctrine:

Henry B. Eyring, "The Power of Teaching Doctrine," *Ensign*, May 1999, 73–75.

Teaching the value of work:

D&C 42:42; 60:13; 68:30–31; 75:3, 29; 88:69, 124.

Kathleen Slaugh Bahr and Cheri A. Loveless, "Family Work," *Brigham Young Magazine*, Spring 2000, 26–34. Online at http://magazine.byu.edu

Thomas S. Monson, "Teach the Children," *Ensign*, Nov. 1997, 17–20.

Boyd K. Packer, "Teach the Children," *Ensign*, Feb. 2000, 10–17.

Additional Resources Correlating with Principle 1: How to Teach

Please see the following for additional reading on:

Teaching by the Spirit:

Joseph B. Wirthlin, "The Unspeakable Gift," *Ensign*, May 2003, 26–29.

Teaching through righteous traditions:

"Family Home Evenings That Work," *Ensign*, Feb. 2002, 21–25.

Russell M. Nelson, "Living by Scriptural Guidance," *Ensign*, Nov. 2000, 16.

James A. Faust, "Enriching Our Lives through Family Home Evening," *Ensign*, June 2003, 3–6.

"Successful Family Home Evenings," *Ensign*, June 2003, 7–10.

"Easy to Prepare," *Ensign*, June 2003, 11.

"Family Home Evening Counsel and a Promise," The First Presidency of the Church, 1915, *Ensign*, June 2003, 12–13.

"Four Tips for Family Home Evening," *Ensign*, Aug. 2003, 69.

Jason Swenson, "Foundation for a Happy Family: Encouraging Family Home Evening," *Church News*, Nov. 2, 2002, 5.

Dieter F. Uchtdorf, "The Global Church Blessed by the Voice of the Prophets," *Ensign*, Nov. 2002, 10–12.

Teaching techniques:

Teaching, No Greater Call: A Resource Guide for Gospel Teaching, Church of Jesus Christ of Latter-day Saints, especially pages 88–95 and 159–184, 1999 edition.

Henry B. Eyring, "We Must Raise Our Sights," *Ensign*, Sept. 2004, 14.

Walter R. Gonzalez, "Teaching as the Savior Taught," *Ensign*, Sep. 2004, 28–31.

ADDITIONAL RESOURCES CORRELATING WITH PRINCIPLE 2:
PARENTAL RESPONSIBILITY INVOLVES BOTH PARENTS

Please see the following for additional reading on:

Parenting Responsibilities:

Carol B. Thomas, "Preparing Our Families for the Temple," *Ensign*, May 1999, 12.

Robert D. Hales, "Strengthening Families: Our Sacred Duty," *Ensign*, May 1999, 32.

Russell M. Nelson, "Our Sacred Duty to Honor Women," *Ensign*, May 1999, 38.

Stephen B. Oveson, "Our Legacy," *Ensign*, Nov. 1999, 29.

Sarah Jane Weaver quoting Gordon B. Hinckley, Church News, Dec. 4, 1999 report of a BYU devotional given Nov. 30, 1999, 7.

James E. Faust, "What It Means to Be a Daughter of God," *Ensign*, Nov. 1999, 100.

James E. Faust, "The Greatest Challenge in the World—Good Parenting," *Ensign*, Nov. 1990, 32.

Loren C. Dunn, "Because My Father Sent Me," *Ensign*, May 2000, 80.

Thomas S. Monson, "Precious Children, a Gift from God," *Ensign*, June 2000, 2.

Neal A. Maxwell, "The Tugs and Pulls of the World," *Ensign*, Nov. 2000, 35–36.

Thomas S. Monson, "Stand in Your Appointed Place," *Ensign*, May 2003, 54–57.

Gordon B. Hinckley, "Loyalty," *Ensign*, May 2003, 58–60.

Spencer W. Kimball, "The Blessings and Responsibilities of Womanhood," *Ensign*, March 1976, 70.

L. Tom Perry, "Called of God," *Ensign*, Nov. 2002, 7–10.

F. Melvin Hammond, "Dad, Are You Awake?" *Ensign*, Nov. 2002, 97–99.

Randal Thatcher, "From 'Me' to 'We,'" *Ensign*, June 2004, 22.

Christy Williams, "The Things of My Soul," *Ensign*, March 2005, 62–63.

ADDITIONAL RESOURCES CORRELATING WITH PRINCIPLE 3:
PARENTING ONE-ON-ONE

Please see the following for additional reading on:

Parenting One-on-One:

Virginia U. Jensen, "Families—It's about Time," given at BYU Women's Conference, April 29, 1999. Online at http://ce.byu.edu/cw/womansconference/archive/1999/jensen_virginia.htm

---

ADDITIONAL RESOURCES CORRELATING WITH PRINCIPLE 4:
KNOW YOUR CHILD'S READINESS STAGES

Please see the following for additional reading on:

Knowing your child's readiness stages:

"Age Characteristics of Children," *Teaching, No Greater Call*, The Church of Jesus Christ of Latter-day Saints, 110–116.

ADDITIONAL RESOURCES CORRELATING WITH PRINCIPLE 5:
BE HUMBLE AND TEACHABLE

Please see the following for additional reading on:

Being humble and teachable:

Neal A. Maxwell, "Repent of [Our] Selfishness," *Ensign*, May 1999, 23.

ADDITIONAL RESOURCES CORRELATING WITH PRINCIPLE 6:
TEACH BY EXAMPLE

Please see the following for additional reading on:

Teaching by Example:

Gordon B. Hinckley, "Keep the Chain Unbroken," BYU devotional, Nov. 30, 1999, in *Speeches of the Year*, 1999–2000, 107–111. Online at http://speeches.byu.edu

Jeffrey R. Holland, "The Hands of the Fathers," *Ensign*, May 1999, 14.

Additional Resources Correlating with Principle 7: Children Learn Best by Encouragement and Positive Reinforcement

Please see the following for additional reading on:

Encouragement and positive reinforcement:

Ezra Taft Benson, "Great Things Required of Their Fathers," *Ensign*, May 1981, 34.

Additional Resources Correlating with Principle 8: Allow Natural and Logical Consequences

Please see the following for additional reading on:

Allow natural consequences:

Robert S. Wood, "On the Responsible Self," *Ensign*, Mar. 2002, 27–31.

Additional Resources Correlating with Principle 9: Correct Children with Love

Please see the following for additional reading on:

Correcting with love:

Susan W. Tanner, "Did I Tell You . . . ?" *Ensign*, May 2003, 73–75.

Gordon B. Hinckley, "Bring Up a Child in the Way He Should Go," *Ensign*, Nov. 1993, 54–60.

Wayne S. Peterson, "Our Actions Determine Our Character," *Ensign*, Nov. 2001, 83–84.

Additional Resources Correlating with Principle 11: Children Need a Sanctuary

Please see the following for additional reading on:

Making your home a sanctuary:

Henry B. Eyring, "The Power of Teaching Doctrine," *Ensign*, May 1999, 73.
Name withheld, "Letting Go without Giving Up," *Ensign*, Sep. 2002, 8–10.
"Hope for Parents of Wayward Children" *Ensign*, Sep. 2002, 11.
Henry B. Eyring, "Always," *Ensign*, Oct. 1999, 7.
Name withheld, "Our Son's Battle with Drugs," *Ensign*, June 2004, 28–33.

Additional Resources Correlating with Principle 13: Involve the Children

Please see the following for additional reading on:

"Family Councils: A Conversation with Elder and Sister Ballard," *Ensign*, June 2003, 14–17.

Additional Resources Correlating with Principle 14: We Are At War

Please see the following for additional reading on:

Lessons from the War Chapters:
N. Eldon Tanner, "Put On the Whole Armor of God," *Ensign*, May 1979, 43.
Henry B. Eyring, "The Power of Teaching Doctrine," *Ensign*, May 1999, 73.
Henry B. Eyring, "Finding Safety in Counsel," *Ensign*, May 1997, 24.
M. Russell Ballard, "Be Strong in the Lord, and in the Power of His Might," BYU fireside, March 3, 2002. see also, "Be Strong in the Lord," *Ensign*, July 2004, 8–15.
Sharon Larsen, "Fear Not: For They That Be with Us Are More," *Ensign*, Nov. 2001, 67.
M. Russell Ballard, BYU Fireside, Mar. 3, 2002.
Carlos E. Asay, "The Temple Garment: An Outward Expression of an Inward Commitment," *Ensign*, Aug. 1997, 19–23.
Boyd K. Packer, "The Father and the Family," *Ensign*, May 1994, 19.
N. Eldon Tanner, "Put On the Whole Armor of God, Fight Wickedness," *Church News*, Nov. 10, 2001, 15.
"Fashion's Battleground," *Church News*, Aug. 25, 2001, 16.

Scriptures referring to the war with Satan:
Ephesians 6:11, 13, 16–17
1 Nephi 15:24
D&C 27:15–18
D&C 3:8
D&C 101

ADDITIONAL RESOURCES CORRELATING WITH PRINCIPLE 15: GRANDPARENTING—ANOTHER CHANCE

Please see the following for additional reading on:

"Family Councils: A Conversation with Elder and Sister Ballard," *Ensign*, June 2003, 18–19.

APPENDIX C
Parenting Principles Scriptural References

Principle 1: The Importance of Teaching
1 Nephi 1:1; 1 Nephi 15:2–3; Jacob 1:19; Jacob 5–6; Enos 1:1–3; Enos 1:9; Mosiah 1:2; Mosiah 4:14–15; Mosiah 18:21–29; Alma 4:17–20; Helaman 5:5–14; 3 Nephi 22:13; Ether 6:17

Principle 1 (Continued): Why and When to Teach
1 Nephi 2:9–10, 14; 1 Nephi 11–14; 2 Nephi 25:11; Alma 36:3; Alma 37:35; Alma 53:20–21; Helaman 5 (entire chapter but especially verses 5–14)

Principle 1 (Continued): What to Teach

a. *Love and Service*

Jacob 5:71; Mosiah 2:20–21; Mosiah 4:14–15; Alma 26:30; Alma 28:8; Alma 29:9; Alma 31:32–36; Alma 34:28; Alma 36:24–25; Mormon 3:12

b. *Gratitude*

2 Nephi 1:1–5; 2 Nephi 4:16–30; 2 Nephi 29:4, 5, 11–13; Mosiah 2:20–21; Mosiah 14:4–6; Mosiah 15:14–19; Mosiah 16:15; Alma 9:18–23; Alma 10:5–6, 22–23; Alma 29:10; Alma 34:38; Alma 49:28; Helaman 5:5–14; Ether 6:30

c. *Agency*

2 Nephi 2:26–29; 2 Nephi 9:25–39; 2 Nephi 10:23; Jacob 4:14; Jacob 5–6; Mosiah 3:19; Mosiah 11:1–2; Alma 3:26–27; Alma 5:39–42; Alma 10:5–6; 22–23; Alma 12 (especially verses 1–6 and 22–37); Alma 14:11; Alma 22:15–18; Alma 29:4–5; Alma 30:8–10; Alma 42:16, 19–23, 27–28; Alma 47; Alma 50:20; Helaman 14:29–31; 3 Nephi 11:33; 3 Nephi 26:4–5; 3 Nephi 27:14–17; Mormon 3:18–19; Mormon 6:21–22; Ether 2:8–9, 12; Ether 2:23 (problem solving); Ether 6:22–24; Ether 10; Ether 13:20–21; Moroni 7:12–14; 17–18

d. *Tolerance*

Mosiah 27:2–4; Alma 30:8–11; Ether 12:34–37

e. *Valuing the Scriptures*

1 Nephi 3:2–4; 1 Nephi 15:24; 1 Nephi 19:23; 2 Nephi 4:1–2; 2 Nephi 7–8; 9:1; 2 Nephi 11:2; 2 Nephi 12–24 (Isaiah); 2 Nephi 25:8; 2 Nephi 29:4–5, 11–13; 2 Nephi 33:2; Jacob 5–6; Enos 1:10, 16; Mosiah 1:2–5; Alma 37:9; Ether 8:25–26

f. *Prayer*

2 Nephi 32:8–9; Mosiah 27:4–17; Alma 6:6; Alma 10:5–6, 22–23; Alma 31:32–35; Alma 34:17–27, 39; Alma 58:10–12; Alma 62:51; 3 Nephi 13:6–13; 3 Nephi 14:7–8; 3 Nephi 17:14–21; 3 Nephi 18:15, 18; 3 Nephi 19:17–28, 31–33; Ether 2:14; Moroni 10:3–5

g. *Obedience*

1 Nephi 9:5–6; 1 Nephi 17:14; 2 Nephi 1:5–9; Mosiah 15:6–7; Alma 53:20–21 (the importance of); Alma 55:31; Alma 57:21; Alma 58:40; Ether 6:16–17

h. *Pure Doctrine*

1 Nephi 13; 2 Nephi 25:13 (Atonement); 2 Nephi 28:31 (compare with the philosophies of men); 2 Nephi 31:20; Moisah 2:41; Mosiah 4 (entire chapter but specifically 9–15); Mosiah 16:15; Alma 11:39–45; Alma 12:22–37 (the plan); Alma 13:27–30; Alma 31:5; Alma 37:33–34; Alma 39–42; Helaman 5:7–12; Helaman 14:15–19; 3 Nephi 12; Ether 11:20 (repentance); Ether 12:3–22 (repentance); Ether 12:6–22, 30–31 (faith); Moroni 7:1 (faith, hope, charity); Moroni 7:25–26, 29; Moroni 8:19–20, 22–23; Moroni 8:25–26

i. *Work*

2 Nephi 5:15–17 (commanded to); Mosiah 6:7 (to serve); Mosiah 27:5 (pleases God); Alma 1:25–28; Alma 53:5 (to be busy and happy); Alma 62:29 (necessity of)

Principle 1 (Continued): How to Teach

a. *Through family traditions*

Alma 18:4–5; (The following are bad examples or wicked traditions, or the results of) Mosiah 1:2–4; Mosiah 10:12; Alma 9:16–17; Alma 24:7; Alma 60:32; Helaman 15:7

b. *Lovingly and patiently*

1 Nephi 8:37; 1 Nephi 15:2–3; 2 Nephi 1:13–28; Jacob 1:7–8; Jacob 2:7–11; Alma 13:27–30; 3 Nephi 11:29–30

c. *By example*

See scriptures listed in Principle 6.

d. *By the Spirit*

1 Nephi 2:9–10, 14; 1 Nephi 10:17; 2 Nephi 1:6; 2 Nephi 25:11; 2 Nephi 25:13; Jacob 1:5–6; Jacob 2:7–11; Mosiah 1:6–8; Alma 4:17–20; Alma 5:43–48; Alma 38:8–9; Alma 39; Alma 40:1; Alma 41:1; Alma 42:1; Moroni 6:9; Moroni 10:8–10

e. *Plainly and age-appropriate*
2 Nephi 25:4, 7; 2 Nephi 31:3; Jacob 5:6; Mosiah 4 (entire chapter but specifically 9–15); 3 Nephi 11:22–28 (specific instructions)

f. *Using appropriate teaching techniques*
Verbal commitments (See Principle 13)
Alma 5, series of "will you" questions
Physical participation (See Principle 13)
Repetition (See Principle 13)
1 Nephi 2:9–10; Helaman 5:32, 33; 3 Nephi 10:4–6; 3 Nephi 11:37–38; 3 Nephi 18:15, 18
Parables, stories, and allegories
1 Nephi 11:9–10; 1 Nephi 18:11–13; Jacob 5–6; 3 Nephi 27:14–15
Incentives
1 Nephi 17:41; 2 Nephi 31:20; 3 Nephi 8; 3 Nephi 9:1–2; 3 Nephi 10:1
Speak softly
Helaman 5:30; 3 Nephi 11:3–6
Liken examples to self
1 Nephi 19:23
Identify the lesson
1 Nephi 17:14

Principle 2: Parental Responsibility Involves Both Parents
1 Nephi 5:1–8 (marital disputes); Jacob 1:19; Alma 56:47–48 (parents must be united); 3 Nephi 11:32

Principle 3: Parent One-on-One
1 Nephi 16:23; 2 Nephi 1:28; 2 Nephi 2–4; Mosiah 27:8–24 (especially verse 14); Mosiah 27:30; Alma 4:17–20 (especially verse 19); Alma 24:8–9; Alma 35:16; Alma 36–42; Alma 40:1; Alma 41:1; Alma 42:1; 3 Nephi 11:15; 3 Nephi 17:9; 3 Nephi 17:21; 3 Nephi 18:36; 3 Nephi 28:1

Principle 4: Know Your Child's Readiness Stages
1 Nephi 14:28; 1 Nephi 15:2–3, 8–9; 1 Nephi 22:25; 2 Nephi 28:30; 2 Nephi 31:3; Mosiah 3:19; Mosiah 21:15–16; Mosiah 29:7–10; Alma 2:17–18; Alma 16:16–17; Alma 27:7, 10–12; Alma 29:8; Alma 39; Alma 40:1; Alma 49:14; Alma 60; 3 Nephi 17:2–3, 5–6; 3 Nephi 18:28–30; Moroni 8:8, 10–11

Principle 5: Be Humble and Teachable
1 Nephi 4:6; 1 Nephi 5:2–6; 1 Nephi 7:4–5; 1 Nephi 13; 1 Nephi 15; 2–3, 8–9; 1 Nephi 16:24–25; 2 Nephi 28:30–31; 2 Nephi 33:2; Mosiah 2:10–11, 26; Mosiah 3:19; Mosiah 4:10–11; Mosiah 23:9–11; Alma 7:23; Alma 12:10–14; Alma 22:15–16; Alma 24:8–9; Alma 24:24; Alma 31:5; Alma 31:32–36; Alma

37:37; Alma 38:8–9; Alma 58:10–12, 33, 40; Helaman 4:13–15; Helaman 12:2–6; Helaman 16:15; Mormon 5:22–24; Ether 6:30; Ether 12:27–28

Principle 6: Teach by Example

1 Nephi 2:16; 1 Nephi 5:2–6; 1 Nephi 9:3, 5, 6; 1 Nephi 10:10; 1 Nephi 11:27; 2 Nephi 2:30; 2 Nephi 10:14; 2 Nephi 31:5–6, 9–13, 17; Jacob 2:34–35; Jacob 3:10; Mosiah 2:14–18; Mosiah 4:14–26 (especially verses 15–16); Mosiah 6:6–7; Mosiah 10:12, 17; Mosiah 12:27–29; Mosiah 19:11–12; Mosiah 24:8; Alma 5:43–48; Alma 48:11–13, 17–19; Alma 59:11–13; Helaman 3:20, 21, 37; Helaman 5:5–7; 3 Nephi 12:48; 3 Nephi 18:16, 24; 3 Nephi 19:17–28, 31–33; 3 Nephi 21:29; 3 Nephi 26:15; 3 Nephi 27:21, 27

Principle 7: Children Learn Best by Encouragement and Positive Reinforcement

1 Nephi 2:1–3; 1 Nephi 2:16; 1 Nephi 11:6; 1 Nephi 12:10; 1 Nephi 15:11; 1 Nephi 15:24; 1 Nephi 17:3, 13; 1 Nephi 17: 31–38; 2 Nephi 1:5–9; 2 Nephi 5:10–11; 2 Nephi 6:12–14; Jacob 3:5–7; Jacob 7:5; Enos 1:5, 10, 12; Omni 1:6–7; Mosiah 5:6–7; Mosiah 7:33; Mosiah 15:1–13; Mosiah 26:15–20; Alma 1:25–33; Alma 3:17; Alma 7:6, 17–20, 26; Alma 8:15–17; Alma 13:3–4, 10, 13–14, 18; Alma 29:9; Alma 38:2–3; Alma 42:31; Alma 44: Alma 48:17–19; Alma 50:23; Helaman 6:9, 11–14; Helaman 10:4–12; Helaman 15:10; 3 Nephi 15:1, 9; 3 Nephi 18:5, 10; 3 Nephi 27:30; 3 Nephi 28:1–15; 4 Nephi 2–5, 7, 10; Mormon 7:7; Ether 3:9–13,15; Ether 9:15–21 (especially verse 20); Ether 9:35; Ether 10; Ether 12 (especially verses 34–37); Moroni 8:2; Moroni 9:22

Principle 8: Allow Natural and Logical Consequences

1 Nephi 8:37–8; 1 Nephi 10:20; 1 Nephi 11:36; 1 Nephi 14:3–4; 1 Nephi 15:32–33; 1 Nephi 17:31–38; 1 Nephi 18:11–13; 1 Nephi 19:13–14; 1 Nephi 22:13–14; 2 Nephi 1:7–12; 2 Nephi 1:20; 2 Nephi 2:5; 2 Nephi 2:11–16, 19, 22–23; 2 Nephi 4:4; 2 Nephi 5:20–25; 2 Nephi 6:15; 2 Nephi 7:1; 2 Nephi 9:25–39; 2 Nephi 15:15; Jacob 3:3–4, 8–9, 11–12; Jacob 4:14; Jacob 5–6; Jarom 1:9–10; Omni 1:6–7; Mosiah 1:13; Mosiah 2:36–39; Mosiah 11:23–25; Mosiah 17:15–19; Mosiah 20:21; Mosiah 26:21–28; Mosiah 26:31–32; Alma 3:6–8; Alma 3:13–19; Alma 3:26–27; Alma 12:13–14, 31–32; Alma 16:9–10; Alma 28; Alma 30:47–50; Alma 37:41–42; Alma 44; Alma 46:35; Alma 50:21–22; Helaman (entire book); Helaman 7:23–28; Helaman 13:18–20; Helaman 14:29–31; 3 Nephi 9:1–2, 10–12; 3 Nephi 15:19–20; 3 Nephi 16:10; 3 Nephi 28:34–35; Mormon 1:13–14, 17; Mormon 2:13–15, 26; Mormon 3:11–15; Mormon 4:5; Ether 8:20–24; Ether 9:28–34; Ether 10:11; Ether 11; Ether 13:20–21; Ether 14:1, 21–25, Ether 15:1–3, 19, 32–33; Moroni 8:27–29

Principle 9: Correct Children with Love

1 Nephi 8:37; 1 Nephi 16:25, 28–29; 1 Nephi 16:39; 1 Nephi 17:41; 2 Nephi

1:13–28; 2 Nephi 10, especially 6–8, 18–19; Jacob 1:7–8; Jacob 2:7–11; Jacob 6:4–5 (see entire chapter); Alma 42:31; Helaman 15:3; 3 Nephi 11:29–30; 3 Nephi 23:7–13; Ether 2:14–16

Principle 10: Listen! Listen! Listen!
Mosiah 5:1; Alma 20:9–16, 26–27; Alma 32:23; Alma 60; Ether 2:23–25; Ether 6:19, 21

Principle 11: Children Need a Sanctuary
1 Nephi 1:20 (support); 1 Nephi 2:2 (protection); 1 Nephi 2:16 (give help/answer plea); 1 Nephi 2:20 (prepared place); 1 Nephi 4:6 (trust); 1 Nephi 7:5 (support); 1 Nephi 8:12–15 (share joys); 1 Nephi 9:3–6 (prepare a way); 1 Nephi 10:3 (don't give up); 1 Nephi 10:10 (make sacrifices); 1 Nephi 10:14 (never give up); 1 Nephi 11:31 (nurture); 1 Nephi 13:30–33 (forgiveness); 1 Nephi 15:11 (support); 1 Nephi 15:19–20 (especially verses 13–20; forgiveness); 1 Nephi 15:24 (guidance); 1 Nephi 16:9–10 (support); 1 Nephi 17:7–10 (support); 1 Nephi 17:24, 27–29 (guidance); 1 Nephi 18:17–20 (give support); 1 Nephi 22:20 (prepare for success); 2 Nephi 1:28 (father's blessing); 2 Nephi 2:30: 2 Nephi 4:3–10 (loving support); 2 Nephi 5:5 (safety); 2 Nephi 5:14–16 (spiritual and physical needs filled); 2 Nephi 6:11 (never give up); 2 Nephi 6:14 (support and safety); 2 Nephi 8 (entire chapter, especially verse 3; comfort); 2 Nephi 9 (entire chapter, especially verse 10; support and safety); 2 Nephi 9:21 (parental sacrifices); 2 Nephi 9:26 (mercy and forgiveness); 2 Nephi 9:53 (offer hope); 2 Nephi 25:16–17 (mercy and forgiveness); Jacob 2:7–11; Jacob 3:1–2 (support and comfort); Jacob 5–6 (entire chapters; never give up); Jacob 6:4 (mercy and forgiveness); Jacob 7:22 (support); Mosiah 4:14–15 (guidance); Mosiah 7:33 (allow repentance); Mosiah 8:18 (support); Mosiah 8:20–21 (never give up); Mosiah 13:34–35 (parental sacrifice); Mosiah 14:4–6 (sacrifices); Mosiah 15:10–13 (parental sacrifice/service); Mosiah 19:11–12 (protection); Mosiah 20:11 (protection); Mosiah 23:9–11 (allow repentance); Mosiah 24:12–15 (support); Mosiah 26:31 (love); Mosiah 27:14, 22–23; (parental prayers); Alma 2:17–18 (support); Alma 2:28 (support); Alma 2:30–31 (support); Alma 3:8 (spiritual protection); Alma 5:33–38 (forgiveness); Alma 5:59–60 (protection); Alma 6:6 (parental prayers); Alma 7:11–12 (compassion); Alma 8:20–21 (prepare for success); Alma 9:16–17 (forgiveness); Alma 12 (entire chapter; leadership, plan ahead); Alma 17:18 (bless); Alma 19:23 (parental prayers); Alma 20:1 (share joys); Alma 31:36, 38 (support, protect, provide for); Alma 32:37–43 (nurture); Alma 34:19–27 (pray); Alma 37:27–29 (spiritual protection); Alma 37:38–40 (support/guidance); Alma 49:4–5 (spiritual protection); Alma 51:52 (spiritual protection); 3 Nephi 15:10–20 (spiritual protection); 3 Nephi 17:5–6 (compassion); 3 Nephi 17:7–8 (parental sacrifices and nurturing); 3 Nephi 17:14–21 (parental prayers); 3 Nephi 18:15–21 (parental prayers); 3 Nephi 18:15–21 (prepare your children); 3 Nephi 18:32

(never give up); 3 Nephi 23, 27–28, 31 (parental prayers); 3 Nephi 21:29 (support); 3 Nephi 22:7–8 (never give up); 3 Nephi 28:19–22 (protection); Mormon 3:12 (love); Mormon 5:1 (never give up); Ether 8:20–24 (warnings); Ether 9:35 (mercy); Ether 11:8 (forgiveness); Ether 12:25–26 (comfort); Moroni 7:47–48 (charity); Moroni 8:3 (parental prayers); Moroni 9:22–26 (specific prayers)

Principle 12: Be Trustworthy, Dependable, Consistent, and Fair
1 Nephi 3:7; 1 Nephi 7:1–2; 1 Nephi 9:22; 1 Nephi 10:18; 1 Nephi 11:5; 1 Nephi 13 (entire chapter, especially verses 3, 5, 13); 1 Nephi 17:3, 5, 13; 1 Nephi 17:5; 1 Nephi 17:31–38; 1 Nephi 22:8, 11, 14, 19–20, 22; 2 Nephi 2:4–7; 2 Nephi 2:11–16, 19, 22; 2 Nephi 9:25–26; 2 Nephi 10:14; 2 Nephi 28 (entire chapter); 2 Nephi 29:7–9; Enos 1:10–11; Omni 1:6–7; Mosiah 2:22; Mosiah 12 (entire chapter); Mosiah 27:30; Alma 37:17; Alma 41:8; Alma 50:19; Alma 58:33; Helaman 8 (entire chapter); 3 Nephi 15:4–5; 3 Nephi 16:1–5; 3 Nephi 17:7–8; 3 Nephi 27:18; 3 Nephi 29 (entire chapter, especially verses 1, 3, 8); Ether 3:12; Ether 4:11–12; Ether 12:6–22, 30–31; Moroni 8:18; Moroni 8:19–20, 22.

Principle 13: Involve the Children and Get a Commitment
1 Nephi 3:2–4; Mosiah 6:1; Mosiah 21:35; Mosiah 29:38–39; Alma 1:1; Alma 5 (entire chapter); Alms 7:14; Alma 17–18 (entire chapters); Alma 24:16–18; Alma 45:2–7; Alma 46:20–22; Alma 46:36; Alma 56:44; 3 Nephi 11:23 3 Nephi 18:1–12; Moroni 4 (entire chapter); Moroni 5 (entire chapter); Moroni 6:2–6

Principle 14: We Are at War
Alma 43 (entire chapter)

Principle 15: Grandparenting—Another Chance
2 Nephi 4:3–10; 2 Nephi 25:8; 2 Nephi 25:21–23; 26–27; 2 Nephi 26, 27, 28; 2 Nephi 33:3–4, 10–15; Jacob 1:1–4; Jacob 4:1–3; Words of Mormon 1:2; Mosiah 1:4; Mosiah 10:12, 17; Helaman 5:6–7; Moroni 10

APPENDIX D
Scriptural Theme Index

Scriptural Reference	Keyword of Principle
First Book of Nephi	
1 Nephi 1:1	Teach
1 Nephi 1:9–10	Teaching technique
1 Nephi 1:16	Teach by example
1 Nephi 1:20	Sanctuary/support
1 Nephi 2:1–3	Positive reinforcement
1 Nephi 2:2	Sanctuary/protection
1 Nephi 2:9–10	Teaching technique
1 Nephi 2:9–10, 14	Teach by the Spirit
	Teaching moment
1 Nephi 2:16	Trustworthy/dependable
	Blessings of the righteous
	Example
1 Nephi 2:20	Sanctuary/support
1 Nephi 3:2–4	Value the scriptures
	Involve the children
1 Nephi 3:7	Be dependable and trustworthy
1 Nephi 4:6	Humble/teachable
	Trust/guidance
1 Nephi 5:2–6	Humble/not defensive
	Example
	Parents be united
1 Nephi 7:1–2	Dependable/planning ahead
1 Nephi 7:5	Support
	Be humble
1 Nephi 8:12–15	Concern for his family
1 Nephi 8:37–38	Teach lovingly
	Teach, then allow agency
1 Nephi 9:5, 6	Wisdom of obedience
	Example
	Lord has a plan
1 Nephi 10:3	Never give up on children
1 Nephi 10:10	Parents make sacrifices
	Example
1 Nephi 10:14	Never give up on children
1 Nephi 10:17	Teach with the Spirit
1 Nephi 10:18	Consistent/dependable

1 Nephi 10:20	Prepare for consequences
1 Nephi 11–14	When to teach
1 Nephi 11:5	Trustworthy
1 Nephi 11:6	Positive reinforcement
1 Nephi 11:27	Example
1 Nephi 11:31	Parental support and caring
1 Nephi 11:36	Consequences
1 Nephi 12:10	Positive reinforcement
1 Nephi 13	Teach eternal principles Be teachable and dependable
1 Nephi 13:30–33	Make a sanctuary
1 Nephi 14:3–4	Allow consequences
1 Nephi 14:28	Know your children
1 Nephi 15:2–3	Continue to teach with love and patience
1 Nephi 15:2–3, 8–9	Know your children Be teachable
1 Nephi 15:11	Support with guidance Reward righteousness
1 Nephi 15:13–20 (especially 19–20)	Never give up
1 Nephi 15:24	Support Reward righteousness Value of the scriptures
1 Nephi 15:32–33	Allow consequences
1 Nephi 16:9–10	Give support
1 Nephi 16:23	Develop a relationship
1 Nephi 16:24–25	Be humble
1 Nephi 16:25, 28–29	Correct with love
1 Nephi 16:39	Correct and forgive
1 Nephi 17:3, 5, 13	Reward righteousness Be consistent
1 Nephi 17:7–10	Give direction
1 Nephi 17:14	Identify the lesson
1 Nephi 17:24, 27–29	Give direction, support
1 Nephi 17:31–35, 38	Be consistent Allow consequences Positive reinforcement
1 Nephi 17:41	Value of obedience Teaching technique Correct, then forgive
1 Nephi 18:11–13	Allow agency/consequences Teaching technique
1 Nephi 18:18–20	Give support

1 Nephi 19:13–14	Allow agency/consequences
1 Nephi 19:23	Value the scriptures Teaching technique
1 Nephi 22:8, 11, 14, 19–22	Consistent/trustworthy
1 Nephi 22:13–14	Consequences
1 Nephi 22:20	Support
1 Nephi 22:25	Know your children

Second Book of Nephi

2 Nephi 1:1–5	Teach gratitude
2 Nephi 1:5–9	Value of obedience Lord blesses the righteous
2 Nephi 1:6	Teach with the Spirit
2 Nephi 1:7–12	Consequences/disobedience
2 Nephi 1:13–28	Teach lovingly Correct with love
2 Nephi 1:17–23	Correct with love
2 Nephi 1:20	Consequences
2 Nephi 1:28	Individual relationship Parental support
2 Nephi 2:2–4	Know each child
2 Nephi 2:4–7	Be just
2 Nephi 2:5	Consequences
2 Nephi 2:11–16, 19, 22, 23	Consequences Be just
2 Nephi 2:26–29	How to use agency
2 Nephi 2:30	Support Personal example
2 Nephi 4:1–2	Value the scriptures
2 Nephi 4:3–10	Grandparenting
2 Nephi 4:4	Consequences
2 Nephi 4:5	Loving support
2 Nephi 4:16–30	A prayer of gratitude
2 Nephi 5:5	Provide safety
2 Nephi 5:10–11	Bless the righteous
2 Nephi 5:14–16	Provide for needs
2 Nephi 5:15, 17	Teach them to work
2 Nephi 5:20–25	Consequences
2 Nephi 6:11	Never give up
2 Nephi 6:12,14	Bless the righteous
2 Nephi 6:14	Support/safety
2 Nephi 6:15	Consequences
2 Nephi 7:1	Consequences

2 Nephi 7–8; 9:1	Value the scriptures
2 Nephi 8 (especially v.3)	Support and comfort
2 Nephi 9 (especially v.10)	Support and safety
2 Nephi 9:21	Parents make sacrifices
2 Nephi 9:25–26	Be just, but compassionate
2 Nephi 9:25, 27–39	Teach responsibility Teach how to use agency Consequences
2 Nephi 9:26	Show mercy and forgiveness
2 Nephi 9:53	Be merciful and forgiving
2 Nephi 10 (especially 6–8; 18–19)	Correct, but with love/mercy
2 Nephi 10:14	Be an example Be trustworthy
2 Nephi 10:23	How to use agency Personal responsibility
2 Nephi 11:2 (chapters 12–24)	Value the scriptures
2 Nephi 15:15	Consequences
2 Nephi 25:4–7	Teach plainly
2 Nephi 25:8	Influence of grandparents Value the scriptures
2 Nephi 25:11	Teach with the Spirit Teach when the Spirit urges
2 Nephi 25:13	Teach eternal principles Teach by the Spirit
2 Nephi 25:16–17	Never give up
2 Nephi 25:21–13, 26–27	Responsibility of grandparent
2 Nephi 26–28	Grandparenting/message to his posterity
2 Nephi 28	Christ consistent/dependable
2 Nephi 28:30	Know your children Be teachable
2 Nephi 28:31	Teach eternal principles Be teachable
2 Nephi 29:1, 7–9	Be consistent and fair
2 Nephi 29:4–5, 11–13	Value of scriptures Teach gratitude
2 Nephi 31:3	Know your children Teach plainly
2 Nephi 31:5–6, 9–13, 17	Teach by example
2 Nephi 31:20	Teach pure doctrine

	Teach plainly
2 Nephi 32:8–9	Power of prayer
2 Nephi 33:2	Value the scriptures
	Be humble
2 Nephi 33:3–4, 10–15	Look after your posterity/grandparenting

Book of Jacob

Jacob 1:1–4	Look after posterity
Jacob 1:5–6	Teach by the Spirit
Jacob 1:7–8	Gentle persuasion
Jacob 1:19	Responsible to teach
Jacob 2:7–11	Teach by the Spirit
	Protect against evil
	Correct with love
Jacob 2:34–35	A bad example/poor parenting
Jacob 3:1–2	Give comfort
Jacob 3:3–4, 8–9, 11–12	Consequences
Jacob 3:5–7	Bless the righteous
Jacob 3:10	Importance of example
Jacob 4:1–3	Responsibility to posterity
Jacob 4:14	Agency
	Consequences
Jacob 5–6 (entire chapter)	Teaching technique
	Allow growth and agency
	Teach plainly
	Allow consequences
	Never give up
Jacob 5:71	Teach love and service
Jacob 6:4	Never give up
Jacob 6:4–5 (entire chapter)	Beseech/teach with love
Jacob 7:5	Positive nurturing strengthens
Jacob 7:22	Support

Book of Enos

Enos 1:1–3	Teach
Enos 1:9	Teach
Enos 1:5, 10, 12	Positive reinforcement
Enos: 1:10–11	Be consistent and dependable
Enos 1:13, 16	Value of the scriptures

Book of Jarom

Jarom 1:9–10	Explain the consequences

Book of Omni	
Omni 1:6–7	Consequences Bless the righteous Be dependable
Words of Mormon	
Words of Mormon 1:2	Look after your posterity/grandparenting
Book of Mosiah	
Mosiah 1:2–5	Teach your children Value the scriptures Unrighteous traditions
Mosiah 1:3–4	Look after your posterity
Mosiah 1:6–8	Bear your testimony
Mosiah 1:13	Allow consequences
Mosiah 2:10, 11, 26	Be humble
Mosiah 2:14–18	Be an example
Mosiah 2:20–21	Teach love and service Teach gratitude
Mosiah 2:22	Be consistent and dependable
Mosiah 2:36–39	Teach about consequences
Mosiah 2:41	Pure doctrine
Mosiah 3:19	Teach about agency Know your child Be humble
Mosiah 4 (especially 9–15)	Teach eternal principles Teach plainly
Mosiah 4:10–11	Be humble
Mosiah 4:14–15 (espcially 15–16)	Provide a sanctuary at home Teach love and service
Mosiah 4:14–26	Teach by example
Mosiah 5:1	Listen to your children
Mosiah 5:6–7	Positive reinforcement
Mosiah 6:1	Get a commitment
Mosiah 6:6, 7	Teach by example
Mosiah 6:7	Work to serve others
Mosiah 7:33	Reward righteous behavior Allow repentance
Mosiah 8:18	Arrange for successful experiences
Mosiah 8:20–21	Have patience/never give up
Mosiah 10:12, 17	A bad example Evil traditions teach evil Power of parental teaching on future generations

Mosiah 11:1–2	Agency
	Good example doesn't always prevail
Mosiah 11:23–25	Allow consequences
Mosiah 12 (entire chapter)	Lord is dependable and consistent
Mosiah 12:27–29	Power of example
Mosiah 13:34–35	Parents make sacrifices
Mosiah 14:4–6	Teach gratitude
	Parents make sacrifices
Mosiah 15:6–7	Obedience brings power
Mosiah 15:10–13	Bless righteousness
	Parental sacrifice
Mosiah 15:14–19	Recognition of blessings
Mosiah 16:15	Teach eternal principles
	Recognition of blessings
Mosiah 17:15–19	Allow consequences
Mosiah 18:21–29	Teach (see also Model of a Righteous Family)
Mosiah 19:11–12	A bad example
	Provide protection
Mosiah 20:11	Provide protection
Mosiah 20:21	Consequences
Mosiah 21:15–16	Know your children
Mosiah 21:35	Outward commitment
Mosiah 23:9–11	Be humble
	Allow repentance
Mosiah 24:8	Poor parental example
Mosiah 24:12–15	Support/endurance
Mosiah 26:15–20	Positive reinforcement
Mosiah 26:21–28	Consequences (good and bad)
Mosiah 26:31–32	Provide a sanctuary
	Consequences
Mosiah 27:2–5	Tolerance
	Work
Mosiah 27:11–17	Power of prayer
	One-on-one relationship (with the Lord)
Mosiah 27:14, 22, 23	Support with your prayers
Mosiah 27:30	Lord knows each child
	He is fair, consistent
Mosiah 29:7–10	Know children's strengths/weaknesses
Mosiah 29:38–39	Get a commitment

Book of Alma

Alma 1:1	Get a commitment
Alma 1:25–28	All worked together
Alma 1:25–33	Righteous are blessed
Alma 2:17–18	Know your children
	Give support when needed
Alma 2:28	Responsive to needs
Alma 2:30–31	Responsive to needs
Alma 3:6–8	Consequences of sin
Alma 3:8	Provide Spiritual protection
Alma 3:13–19	Sin provides Consequences
Alma 3:17	Protect righteousness
Alma 3:26–27	Teach agency
	Consequences
Alma 4:17–20	Teaching/important calling
	Bear testimony to children
	Know children's weaknesses
Alma 5 (entire chapter)	Teaching technique/questions
	Involve the children
Alma 5:33–38	Never give up/forgive
Alma 5:39–42	Teach about agency
Alma 5:43–48	Bear testimony
	Teach by example
Alma 5:59–60	Provide spiritual protection
Alma 6:6	Teach children to pray
	Support children with prayer
Alma 7:6, 17–20, 26	Positive reinforcement
Alma 7:11–12	Be willing to sacrifice
Alma 7:14	Baptism an outward commitment
Alma 7:23	Pure doctrine
	Be humble
Alma 8:15–17	Positive reinforcement
Alma 8:20–21	Parental support
Alma 9:16–17	Unrighteous traditions
	Forgiveness
Alma 9:18–23	Teach gratitude
Alma 10:5–6, 22–23	Recognize blessings
	Wise use of agency
	Teach prayer
Alma 11:39–45	Teach eternal principles
Alma 12 (entire chapter)	Have a plan
Alma 12:1–6	Agency
Alma 12:10–14	Be humble and teachable

Alma 12:13–14, 31–32	Consequences of sin
Alma 13:3–4, 10, 13–14, 18	Bless righteousness
Alma 13:27–39	Teach eternal principles Teach lovingly and patiently
Alma 14:11	Agency
Alma 16:9–10	Rewards of wickedness
Alma 16:16–17	Know your children
Alma 17:9–10	Support and comfort
Alma 17:18	Bless your children
Alma 18:4–5	Righteous traditions
Alma 19:23	Parental prayers
Alma 20:1	Share joys with family
Alma 20:9–16, 26–27	Take time to listen
Alma 22:15–16	Use of agency Be humble/repent
Alma 24:7	Evil traditions
Alma 24:8–9	Communication Be humble
Alma 24:16–18	Get a commitment
Alma 24:24	Be humble
Alma 26:30	Joy of service
Alma 27:7, 10–12	Know your children's hearts
Alma 28 (entire chapter)	Consequences of sin
Alma 28:8	Teach love and service
Alma 28:15–17	Bless the righteous
Alma 29:4–5	Teach use of agency
Alma 29:8	The Lord knows His children
Alma 29:9	Joy in service Show trust in children
Alma 29:10	Remember blessings/gratitude
Alma 30:8–10	Explain agency
Alma 30:8–11	Teach tolerance
Alma 30:47–50	Consequences
Alma 31:5	Teach eternal principles Be humble
Alma 31:32–36	Parents be humble/pray Example of love and service
Alma 31:36–38	A parent responds to plea
Alma 32:23	Listen to your children
Alma 32:37–42	Children need emotional and spiritual nourishing
Alma 34:17–27, 39	Teach them to pray Pray for your children

Alma 34:28	Teach love and service
Alma 34:38	Teach gratitude
Alma 35:16	One-on-one interviews
Alma 36–42 (all chapters)	Parental interviews
Alma 36:3	Teach the very young
Alma 36:24–25	Joy in service
Alma 37:9	Value the scriptures
Alma 37:17	Be trustworthy
Alma 37:27–29	Protect from evil
Alma 37:33–34	Teach eternal values
Alma 37:35	Teach while they are young
Alma 37:37	Be humble
Alma 37:38–40	Give guidance
Alma 37:41–42	Consequences
Alma 38:2–11	A good teaching sequence
Alma 38:2–3	Positive reinforcement
Alma 38:8–9	Learn from mistakes
	Bear testimony
Alma 39 (entire chapter)	Teach as the Spirit directs
	Know your children
Alma 39–42 (all chapters)	Teach eternal principles
Alma 40:1	Let the Spirit direct you
	Relate to child personally
	Know your children
Alma 41:1	Let the Spirit direct you
	Relate to child personally
Alma 41:8	Be consistent
Alma 42:1	Let the Spirit direct you
	Know child's concerns
Alma 42:16,19–23, 27–28	Teach agency
Alma 42:31	Show trust
	Correct, then forgive
Alma 43 (entire chapter)	How to win the war against Satan
Alma 44 (entire chapter)	Consequences of sin
	Bless the righteous
Alma 45:2–7	Get a commitment
Alma 46:20–22	Get a commitment
Alma 46:35	Consequences
Alma 46:36	Remind of commitments
Alma 47 (entire chapter)	Poor use of agency
Alma 48:11–13, 17–19	Teach by example
	Positive reinforcement
Alma 49:4–5	Spiritual fortification

Alma 49:14	Know your children
Alma 49:28	Teach gratitude
Alma 50:18–23	Blessings of the Righteous
Alma 50:19	Lord is consistent
Alma 50:20	Explain agency
Alma 50:20–22	Consequences of sin
Alma 51–52	Fortify your home against Satan Contention in the home
Alma 53:5	Value of work
Alma 53:20–21	Obedience Teach them in their youth
Alma 55:31	Obedience yields blessings
Alma 56:44	Get a commitment
Alma 56:47–48	Mother's influence important
Alma 57:21	Teach safety in obedience
Alma 58:10–12	Teach the power of prayer
Alma 58:11–12; 33, 40	Seek the Lord's council
Alma 58:33	Be trustworthy
Alma 58:40	Teach safety in obedience
Alma 59:11–13	Leadership a poor example
Alma 60 (entire chapter)	Know your children's abilities Listen before concluding
Alma 60:32	Evil traditions
Alma 62:29	Value of work
Alma 62:51	Pray continually

Book of Helaman

The whole book of Helaman is full of consequences—blessings for the righteous and destruction for the proud and haughty.

Helaman 3:20–21,37	Results of a good example
Helaman 4:13–15	Lord teaches humility
Helaman 5:5, 13–14	Teach your children Gratitude When to teach
Helaman 5:5–7	Follow ancestors example Importance of grandparents
Helaman 5:6	Why we must teach Teach gratitude Importance of a good example
Helaman 5:7–12	Pure doctrine
Helaman 5:30	Technique/speak softly
Helaman 5:32	Technique/repetition

Helaman 6:9, 11–14	Blessings of righteousness
Helaman 7:23–28	Consequences of sin
Helaman 8 (entire chapter)	The Lord is consistent
Helaman 10:4–12	Recognize righteousness
Helaman 12:2–6	Teach humility
Helaman 13:18–20	Consequences
Helaman 14:15–19	Teach eternal principles
Helaman 14:29–31	Use of agency
Helaman 15:3	Chastise with love
Helaman 15:7	Overcome evil traditions
Helaman 15:10	Blessings of righteousness
Helaman 16:15,22	Be humble

Third Book of Nephi

3 Nephi 8 (entire chapter)	Technique/get their attention
3 Nephi 9:1–2, 10–12	Consequences of sin
3 Nephi 9:1–2; 10:1–2	Technique/Get their attention
3 Nephi 10:4–6	Technique/repetition
3 Nephi 11:3–6	Technique/speak softly
3 Nephi11:15	One-on-one relationship
3 Nephi 11:22–28	Teach plainly and clearly/outward commitment
3 Nephi 11:29–30	Stir not up contention
3 Nephi 11:32	Parents must be unified
3 Nephi 11:33–34	Teach agency
3 Nephi 11:37–38	Technique/repetition
3 Nephi 12	Eternal principles
3 Nephi 12:48	Perfect example
3 Nephi 13:6–13	Teach children how to pray
3 Nephi 14:7–8	Prayer
3 Nephi 15:1, 9	Blessings of righteousness
3 Nephi 15:4–5	Be consistent
3 Nephi 15:10–20	Prepare a sanctuary
3 Nephi 15:19–20	Consequences of sin
3 Nephi 16:1–5	Be fair
3 Nephi 16:10	Consequences
3 Nephi 17:2–6	Know your children
3 Nephi 17:5–6	Have compassion
3 Nephi 17:8	Be willing to serve them Be fair
3 Nephi 17:9	One-on-one relationship
3 Nephi 17:14–21	Parental support Teach children to pray

3 Nephi 17:21	One-on-one relationship
3 Nephi 18:1–12	Physical involvement
3 Nephi 18:5, 10	Give praise/ responsibility
3 Nephi 18:15, 18	Technique/repetition Teach them to pray
3 Nephi 18:16, 24	Teach by example
3 Nephi 18:18–21	Prepare your children
3 Nephi 18:28–30	Know your children
3 Nephi 18:32	Never give up/have charity
3 Nephi 18:36	Touch as you teach
3 Nephi 19:17–28; 31–33	Teach them to pray Teach by example
3 Nephi 19:20, 23, 27–28, 31	Support with your prayers
3 Nephi 21:29	Example Support
3 Nephi 22:7–8	Show mercy
3 Nephi 22:13	Teach your children
3 Nephi 23:7–13	Correct with love
3 Nephi 26:4–5	Teach how to use agency
3 Nephi 26:15	Teach by example
3 Nephi 27:14–15	Technique/use analogies
3 Nephi 27:16–17	Teach them their choices
3 Nephi 27:18	Be consistent, trustworthy
3 Nephi 27:21, 27	Teach by example
3 Nephi 27:30	Positive reinforcement
3 Nephi 28:1	Find out from children
3 Nephi 28:1–15	Blessings of righteousness
3 Nephi 28:19–22	Support your children
3 Nephi 28:34–35	Consequences
3 Nephi 29:1, 3, 8 (entire chapter)	Keep your promises

Fourth Book of Nephi

4 Nephi 1:2–5, 7, 10	Blessings of righteousness

Book of Mormon

Mormon 1:13–14, 17	Consequences of sin
Mormon 2:13–15, 26	Consequences of pride
Mormon 3:11–15	Consequences
Mormon 3:12	Example of love and service Give support
Mormon 3:18–19	Agency

Mormon 4:5	Consequences Teaching technique
Mormon 5:1	Never give up
Mormon 5:22–24	Be humble
Mormon 6:21–22	Agency
Mormon 7:7	Blessings of the righteous
Book of Ether	
Ether 2:8–9, 12	Agency
Ether 2:14	Importance of prayer
Ether 2:14–16	Correct errors with love
Ether 2:23–25	Problem solving Ask and listen
Ether 3:9–13, 15	Positive reinforcement
Ether 3:12	Be dependable
Ether 4:11–12	Be trustworthy
Ether 6:16–17	Teach humility and obedience
Ether 6:19, 21	Family council
Ether 6:22–24	Allow agency
Ether 6:30	Be humble Teach gratitude
Ether 8:20–24	Consequences and spiritual protection
Ether 8:25–26	Value of the scriptures
Ether 9:15–21	Blessings of righteousness
Ether 9:28–34	Consequences
Ether 9:35	Blessings of righteousness Offer forgiveness/charity
Ether 10 (entire chapter)	Examples of agency exercised Positive reinforcement
Ether 10:11	Consequences
Ether 11 (entire chapter)	Consequences of sin
Ether 11:8	Offer forgiveness
Ether 11:20	Teach repentance
Ether 12:3–22	Teach eternal principles
Ether 12:6–22, 30–31	Parents must be dependable
Ether 12:25–26	Parental support
Ether 12:27–28	Be humble
Ether 12:34–37	Teach charity Positive reinforcement
Ether 13:20–21	Agency Consequences
Ether 14:1, 21–25	Consequences of sin
Ether 15:1, 3, 19, 32–33	Consequences of sin

Book of Moroni

Moroni 4–5	Frequent participation
Moroni 6:2–6	Get a commitment
Moroni 6:9	Teach with the Spirit
Moroni 7:1, 25–26, 29	Teach eternal principles
Moroni 7:12–14, 17–18	Teach how to use agency
Moroni 7:47–48	Show charity
Moroni 8:2	Positive reinforcement
Moroni 8:3	Support through prayers
Moroni 8:8,10–11	Know children's abilities
Moroni 8:18	Be consistent and fair
Moroni 8:19–20, 22–23	Teach eternal principles
Moroni 8:25–26	Teach eternal principles
Moroni 8:27–29	Consequences
Moroni 9:22	Positive reinforcement
Moroni 9:22–26	Give loving direction/pray
Moroni 10 (entire chapter)	Responsible for posterity
Moroni 10:3–5	Teach prayer
Moroni 10:8–10	Teach by the Spirit

About the Author

Geri R. Brinley was born in Galesburg, Illinois, but raised and educated in Logan, Utah. She has a bachelor's degree in Child Development and Elementary Education and a master's degree in Child Psychology, both from Utah State University. She has written several articles for the *Ensign* and *New Era* and has served on the curriculum writing committee for the Church. She has served in all the Church auxiliaries, but her favorite assignment was being a "mission mom" while her husband Doug served as president of the Texas Dallas Mission. She and her husband are the parents of six children.